OMT Insights

SIGS Reference Library

Donald G. Firesmith
Editor-in-Chief

Additional Volumes in Preparation

OMT Insights

Perspectives on Modeling from the Journal of Object-Oriented Programming

James Rumbaugh

Rational Software Corporation

SIGS
BOOKS

New York • London • Munich • Paris • Cologne

Library of Congress Cataloging-in-Publication Data

Rumbaugh, James.
  OMT insights : perspectives on modeling from the Journal of Object-Oriented
Programming / James Rumbaugh.
      p. cm. -- (SIGS reference library series : 6)
    Includes bibliographical references and index.
    ISBN 1-884842-58-5 (pbk. : alk. paper)
    1. Object-oriented methods (Computer science) I. Title. II. Series.
  QA76.9.O35R88   1996
  005.1'1--dc20   96-18006
                                                                                  CIP

PUBLISHED BY
SIGS Books
71 W. 23rd Street, Third Floor
New York, New York 10010
http://www.sigs.com

Design consultation by Susan Culligan, Pilgrim Road, Ltd.
Composition by James Rumbaugh. Set in Minion.
Cover design by Brian Griesbaum.
Printed on acid-free paper.

SIGS Books ISBN 1-884842-58-5
Prentice Hall ISBN 0-13-846965-2

Printed in the United States of America
00 99 98 97   10 9 8 7 6 5 4 3 2
First Printing October 1996

For Madeline, Nick, and Alex

Contents

Contents

About the Author

JAMES Rumbaugh is a Fellow with Rational Software Corporation in Santa Clara, California, where he investigates the methodology of software development. Recently he has been working with Grady Booch and Ivar Jacobson to bring together the best ideas in object modeling into a single Unified Modeling Language.

Before joining Rational in 1994, he was a Computer Scientist for 26 years at the General Electric Research and Development Center in Schenectady, New York. At GE Dr. Rumbaugh worked on a wide variety of projects, including the design of one of the first time-sharing operating systems, an early transaction management system, algorithms for reconstruction of x-ray tomographic images, parallel generation of 3-D pictures, a computer-aided design system for VLSI chip layout, a generic graphics support framework, an object-oriented programming language, and an interactive graphic editor for object-oriented modeling. Dr. Rumbaugh's work in object-oriented modeling grew out of his experience on many different kinds of projects and from his life-long interest in computational modeling.

He received a bachelor of science degree in physics from the Massachusetts Institute of Technology in 1967 and a master of science degree in astronomy in 1968 from the California Institute of Technology. He received a doctor of philosophy degree in Computer Science in 1975 from the Massachusetts Institute of Technology. During his doctorate study at M.I.T. he worked in the Computation Structures Group under Professor Jack Dennis. His thesis involved the design of a highly parallel computer architecture using data flow principles.

He has been active in the object-oriented area since the early 1980s, developing first the DSM language and then the OMT method of software development in conjunction with colleagues at GE and Calma Corporation. He is author (with four former colleagues) of *Object-Oriented Modeling and Design*. He has written a regular column in the *Journal of*

Object-Oriented Programming since 1991 and has contributed papers to a number of jour-
nals and conferences. Dr. Rumbaugh is a member of the ACM and has served on several
program committees for conferences. He has spoken widely around the world at conferences and seminars.

Foreword

I N Western culture, we tend to believe that what is written is true. We perhaps hold this value most strongly for the literature of the hard sciences, such as biology, and for the cousins of hard science, such as computer science. This value holds sway even in subjective areas like process and method, which have gravitated in recent years from an oral culture to a written culture. It is in part this value and in part the fact that nature abhors a vacuum that have propelled the success of early design methods.

We have never lacked literature to satisfy the hunger for methodological guidance; there are now at least 75 books in print on object-oriented methods alone. There have been method wars, debates, and campaigns to establish which of these methods is closer to truth and beauty than the others. At any point in time, we can compare any two of these methods, make an assessment, choose, and move forward with our choice. We learn as we apply these methods. Sometimes the learning leads practitioners to customized variations on the methods; these reflect progress, and it's sad that practitioners so often view them as heresies. Sometimes these lessons make it all the way back to the original methodologist, who publishes a new book or creates a new tool and propels the work a step forward into the industry.

Over many years, the industry as a whole has learned from these experiences. But the learning has been slow and expensive. New methods rarely come with **diff** marks that show what has changed from one version to the next. To include them would cast doubts on the credibility of earlier published work, which would violate our cultural touchstone of *what is written is true.* Methodologists rarely recant old stances. Few methodologists cite their competitors' products or their own failures as a source of inspiration. Even if we do have the diff marks, we are rarely told the insights behind them. Such insights fuel true learning; they can broadly be disseminated and can lift the industry as a whole.

Software disciplines may be reaching a stage of maturity that provides enough perspective to humble even the firmest stances; modern hindsight supports compelling arguments against yesterday's subjective truths. One recent example is Brooks's admission that Parnas was right and that he—Brooks—was wrong about information hiding. Brooks *learned* something, and when *he* says he learned something, I listen!

It is a priceless and rare artifact that takes us on a journey through the learning process of a brilliant methodologist. This book, which is in part a distillation of Jim Rumbaugh's current vision of OMT, also shows us how a fledgling set of constructs matured through practical learning. Think of this book as OMT with **diff** marks. It captures Jim's thoughts, as conveyed in his journal columns, at important points on the time line of insight. And it conveys the learning that drove changes in thinking and method.

What did Jim learn over the years? Sometimes he tells us explicitly, but there are also subtle nuggets in the manuscript awaiting discovery by the discerning reader. For example, we find Jim saying on page 8 that *any attempt to standardize across many different methods is a hopeless idea, similar to trying to standardize a common language from C++, Smalltalk, and Lisp.* Then, on page 315, he turns optimistic about the prospects for a universal modeling language: *The UML serves as a basis for representing most methods using a common set of modeling constructs and common notation.*

A shallow reading or a shallow reader would fault the author with inconsistency. The differences demonstrate learning and their publication documents a recognition and celebration of that learning. The book derives much of its power from just such differences, because they tend to reflect broad changes in thinking that have crept up on us over the years. Those who don't notice these fail to notice what they've learned. By failing to reflect on what we've learned, we forget how to learn. Such learning brings a crucial perspective to contemporary software development trends. In particular, it puts the UML in sharp perspective and focus, just as Jim's whimsical aside about languages gives one pause and leads one to think about Java.

As the writings mature (and as they benefit from recent annotations added for this volume), we clearly see the learning process in the context of other schools of thought. The influence of other key methodologists is freely acknowledged. As a UML aficionado might expect, there are frequent references to Grady Booch and Ivar Jacobson. But we find additional references to Harel and to many others. Perhaps it doesn't take ideas from all 75 of the published method books, but a good smattering, nonetheless. This book is about more than Jim

Rumbaugh's knowledge—it's about industry progress in method. The book doesn't defend one method against others, but takes the high road and follows an inclusive approach.

Those who follow the pattern discipline will enjoy both the explicit and implicit pattern insights. **Controller** is a recurring theme, or pattern, in the discussions on design. Many early columns explicitly point to recurring design constructs (like **Singleton**) that would be born anew and christened in the Gang of Four book. Slightly newer columns reflect a primitive notion of pattern that was widely held a few years back, namely, that patterns were basically about structure. Jim has annotated this volume to explain the interworkings between contemporary understanding about patterns and their relationship to general-purpose methods, and he does it well. He even makes frequent—often casual—use of patterns that have yet to gain wide acceptance in many programming cultures, such as reification.

And the author encourages the practitioner to learn, and he leaves open the door for further evolution in his own thinking and method. There is little dogma here. Jim encourages us to not be hung up on notation. He relates the (now almost perfunctory) caveats about the inability to cleanly separate development activities (analysis, design, implementation) in time. Except for the very rare (and seemingly perfunctory) wry asides on programming language, he largely avoids language wars or syntactic detail: I think the book has fewer than 50 lines of code in it.

Even by avoiding code, the book does not escape the Whorfian hypothesis: it embraces it. He acknowledges that each language will implement a given model using different structures and patterns. He accommodates low-level language features in the notation. He emphasizes the iterative development cycle that may lead to modeling changes driven by implementation challenges. But beyond these, OMT is a language in its own right, and Jim shows us how it captures what he wants it to capture, which is most often the *what* of a system apart from the *how*.

This book makes me wonder about just where our industry is now in its understanding of the broad issues of paradigm, design, and systems thinking. It makes me wonder how we'll learn as we go forward with UML. It gives me hope that we can go forward, consciously documenting both our progress and regress so that we can share experiences like these with others and learn as an industry. This book captures such experience and hints at a broader vision (or at least a model) of how we can go forward as a learning discipline.

James Coplien
Wheaton, Illinois
September 1996

Preface

I HAVE been writing the column "Object-Oriented Modeling and Design" for the *Journal of Object-Oriented Programming* (JOOP) for five years now. I accepted the offer to write the column because I realized that it would give me the opportunity to explore topics in greater depth than is possible in a textbook such as *Object-Oriented Modeling and Design*. Columnists enjoy the privilege of writing anything they want without having to worry about whether the article will be accepted. Original journal articles have to be original, which keeps them interesting but also eliminates many areas that would be useful to readers. Columnists are not bound by this restriction. In fact, one of the benefits of columns is that they can explain existing material, give examples, and teach without having to constantly cover new ground. Sometimes I used this privilege to cover some small topic in detail, with plenty of examples; sometimes I examined the whole modeling enterprise from a high level; and sometimes I used the forum to propose some new and untried idea. Not all of the new ideas survived to become a permanent part of the OMT method, but the opportunity to obtain feedback from readers was invaluable.

Another privilege of columnists is fast turnaround. Authors who submit an article to a journal or magazine must sometimes wait up to a year for publication, if the article is accepted. My work is in the hands of readers less than two months after a floppy disk leaves my computer in a Federal Express package for the SIGS offices. And I never have to worry about having it accepted. There is a cost to this, however. Every month I am faced with an impending deadline without a clear idea about what to write. Eventually an idea comes to me, sometimes from some new topic I am working on, sometimes from a question I receive from a reader via e-mail, and after several drafts a column is born. I have learned a great deal by writing these columns. It is an old adage, but a true one, that you don't know something unless you can explain it to someone else. Having to take rough new ideas and put them on paper has forced me to refine and sharpen the ideas in ways that I did not always imagine when starting to write the articles.

Writing JOOP articles has enabled me to evolve the OMT method in an unusual way, through the pages of a magazine. From the publication of the *Object-Oriented Modeling and Design* book in 1990 until its merger into the Unified Modeling Language and Unified Method in 1995, the OMT method evolved considerably to handle more complex problems worked on by larger teams. Readers of my column were able to trace the evolution of the method and reconstruct an updated version of the OMT method from a distributed source. This is perhaps not the best way to document a method, but I did not feel that things were stable enough for me to write a new book. Now that OMT has merged into the Unified Method, I felt it would be useful to summarize the evolved version of OMT as well as make available much of my writing clarifying different points.

Many readers do not have access to the early issues of JOOP, and in any case it is inconvenient to read articles scattered across many different issues. This book is a collection of my columns in JOOP. I have eliminated the weaker articles and organized the rest according to topic. I have made minor changes to articles to update them with the benefit of hindsight. However, I have not attempted to make major revisions or rearrangements to the original articles.

I have organized the articles by theme into seven groups. For each group I have written a short introduction describing the articles in the group. The themes are as follows:

Methods—Discussions about methods in general, their purpose and contents.

Modeling Concepts—In-depth treatments of various specific modeling constructs.

Modeling Conundrums—Modeling problems that frequently cause trouble for modelers.

Behavior Modeling—Modeling behavior and computation.

Case Studies—Samples of complete models that put it all together.

Design Process—The development steps to build a model.

OMT Summary—A brief but complete summary of OMT up to the time it merged into the Unified Modeling Language.

Every article cannot be cleanly assigned to a single group, but I have arranged them as best I could. Remember that this is an anthology and not a textbook, so don't expect a smooth flow from article to article or complete coverage. By reading these articles you will get a good idea of the overall sweep of the OMT method and of many of its key elements, although you won't get uniform coverage of every detail.

This collection is not meant to be an introduction to OMT. If you are totally unfamiliar with it, you should first read the original OMT book, *Object-Oriented Modeling and Design*, or later a book on the Unified Modeling Language. The purpose of the articles can be summarized by the preface to my first column:

> In writing this series of columns, I hope to show the value of an object-oriented analysis and design methodology and to show how to apply it to the solution of problems. I want to show that object-oriented technology is more than just programming and languages. For the most part, I intend to give examples that illustrate various aspects of analysis and design, as I have found that a single concrete example is often more illuminating than a broad but abstract theoretical presentation. In presenting these examples, I will use the OMT methodology and notation developed by my colleagues and me and described in the book *Object-Oriented Modeling and Design* published recently by Prentice Hall. In the process our philosophy of design should become clear, as will both similarities and differences in outlook between us and other authors. Keep in mind that developing software (or anything else) is a complex creative task, and there is no one best way to do it. Neither our methodology nor any of the others is the final word; they will all evolve as new ideas and new combinations of old ideas are developed. My goal is to get you to use some methodology of analysis and design rather than just sitting down and starting to program.

This is not a textbook. I cover some topics in depth and omit others entirely. The inclusion or exclusion of a topic is no reliable guide to its ultimate importance. The repeated inclusion of certain topics may indicate, however, that they are tricky or potentially confusing and require more explanation.

OMT has now been absorbed into the Unified Modeling Language (UML) and Unified Method developed by Grady Booch, Ivar Jacobson, and myself. OMT fans should not worry, because the UML captures all of the important concepts from OMT and most of the less important concepts, and even the notation is mostly familiar. At the same time, the merger of OMT with the Booch Method, the OOSE method of Jacobson, and the concepts of many other methodologists has resulted in a stronger, more capable method with little lost and much gained.

Most of the ideas in these articles, however, apply generally to most varieties of object-oriented modeling, so the choice of method is not critical (although naturally I think that mine is good). What I have tried to teach is a certain style of thinking about problems that leads to accurate and robust models and designs. I hope that you will find the articles useful.

Acknowledgments

W HEN I and my colleagues at the GE Research Center began writing the *Object-Oriented Modeling and Design* book in 1988, we hoped that we would finish it in nine months and that we would sell over 10,000 copies. We were far short on both estimates: the writing took 2½ years but the sales have exceeded our wildest dreams by more than an order of magnitude. For the success of the book and OMT I must thank my colleagues and coauthors, Mike Blaha, Bill Premerlani, Fred Eddy, and Bill Lorensen. Our discussions were often loud and lively, but always friendly, and by working together we accomplished much more than any one of us could have done alone. I have gained much benefit from OMT and I want to remind everyone that it was truly a joint work.

When they worked for the Calma Company, Mary Loomis and Ashwin Shah worked with me to develop the original OMT notation. I had a somewhat awkward notation for my object-oriented language, DSM; Mary had an elegant notation that was specific to data bases. Together the three of us developed a notation that was both elegant and general purpose, and Calma became the major (indeed the only) user of DSM. We learned a lot about object-oriented design by doing it. I only regret that we didn't push DSM harder; maybe we could have stopped the C++ tide and spared the world some of its excesses, although I doubt it.

I want to thank the management at GE R&D Center for their support over many years. We had a unique opportunity to advance object-oriented technology without having to follow short-range schedules. In particular I want to thank Peter Dietz, Bob Salemme, Art Chen, and Norm Sondheimer. We were able to apply OMT to many different areas within GE, which strengthened OMT enormously and gave us an advantage that few people in software development companies had. I also want to thank the programmers who developed the OMTool with me: Peter Halverson, Carl Hansen, and Chris Roffler. They showed that development tools can be both intuitive and powerful.

I want to reach further back and thank several individuals who helped me learn how to think. I did my doctorate work in Professor Jack Dennis's Computation Structures Group at MIT. There I worked with an outstanding group of people who were exploring modeling years before it became fashionable. Jack had a unique ability to inspire people to creativity, and I still benefit from the thought patterns I learned during my work in his group. I also want to thank Robin Kerr, the leader of the team that developed the GE R&D Operating System. We built one of the first time-sharing operating systems. I was just a young college kid and I became part of a great team. It was the best project I ever worked on and one of the most fun. I want to thank Dick Shuey and Phil Lewis for their support at GE. I also want to recall two of the most colorful and creative people I knew at GE, neither trained as a computer scientist, and both sadly now dead: Bob Macdonald, a chemist and my first boss at GE R&D, who had automated his chemistry lab so that we could be the first hackers to crack the security on the GE Mark-II Time Sharing System; and Henry Hurwitz, a physicist and original thinker whom I helped to disprove conventional theories of x-ray tomographic reconstruction algorithms with huge doses of linear algebra and supercomputer time.

I want to thank several other groups for help in spreading OMT: the GE/Martin-Marietta/Lockheed-Martin Advanced Concepts Center, Prentice Hall, the Aerospace Division of GE, and, of course, the many people who shared their experiences using OMT to make it better.

I have enjoyed developing OMT, but everything gives way to something else eventually, and the UML is now replacing OMT. I have enjoyed working with Grady Booch and Ivar Jacobson in developing the UML. We have had a few stormy moments, but I have also learned a lot from both of them, and I think that the result is better than any of our individual efforts. I want to particularly thank Mike Devlin for convincing me to come to Rational to work with Grady and later with Ivar and to build the UML together. Sometimes the time is ripe for a consolidation, but a person of vision has to make it happen, and Mike was that man of vision.

Finally and most importantly, I want to thank my wife, Madeline Morrow, and my children, Nick and Alex, for their support and patience over the years. Writing the original OMT book took many nights and weekends for which they paid the price. Later I traveled a lot while they were stuck at home, so I thank them for persevering through some difficult times and giving me the time that I needed to complete the work. No creative work is the product of one person. Over the years I have been lucky to be in the right place at the right time, and I thank all of those people whom it was my fortune to know when I needed them.

Methods

OBJECT-ORIENTED modeling and design is a systematic way to understand systems and build software applications. It is a *method* for software development. What is a method and what are its characteristics? This first group of articles addresses that broad question.

Many people equate methods with notation, "bubbles and arrows," but that is an unnecessarily limited view. *What is a Method* outlines the components in a complete method: concepts, notation, process, and patterns. No method yet incorporates all these elements fully, but this article presents a goal to strive for.

The Waterfall Model was characteristic of an earlier generation of "traditional" software development methods. (How quickly "traditions" evolve in the computer field!) That early method proposed a linear development path that required a large, perhaps unrealistic, amount of foresight. Real problems are difficult because they require iteration on several simultaneous dimensions. *Over the Waterfall and into the Whirlpool* describes six dimensions of iteration during development. This is an early article and the details of actually doing the iteration have been expanded in the next article in this collection.

A model changes its character as the development process continues through the life cycle. In *Layered Additive Models* I argue that the goal of a model is to capture design decisions as directly as possible, and the best way to do this is to evolve the model by adding elements, rather than by replacing them. A good modeling language is constructed as a set of layers that add successive details as the life cycle progresses. This kind of seamless development supports iterative design because different parts of the model can be at different life cycle stages yet coexist within a single model, in contrast to a development process that imposes rigid translation boundaries.

Some support tools allow an entire team to share a single workspace that contains the model being developed. Although the ability to share a single model is desirable, it is not sufficient. *A Private Workspace* shows that developers also need private workspaces in which they can work without being disturbed by constant changes from other developers. In this article I describe the parallel iterative development process that is most applicable to development of complex systems.

What Is a Method?

October 1995

Methods and Other Development Guides

There are a lot of books about analysis and design methods. There are also a lot of books about computer science principles, software engineering, and systems science. There are a lot of books telling you how to use various programming languages with various degrees of elegance. Recently there have been a number of books about patterns as a new approach to design. How does all of this stuff fit together and what is the role of a method?

A method is a generic guide to help people perform some activity. A method must apply to many different situations for many different people. There are methods for teaching skiing, doing accounting, or making sales. More particularly in the software business, we want methods for developing complex software. A method provides a framework for software development. But the term can't be so broad that it includes everything that one does during software development. It must be bounded. It is bounded on the generic side by the general principles of computer science and software engineering. It is bounded on the specific side by case-specific knowledge such as patterns, conventions, and domain experience. A method is the engineering practice in the middle.

What's in a Method

A method is a mixed bag of guidelines and rules, including the following components:

◆ A set of fundamental *modeling concepts* for capturing semantic knowledge about a problem and its solution. The modeling concepts are independent of how they are visualized. They are the inputs for semantic tools, such as code generators, semantic checkers, and traceability tools.

◆ A set of *views and notations* for presenting the underlying modeling information to human beings which allow them to examine and modify it. Normally the views are graphic, but multimedia interfaces are feasible with current technology. Graphic views use geometric arrangement and graphic markers to highlight portions of the semantic information. Usually each view shows only a part of the entire semantic model and different views may present the same semantic information in different forms.

◆ A step-by-step iterative *development process* for constructing models and implementations of them. The process may be described at various levels of detail, from the overall project management down to the specific steps to build low-level models. The process describes which models to construct and how to construct them. It may also specify measures of goodness for evaluating proposed designs.

◆ A collection of hints and rules-of-thumb for performing development. These are not organized into steps. They may be applied wherever they make sense. The concept of *patterns* is an attempt to describe case-based experience in a uniform way. Patterns represent specific design solutions to recurring problems. These may apply at various levels of detail, from large-scale architecture down to low-level data structures and algorithms.

Sometimes methods are criticized for being "just lines and bubbles." That is a simplistic view by people who just see a part of the picture (such as the notation). A balance between the different components is important. The test of a method is its ability to help people get correct results efficiently.

Modeling Concepts

The ultimate job of a method is to capture knowledge about a problem and build a solution to it. A model is a formal representation of a system at some level of abstraction. Models can be at different levels of abstraction. During requirements specification or analysis, the abstraction level may be high and implementation details may be omitted. During design and implementation, detail must be sufficient to actually construct a program.

Any model is built out of a collection of modeling concepts. Often people think of notations when they think of models, but underlying any notation is a set of logical modeling concepts that capture the semantics of the model. For example, important modeling concepts in OMT include classes, associations, generalizations, states, events, and other things. A usable method requires a "universal set" of modeling concepts—a sufficient set of concepts to model any system. Not all methods have a sufficient set of concepts. For example, many methods have relationships of aggregation and inheritance but no relationship of association; they are deficient and can't model things fully. A good method should have a small set of modeling concepts, but not so spare that it becomes tortuous to model common things. Set theory and most formal specification languages, although formal and universal, are too spare in practice for anyone but mathematical masochists.

The same model can be visualized in many different ways without changing its meaning. For example, a circuit diagram may be drawn using various electrical symbols, but the underlying meaning is the same—certain electrical components are connected together in particular ways. A circuit model can be subjected to various kinds of semantic analysis, such as computing current flows through the various components.

The modeling concepts in an object-oriented software development method include things such as classes, associations, inheritance, states, events, and functions. These all represent well-defined concepts with crisp definitions. They can be analyzed for correctness and for goodness of design. They can be mapped to and from code. They convey the meaning in the design. A code generator, for example, depends on the semantic model and doesn't care at all about the graphic notation.

The semantics of a model do not depend on the way it is drawn on a diagram. There are a lot of notations that use many different symbols for classes, associations, inheritance, and other modeling concepts. There is a wide variation in the appearance of the notations. Under the surface, however, the modeling concepts from most of these methods are fairly similar. Most methods mean the same thing by a class, for example. The superficial differences in notation can obscure the deeper similarities in notation. Grady Booch and I began working to unify our two methods after we discovered that the fundamental modeling concepts were almost identical, although the surface symbols were different.

Metamodels

A metamodel is a model that describes other models. A metamodel for a method model describes the concepts in the method and their relationship to each other. It defines and restricts how atomic concepts can be connected to form complex constructs. It defines the legal models that can be constructed within the method. It describes the information that must be captured by computer-aided software engineering (CASE) tools to support the method.

Because methods have both modeling concepts and notation, a metamodel for the method needs to describe both. The metamodel should first describe the underlying semantic model. Then it should describe the mapping between the semantic model and the various views. Usually the views closely mirror the semantic model, so it may be unnecessary to actually draw the metamodel for the views. Instead the metamodel can describe the graphical syntax of diagrams and explain how to map diagrams into logical models.

Because a metamodel is itself a model, a method can describe itself. This can be a bit confusing for most people, because the same concepts appear in the metamodel more than once at different semantic levels: we can describe a modeling concept using itself and other modeling concepts, which can sometimes make the head spin.

Notation

People need notation to construct, examine, and manipulate models. People can't interact directly with a logical model. Any model has to be represented somehow, if only by a text description or table. Most methods provide a graphical visualization of most of the key models. Various shapes, lines, arrangements of symbols, and graphic marks represent the underlying semantic information. This is what people see first about most methods, and they can get excessively attached to a particular notation which is intended after all to be a pipeline to the underlying concepts. The same model can be drawn in many different ways using different symbols, even though they all mean the same thing. Whether classes are drawn as rectangles, clouds, ellipses, or other shapes, they all have the same meaning. Don't lose the model for the icons!

A diagram is more than a simple mapping from a model. A diagram adds information, but it is not semantic information. All the semantic information comes from the semantic model. A diagram selects, organizes, and displays information to highlight things of interest and suppress less important things. A diagram is a *projection* from a model; it doesn't have to include everything. It may require several diagrams to show all the information in a model. This is all right; you don't need to see it all at once, and if you did, it would be too confusing.

Text formats are views too. A language, a table, a set of records are all ways of presenting semantic information to people. The same kinds of model-view mappings can be used to handle graphic and text views.

The geometric organization of a diagram adds an aesthetic component to the model. The geometric arrangement of symbols can be used to emphasize things that are closely related, but the criteria for affinity are left up to the person. Graphic markers, such as density, color, texture, fill patterns, multiple lines, text fonts, size, etc., can be used to convey various kinds of information for quick apprehension by humans. The trick is to avoid trying to show too much at one time.

Different people may adopt different conventions to format their diagrams, just as programmers may follow different indentation rules in writing C++ code. For example, the use of orthogonal lines in OMT diagrams is just a formatting convention. A convention is a way for an individual to tailor a notation to individual taste. It is not part of the method itself, but I think of it as part of the penumbra (shadow) of the method.

Artifacts

Models and diagrams are the artifacts of the development process. These are the documents that developers, domain experts, managers, and customers can examine, argue about, and criticize. These are the deliverables that measure progress. These are the artifacts that tools must produce. These are the files that can be exchanged among people and among tools. The final system is just a very complete model that includes code among its components.

Artifacts are what are exchanged, so artifacts are the things that need to be standardized. It is not so important to standardize the development process itself, because different people can get the same results in different, equally valid ways, but the results themselves must be represented in some well-defined format so that people can understand them and tools, including CASE tools as well as compilers and GUIs (graphical user interfaces), can manipulate them. Not only the content of the artifacts but their physical format must be standardized to permit interchange among tools supporting a single method.

However, any attempt to standardize across many different methods is a hopeless idea, similar to trying to standardize a common language from C++, Smalltalk, and Lisp. One of the most important aspects of any method is the choices it makes about which concepts are important and which can be omitted. It is balance that makes a successful method, not a checklist of features. The idea of a common core method is misguided, not because it is undesirable, but because it is impossible. Any "core" method is inevitably yet another method, with its own choice of concepts, notation, and priorities, subject to the same evaluation criteria as any other new method. There is no evading the necessity to make choices.

Process

Artifacts (models and diagrams) are target points on the development map; the process is the path taken to get to them. Like routes on a roadmap, there are many possible processes that produce the same results. The choice between them may depend on personal taste as much as whether one is "better."

·A process is a guide telling how to produce a model. It provides a framework for development, describing the artifacts to be produced and the steps for producing them. At the top level, a process describes the development lifecycle and the iteration steps within it. At a lower level, a process provides a framework for producing models: steps to construct the model, guidelines for discovering components of it, design principles to be followed, measures of goodness, cross-checking and consistency rules, and red flags for possible problems.

You can't expect a method to tell you everything to do. Writing software is a creative process, like painting or writing or architecture. There are principles of painting, for example, that give guidelines on composition, color selection, and perspective, but they won't make you a Picasso. You still have to select your subject and decide on your approach. Software development is the same. You can't follow a recipe without having to think. Some methods claim to fully automate the process, to tell you every step to follow so that software design is painless and faultless. They are wrong. It can't be done. What can be done is to supply a framework that tells how to go about it and that identifies the places where creativity is needed. But you still have to supply the creativity. A process can give guidelines for identifying objects, for example, but you still have to use your judgment to select the objects from the problem.

A process can operate at several levels: the high-level management process, which describes the course of the entire project, focusing on deliverables and task planning; the middle level technical macroprocess, which describes the software lifecycle and the iterations needed to produce a design; and the lower level technical microprocess, which describes the actions needed to construct pieces of the detailed design. The upper levels can be prescriptive enough, outlining a step-by-step plan for development; but the steps are large and somewhat fuzzy. At the lower levels it is much less realistic to expect a rigid step-by-step process. Instead what can be offered is a set of guidelines to be applied and rules for when to apply them. The sequencing of the guidelines is usually fairly open.

In my work on OMT I have outlined two levels of technical process. I have left the management process for others. There is more scope for tailoring the process than the notation. If you want to do things differently than I recommend, then go ahead, provided you don't blame me if things go wrong.

Patterns

Over time many people have observed that there are good solutions to certain problems that come up repeatedly in good designs. Over the years in any creative craft, the practitioners learn good ways to solve certain kinds of problems, and the good solutions tend to be reused. Rather than create a brand new design from first principles each time, expert designers save a lot of work by incorporating these "canned solutions" into their own designs. House builders have conventional solutions to building windows, running plumbing, or laying out kitchens. These standard solutions may not be optimal in every respect, but they are good, serviceable designs that have been validated by years of experience. These "solutions waiting for problems" are called *patterns*. Architects, tailors, cabinetmakers, and other craftsmen have traditionally kept pattern books that showed good solutions to many design problems. Novice craftsmen learn from the experts by examining their patterns.

Software people have had a great handicap in learning to design. There are no "program museums" where you can examine great programs to emulate. At best, novices can undergo an apprenticeship by working with experts and learning their tricks. At worst, new designers are on their own, and the results often show it.

Methods have helped by supplying a framework and general principles for development, but what has been missing is the case-based experiential knowledge that exists in engineering, for example. Recently the Patterns Movement has sprung up to fill this gap. People have begun collecting, cataloging and explaining useful patterns so that other designers can learn from them. Books such as *Design Patterns* by Gamma, Helm, Johnson, and Vlissides [1] contain lists of low-level design patterns. These patterns are the heart of the detailed design process. They are the proven solutions to frequently-encountered problems.

Rules of Thumb

Many method books have contained rules of thumb for building designs. But what is a rule of thumb but a pattern in a less formal presentation? So software patterns have actually been around for a long time. Does this mean that the Patterns Movement is just a gimmick? Not at all, any more than the Object Movement is a gimmick. There is virtue in identifying a general approach to capturing and representing knowledge, and patterns are a good way to describe this kind of knowledge.

I find that I can recast some of my own advice as patterns. For example, I recommended trying to reify (turn into an object) operations that can have variant implementations or algorithms so that the implementations are easy to change without having to change client code. This is described in *Design Patterns* as the Strategy pattern.

I have other rules that do not appear in the *Design Patterns* book, but they could be stated as patterns. For example, a pattern to add redundant associations to optimize frequently traversed paths could be called "Redundant."

Other rules of thumb are not so easily cast as patterns, however. Advice to "keep methods small" seems best expressed as a rule. Perhaps there is room for both patterns and more general rules without specific implementations (or perhaps I just haven't seen how to write them as patterns).

Process and Patterns

What's the relationship between process and patterns? Should a method contain patterns or are they separate?

I would distinguish three kinds of how-to-do-it components for methods: process, general design rules, and patterns. A process provides a time-sequence-oriented framework for work. It may not be rigidly ordered, but it is normally procedural, with advice of the form "do this, then do that, until such and such is true." A process is a kind of recipe to follow, although the steps may be complex and some of them may require application of patterns.

Although a process can be tailored or extended over time, it is not really intended to be open-ended the same way that a pattern book is.

General design rules state properties to achieve or avoid in the design or general approaches for proceeding. "Each class and each operation should do one thing well" is a useful rule (as well as a red flag when it is violated) but I don't think I would want to state it as a pattern. "Divide and conquer" is a general design strategy applicable to almost any complex system, but I don't think I would want to make it a pattern either.

Patterns summarize open-ended case-based experience. They propose mechanisms that solve some problem in a reusable way. They need not fit into a general framework or be organized into a full taxonomy, although they will be easier to find if they have some organization. The *Design Patterns* authors have tried to organize their patterns in several different ways.

Implementing Patterns

There is a different way in which patterns and methods interact. Patterns have to be described and implemented within some method. Describing patterns is not so difficult. Any all-purpose notation will do. For example, the patterns in the *Design Patterns* book were described using OMT notation. Of course, some methods lack essential concepts such as general associations, so they might have some trouble representing patterns.

We don't expect to find patterns preexisting in a method notation. All we need to do is *implement* the pattern using the notation. There is no need for the notation to make explicit provision for particular patterns; it just needs to model patterns in general. Indeed, it would defeat the very purpose of a pattern book to expect the patterns in the book to be already present in a generic language or notation (although certain basic ones might be provided for). But the nice thing about patterns is that you can add new ones without having to extend the notation.

There is another way that patterns interact with processes. A pattern must be selected and applied to the design at some point. The process might specify when to consider applying various kinds of patterns. The process doesn't have to give rules for applying individual patterns—patterns contain their own criteria for applicability—but the process might say when to examine certain sets of patterns.

In addition, the application of patterns has to fit with the rules of the process. This is not such a difficult thing, but some processes are totally driven by external requirements, for example, and don't have any place for an optimization step.

Toward a Theory and Practice of Design

All the software engineering, methods, and pattern books are incomplete today. They each cover a portion of the entire problem, but no one level is complete. A practicing software professional needs the experience of all three levels. In constructing electrical power systems, for example, electrical engineers learn to use laws of physics, electrical engineering principles, and design handbooks to construct designs. Knowledge of all levels and when to use each one is essential to success. The same thing applies to software development, but currently the levels are loosely integrated. One of the challenges of the future is to integrate software engineering practice to the same extent as other engineering disciplines. I intend to work on that challenge.

References

1. Erich Gamma, Richard Helm, Ralph Johnson, John Vlissides. *Design Patterns: Elements of Reusable Object-Oriented Software.* Addison-Wesley, Reading, Mass., 1995.

Over the Waterfall and into the Whirlpool

May 1992

Waterfalls

Most software development methodologies (including mine) have been properly criticized for presenting an overly simplistic picture of the phases in the development process. The problem is that in books and in courses the information must be presented in some linear order. In addition, people like to have a nice step-by-step process that spells out all the decisions that have to be made. Real development is much messier, of course, and involves the use of judgment. In this article I hope to paint a truer picture of the multiple interrelated iterations involved in realistic development.

The "traditional" phases of software development are summarized by the famous (or infamous) Waterfall Model. The exact breakdown among phases varies from author to author, but the basic idea is that development consists of a number of phases that are performed one after the other. For example, we might identify the phases as Conceptualization, Analysis, System Design, Object Design, Implementation, Testing, Deployment, and Maintenance (feel free to add your own favorites). Each phase has its own particular concerns and notation and must be completed before the next phase is begun. Because development always proceeds from one phase to the next, it is like a waterfall that always flows downward.

The Waterfall Model has a number of appealing properties. The status of a project can be summarized by a single parameter, its current development phase (we could think of having completed 75% of the analysis, for example). Because the phases are performed in strict order, each phase can be carried out with the full information developed during the previous phase. There is little wasted effort because development proceeds inexorably forward. It is not so hard to decide the order in which to do things.

Unfortunately, real projects are not usually so accommodating. It is hard to foresee all the consequences of a design decision before going on to the next phase; you often have to go back to a previous phase and revisit a decision that did not work out well. All methodology books that I have seen admit that development is not purely linear, but this message has not been understood by all of the users of the methodologies. Even the original Waterfall Model (developed by Win Royce) was not presented as a one-way flow, but many people think that it is. The "Myth of the Waterfall" says that development should proceed in a strictly linear fashion as an accumulation of documents from successive phases with no opportunity to revise previous phases. In reality, development involves many dimensions of iteration that proceed simultaneously.

Multiple Iteration

The Waterfall Model assumes one dimension of iteration: the phase of the design process. I can think of at least six dimensions on which a design can iterate (there may be others):

1. *Breadth:* the content or size of a design, that is, the number of individual elements in it. Even a simple system consists of some number of components each of which must be designed and fit together with the other components. In a "flat" design components are specified directly in terms of primitive concepts. Breadth is implicit even in the Waterfall Model, as each phase must obviously iterate over the design elements.

2. *Depth:* the level of abstraction or detail. Large systems require hierarchical organization (depth) to keep the size of any one module small enough to understand. Any large complex system can be viewed at different levels. At a high level, there are fewer details but the entire system can be viewed at once; at a low level, all details are explicit but only part of the system can be viewed at once. For top down design, the entire system is first sketched out containing only major subsystems with few details; the design process is iterated at lower levels adding more and more details.

3. *Maturity:* the degree of completeness, correctness, and elegance of something. Most system elements are not written down in their final form at the first try. It takes some refinement and rework to get things right. After a system design

is logically correct, it can still be reworked further to make it cleaner, easier to maintain and extend, and more efficient. This represents iteration in maturity.

4. *Phase:* the stage of design, such as analysis, system design, object design, or implementation. It is not necessary that all design elements be at the same phase at the same time, but for any given element you have to understand (analyze) it before you build (design and implement) it. Any particular system element therefore undergoes an iteration in phase.

5. *Alternative:* different possible solutions to a design problem. There are usually many ways to solve a problem; the designer's job is to pick the best one. Engineers are more apt than software people to actually try out alternate solutions, but even software solutions are occasionally "breadboarded" and compared, and parts of a completed design are often reworked to fix performance problems.

6. *Scope:* the goals and purposes of a system; the requirements. Many designs are produced with the assumption that the requirements of the system have been determined and will not change. Sadly, this is rarely the case, and changes to system functionality after a project is well underway can be very costly. Changes occur not just because things have been forgotten; some things prove too hard to do and must be abandoned, whereas others prove so easy that the temptation to add functionality cannot be avoided. Furthermore, working on the design usually increases understanding of the system and its requirements and causes changes in them. Iteration in scope is a real if unpleasant part of the design process, so we must organize a design such that changes will not be fatal.

The multiple dimensions of design iteration can be traversed in many different ways. A simple waterfall approach would iterate on the following dimensions in the following nested order:

> phase
>> maturity
>>> breadth

In other words, complete an entire phase at a time; within a phase, make one or more passes over the system elements at increasing design maturity until the design is satisfactory. We ignore the other dimensions for now because they are not covered by the basic approach, but we will consider them later.

Iteration Order

Even two dimensions are enough for complex possibilities. Consider just depth and breadth. There are several ways to traverse the entire set of elements, including:

1. *Successive refinement.* Scan all the elements at a given depth before proceeding to the next lower level. This has the virtue of viewing the entire system from successively more detailed viewpoints, but having to treat an entire level at a time prevents partitioning the system and working in parallel.

2. *Depth first.* Expand the design of a component to full depth before designing sibling components. This scan order keeps modules and their contents together in the design process. In practice a single designer would be unlikely to do this, because the constant shifting in level of detail would be confusing. More realistic would be allocating different components to two or more designers or teams to design in parallel. If the designers work independently, the design is effectively depth first.

3. *Bottom up.* Create systems by first building individual small elements and then assembling them into larger and larger components. This may work well enough for tailoring new versions of previously-designed system from a library of parts, but it is not very useful for a very large system.

In practice, you often see a mixture of top-down and bottom-up approaches. The scan order can vary by phase. Many systems are *designed* from top down and *implemented* from bottom up. Variations such as "middle-out" have also been proposed. The remaining approach takes a more selective attitude toward filling out the design:

4. *Skeleton.* On the first pass through design work top down, but at any given depth only complete the most critical elements and one or two typical elements from any enumerated list. For example, from a list of many shapes in a

system we might design Rectangle and Circle as well as the general-purpose classes Screen and Window. The objective is to design and implement a complete but stripped-down system with a representative sampling of functionality so that the entire system can be exercised and integrated. It is important to include the "infrastructure classes" and a few typical application classes to exercise the mechanisms and protocols. Then additional elements are completed incrementally and fitted in. The process has somewhat of a fractal nature as pieces of the system are gradually added in. This approach is perhaps most useful if it is carried through to implementation.

The discussion of top down and bottom up approaches has assumed that the design elements form a tree. Usually there is some sharing of common elements, so we have not a tree but rather a partial order graph. This does not change the iteration possibilities much.

The design process is complicated enough with just two dimensions, depth and breadth. If we now consider maturity, it gets very complicated indeed. For example, we could perform a successive refinement by layers to obtain a first cut at a design. Then we could repeat the same process again to obtain a better design. During the second pass, the context of each design element would be clear. Another possibility is to make the first pass from top to bottom, then reverse the scan order and revise the design from bottom to top. This approach is highly modular, because each subsystem at any level is designed and revised independently of other subsystems at the same level.

Decomposition Bases

In discussing iteration order over depth and breadth, I have written as if the system structure were predefined and merely needs to be scanned in some fixed order during the design process. In reality the most important part of the design process is to decide how to organize a system into parts, that is, how to decompose each component into subcomponents. The iteration process over depth and breadth must create a good system decomposition. The most natural approach is to work top down, recursively decomposing each subsystem into smaller subsystems, until the leaf subsystems are small enough to comprehend and design directly from primitive elements or library components. But *what* are we decomposing? The "traditional" approach is to decompose functions into finer and finer units, but this is not object-oriented. The problem with decomposition of functions is that the resultant organization is critically dependent on the exact definitions of the top-level functions. If the functions change (iteration in scope) then the decomposition may change radically.

In contrast an object-oriented approach organizes a design around object classes, not the individual functions that they collectively embody. Changing the exact definition of a function or adding or deleting functionality to a class does not invalidate the classes or their relationships to each other (up to a point, anyway). In practice, the functions are much more volatile than the object classes that contain them.

Classes should be grouped into recursive packages called subsystems or modules or packages. There are several possible bases for decomposing a system into subsystems and allocating the classes among them. These include:

1. *Functionality.* What is the main purpose of the class, that is, what kind of functionality does it support? For example, a graphics editor might be divided into modules for geometry, for user interactions, for managing windows, and for storing persistent information. Classes such as Ellipse, Polygon, Line, and Spline would belong to the geometry module. The user interaction module would contain classes such as Menu, Command, Form, and MouseEvent. Use cases are a good way to identify functionality groupings.

2. *Generalization.* If a module represents a generic capability with many specific enumerated cases, then it can be decomposed into submodules for major abstract classes or classes with many details. For example, a Geometry module could be decomposed into modules for 0-dimensional (points and iconic markers), 1-dimensional (lines and curves), and 2-dimensional (areas) figures. Often the high-level behavior of the system does not depend on the specific low-level classes (this is the point of abstract classes and methods). Generalization decomposition is usually not performed at the top level of the system but at the second or third level.

3. *Association coupling.* If a system contains a set of classes, it is good to group tightly-coupled classes into categories. Classes are tightly coupled if there are many associations between them. Classes in different categories should have few associations. This basis is more useful for bottom-up consolidation of designs into categories rather than top-down decomposition, because it is usually hard to determine the coupling between classes in advance.

4. *Execution phases.* Many batch-like computations can be performed as a sequence of execution phases, in which each phase has its own set of object classes. For example, a compiler can be divided into lexical analysis, syntax parsing, semantic analysis, code generation, and optimization phases. Each phase requires object classes, many of which are used only within the phase or by a neighboring phase. For example, the lexical phase produces Token objects whereas the syntax phase produces ParseTree objects.

5. *Implementation units.* If a system is to be built from physically distinct hardware units, such as CPUs, tanks, or telephones, then the top-level system decomposition should usually correspond, otherwise lower-level design decisions will cross physical boundaries. Sometimes functionality does need to cross boundaries, but physically-distinct units are often designed independently, so it is better that the software not contain unnecessary interdependencies. For example, in a satellite communications system, the first decomposition should probably be into Satellite and GroundStation modules.

Note that I propose to decompose sets of object classes into modules according to various bases. In particular, decomposing a system by functionality does *not* mean producing a tree of functions decomposed into supporting functions as in the traditional functional decomposition approach. It is the classes that we organize according to the kinds of functions they support, but the exact details of the functions are not crucial. One function more or less on a class does not make much difference to the meaning of the class.

To clarify, in the traditional approach we might start with a function, such as creating a polygon, and decompose it into its parts: reading input points, drawing rubberband lines to input points, creating and inserting a data structure for the completed polygon, and drawing the polygon on the screen. This approach mixes together functions of quite different character.

In the object-oriented design approach the *create polygon* function would be attached to a *Command* class in the *UserInput* module; creating a data structure and rendering a figure would be part of a *Polygon* class in the *Geometry* module. The *create polygon* function would use the services of the classes in the *Geometry* module, but that decision would not have to be made when defining the initial breakdown into modules. The class-based decomposition along functional lines is much more stable with respect to changes in functionality than decomposition of functions themselves.

Defining the High-Level Architecture

The following approach can be used to perform the decomposition process of a system:

1. Define the functionality and bounds of the entire system, taking into account knowledge of the application domain as well as the specific application.

2. Decompose the system into top-level subsystems on the first applicable basis from this list:

   a. Physical execution units. These usually take precedence because physical boundaries are obvious targets for parallel development by different developers.

   b. Execution phases. Coupling within an execution phase is usually much stronger than coupling between phases.

   c. Functionality. If the previous two cases don't apply, then the top-level decomposition should usually be based on broad categories of functionality.

3. Now drop down one level of detail and repeat the decomposition for each top-level module. Decomposition according to generalization is often appropriate at this level. For example, a top-level module may support geometry functionality. At the next level we would enumerate the various geometrical shapes.

4. Except for very large systems, two levels of decomposition are probably enough. At this point use association coupling and generalization to further group the existing classes in the bottom-level modules. Add new modules as convenient for grouping.

5. Additional consolidation and restructuring can often be done by reversing the process and going from bottom to top in depth. Don't be afraid to move classes between modules during consolidation.

Phases

I have gone into a lot of detail on variations in iteration order among the dimensions of depth, breadth, and maturity. Let us now add iteration over the development phases. We have seen that iteration over depth, breadth, and maturity can be performed in many possible ways. The Waterfall approach can be summarized as:

1. Do all the analysis.

2. Then do all the design.

3. Then do all the implementation.

Iterate within each phase according to your favorite decomposition method.

A more realistic approach would be:

1. Do all the analysis.

2. Start the design.

3. Discover some problems, go back and modify some of the analysis, then drive forward again until the design is done.

4. Do the same thing for implementation.

Iterate within each phase according to top-down decomposition, but go back to the previous phase and regroup if problems are discovered.

Iterative Development

The design process is further complicated by iteration in scope (changes in requirements) and in alternative (alternate design trade-offs). User interfaces are an area in which it is hard to get requirements right just on paper; you have to see it work to evaluate a user interface properly. One approach to dealing with this complexity is to use iterative development:

1. Identify those areas of functionality and behavior most at risk to change. Perform a skeleton analysis (depth and breadth) including critical areas and ignoring or glossing over less critical areas in the system.

2. Drive the system through design and implementation (phase) on the selected skeleton using the simplest possible design and implementation (alternative).

Other portions of the system are simulated by stubs or canned procedures. Many commands are simply omitted in the rapid prototype.

3. Run the system and evaluate the observed behavior. Modify the requirements as desired (scope) and repeat the skeleton implementation until the functionality is correct.

4. When the functionality is satisfactory, go back and redo the entire system in full detail (depth, breadth, phase) using a more efficient and robust approach (alternative and maturity).

5. When the entire system is done, go back and clean it up for greater elegance and maintainability (maturity).

We see from this description that rapid prototyping involves iterations in all dimensions, frequently simultaneously. It is a much more complicated design strategy than the simple waterfall approach. This is not unexpected, as we could regard it as an optimization of the design process, and any optimization is more complicated than a simple but straightforward approach.

The Whirlpool

We have seen that realistic software development is more like a whirlpool than a waterfall. There are many different cycles at various scales and on various dimensions. Development is more of a fractal process than a linear one. Nevertheless simple, well-nested linear processes, such as the waterfall model or top-down decomposition by layers are useful guides to the development process. They represent idealized models of the development process itself, just as any design is an idealized model of an actual system. You can think of the actual multicyclic development process as a transformation of the idealized linear process. The waterfall gives rise to the whirlpool.

Layered Additive Models
Design As a Process of Recording Decisions
March 1996

Layered Decisions

I feel that a model should represent design decisions as layered properties that are made at various stages in the design process. My basic argument is that the development process is a series of decisions. The best kind of model is one in which the individual design decisions are captured directly in an *additive* form, that is, successive decisions are represented by separate modeling elements that add to, rather than replace, modeling elements representing earlier design decisions. I will first outline the argument briefly.

Additive Models

A development process is a series of decisions of various kinds. The purpose of a model is to capture design decisions and use them to produce an implementation in some language. To be able to easily understand and modify the implementation, the design decisions should ideally be represented one-to-one by model elements. This can best be accomplished by organizing the design decisions into several layers according to the order in which the decisions normally occur for a given component. Roughly, we can identify the development phases of analysis, design, and implementation, but the lines between them are neither rigid nor fundamental. These layers apply to each system component, but all components of the system need not progress at the same rate. More specific decisions made later in the life cycle should *add to* and *layer on top of* more general decisions made earlier in the life cycle, rather than replacing elements with other elements. This kind of layering preserves traceability and permits changing individual decisions with minimal impact on the rest of the model.

It is desirable to spread out the decisions across the development lifecycle so that all the work need not be done at once. It is not always possible to go "forward" in the life cycle of a component; some rework is necessary and the model should propagate the effects of changes to remain consistent across levels.

The text of actual programming languages depends on internal language features and is not usually well-matched to showing design decisions. The best approach is to generate as much code as possible from the model. Tools can use the layered properties of components in the model to parameterize the code generation process. Some parts of the code are easier to write directly as text rather than to model in some other way. Because the developer must eventually work in the language domain, the effects of code generation must be predictable and controllable.

To summarize: A model should be built by adding separate properties corresponding to successive design decisions. The additive properties of the model are used to parameterize the generation of code that the developer completes by writing additional code text directly. Changes to decisions are made directly to the affected component and their effects are propagated; in a layered additive model other model properties may be unaffected but the generated code may change considerably. These ideas require explanation, so I will expand on them in the rest of the article.

Layered Decisions

A development process takes time. It encompasses a number of decisions of many different kinds, including what to do (requirements), what the real-world and the user's view of the system look like (analysis), what kinds of strategies to use (design), and how to realize the system in some medium (implementation). A method should supply guidance on how to make the decisions (the design *process*) and should provide ways to capture the decisions so they are not lost (the design *model*).

Many different processes have been proposed for carrying out software development. These range from a linear *waterfall* approach to an involuted *iterative* approach. I lean toward an iterative approach as being more flexible for development of complex systems, but that is not crucial to my remarks here; an iterative approach or a waterfall approach or something else are equally applicable.

Any kind of process represents a series of decisions. It is possible to keep the decisions inside the head of a developer, but then valuable information is lost that would be useful for understanding the structure of the final system and particularly for understanding why each component is there. This information is important when you want to modify the system. Some components can be changed with little consequence, but others are the result of complicated decision processes. If you don't capture this information, then you have to reconstruct it later, and there is a high probability of overlooking something. So I claim that the main purpose of modeling is to capture design decisions at every step of the process.

The goal of the design process is to produce a *product*, such as a workstation application or a piece of hardware. It is *possible* to do design without keeping track of the decisions. The product embodies the *results* of the decisions but the decisions are not necessarily explicit within the product. This is fine as long as the product will never be changed, but most products are modified or extended many times. If you don't record the design decisions and you later want to modify the product, then you must either repeat the entire design process, or try to remember the decisions, or reverse engineer the product to reconstruct them. All of these approaches are costly and dangerous. Better to keep track of the decisions as they are first made!

Note that the code for a system is a kind of product, as it does not directly embody decisions. There may in fact be a series of intermediate products before the ultimate product: program code, compiled binary files, executable code. Each level has less and less explicit design information. Later levels can be regenerated from earlier levels, but an earlier level can only be reverse engineered from a later level at great cost and with marginal results.

An *additive model* is simply the sum of all the design decisions. To be useful, however, the decisions have to be fairly clear and separable; if you have to go through a complicated analysis to reconstruct the decisions, then the model is not of much use. So to be most useful, a model must capture individual design decisions in a direct manner and keep them from getting mixed up. Ideally we would like a one-to-one match between design decisions and model elements. This is not always possible but it is a goal to strive for.

It is important not to destroy information. If a later decision destroys the record of an earlier decision, then valuable information is lost. I don't mean that you can't change your mind, but that an optimization, for example, should not destroy the underlying model beyond recovery. (There is an argument that even bad decisions should be recorded so that they will not be repeated later. There is some merit to this argument, but it makes things much more complicated, so I will not include it in the present discussion.)

Example

For example, suppose we are making a phone book. The phone book consists of a set of listings. Each listing has a name, an address, and a phone number. We choose to implement the phone book as an array of entries sorted by name and to use a binary search to find entries.

The decisions are as follows: the phone book is a set of entries; an entry is a record containing a name, address, and phone number; the set is implemented as an array sorted by the name field in each entry; names are found by binary search. Some of the decisions depend on previous decisions, but each decision is distinct.

On the other hand, the code to implement the application might lose some of the decisions. Suppose we just have a **PhoneBook** class with the operations **addEntry** and **findEntry**. The **addEntry** operation adds a new entry in alphabetical order. The **findEntry** operation finds an entry by binary search. Now the fact that the phone book is just a set of entries has been lost. The sorted data structure is part of the code, and there is no indication that it is not essential. We don't know that it is just a design optimization to speed the search. It would be difficult to organize the entries by phone number instead or to use a hash table instead of an array. The code has optimized away the separate decisions.

Constrained Decisions

Decisions are not independent, however. Many later-stage decisions are constrained by earlier decisions, and the relationships among them are important facts to record. For example, it is impossible to use a binary search for the phone book unless it is sorted. A hash table would not require or permit a sorted order; it has its own data structure.

One has to be realistic about this. The level of detail has to be correct; you don't want to get bogged down in minutiae. We want to keep track of decisions that are large scale or difficult to extract from the final system. A localized decision that can easily be redone is not important to record.

We should note another thing. It is not desirable that all the decisions are made at once. Making decisions takes time; that is what development is all about. We want the decisions to be spread out evenly across the whole development lifecycle. For example, during coding we specify iteration loops in detail; earlier you can state the need for iteration but omit the loop variables and loop mechanisms. Otherwise you have to do all the work at once. This means that you don't expect to know everything after analysis, such as performance details or even dependencies among classes, because there is still a lot of work to do. We expect to gradually complete the design process over a period of time. Otherwise you aren't working productively at each stage.

This implies that you cannot have a complete model of a system, a fully executable model, until you are done with it. The earlier versions of the model can capture certain important aspects of the system but not all its details. Our goal in building models and in building metamodels is to identify the important high-level aspects and model them first. So "full simulation" of a system based on early models is impossible, but "partial simulation" to reveal certain aspects of the system behavior is possible, but it may require some assistance from the developer to fill in the unimplemented details.

The conclusion from this discussion is that design models should be *additive* rather than *transformational*. In other words, we would like to capture successive design decisions as separate elements of the model, whose relation in the model captures the constraints of the decisions themselves. However, we also have to end up with an implementation, preferably one that is easily extracted from the final model. This means that the model must take on the shape of the final system (more or less) but the various design decisions must fit into it so that they keep their identity and preserve their connections.

I propose that the best way to do this is to build a *layered model*. Each layer captures design decisions made at a particular stage in the lifecycle of a particular system element. For convenience, I will use the stages of *analysis, design,* and *implementation*. These are not rigid terms but I feel they are useful enough. Analysis includes decisions about *what* to do. Design includes decisions about *how* to make it work. Implementation includes decisions about the *exact form* of the system. Each stage obviously depends on the previous stages.

Note that each individual element goes through an evolution but that the different elements may progress at different rates, that is, I do not assume a waterfall process, in fact, I recommend an iterative process. Changes to all levels are inevitable, so we may have to revisit decisions about an element even after subsequent decisions about it have been made. One of the strengths of an additive model is that individual decisions can be changed without having to change the entire model or map between multiple models, such as a distinct analysis and design model. For example, if we change the entry in the phone book to also contain an e-mail address, we do not have to revisit the decisions about sorting.

Now the catch is that the various decisions that affect an element are not independent. For example, design decisions depend on the analysis decisions for an element. A decision to implement the phone book as a lookup table sorted in alphabetical order by entry name depends on the understanding that a phone book is a set of entries with no externally imposed ordering. However, it is not essential to use a lookup table; we could use a b-tree, for example. Later decisions obviously depend on some of the earlier ones; the decisions are separate but *layered.* In the Unified Notation, we capture the decisions in distinct modeling actions: first a one-to-many (or many-to-many) association between classes **PhoneBook** and **Listing;** the specification of the attributes of **Listing,** an annotation **sorted(name)** on the **listing** role of the association, and finally an annotation (usually in the background of a tool, rather than on the diagram) on the association to indicate the use of class **LookUpT-able<Name,Entry*>** to implement the association in C++.

If the decisions affecting a single design element are layered and separate from decisions affecting other elements, then the effects of a change are clear and local. Design decisions can be changed without affecting analysis decisions, for example. If the model is additive, then a design annotation cannot be incompatible with an analysis decision, but at worst irrelevant. For example, whether an association is ordered or unordered is irrelevant if the multiplicity is one, but the choice of *ordered,* for example, causes no problems and might be useful if the multiplicity is changed back to *many* in the future. We could consider this a *latent decision,* one that has no effect at a given moment but has a meaning if certain other decisions are changed.

Development Process

So far my statements have been fairly general and would apply to most processes. Now I am going to make some specific proposals: Start with the real-world objects and capture them in a class model. This forms the core of the *domain model.* In parallel, write use cases to capture the behavior of an application. The domain model and use case model are separate but related; each one can help to validate and suggest omissions in the other. The use cases must deal with the domain objects. The domain model must be augmented with application objects from the use cases. Together the class model and use cases define the *analysis model.*

Although I have described the construction of the analysis model as a waterfall process, it need not be built at once. In an iterative process you would construct *some* of the analysis model, usually the high-level parts and some typical parts from lower levels, and then proceed to design and implement part of the system. On a subsequent iteration extend the analysis model.

The analysis model forms the first layer of the layered model. Even when the design is complete, the analysis model remains at the center of the model and can be extracted from it.

Design is the process of elaborating an analysis model until it specifies enough detail to construct an executable program. During the design part of development, the class model is augmented by additional classes and additional behaviors for existing classes. Most of the work is in writing methods to do the work of implementing the top-level externally-visible methods.

How can the internal and external methods and other elements be indicated? They can be marked with a property to indicate the phase of the life cycle: analysis, design, or implementation. Therefore the analysis model can be projected out from the entire life model, even if it was constructed in stages as part of an iterative process.

Traceability

It is all well to be able to project out the various parts of the model, but what about making changes to it? The bane of most multimodel approaches in the past was the difficult of keeping multiple models synchronized. Analysis models could be used to generate design models, but generally changes to the design models never got put back in the analysis models. It was too difficult or too much bother. Experience over 40 years has shown that people cannot keep a series of models synchronized.

Therefore it is necessary to keep everything within a single connected model. It must be possible to change either the analysis parts of the model or the design parts without breaking the synchronization of the parts. If most of the features are additive, this is not a problem. The various stages will use different properties that do not conflict.

In most cases traceability is direct: the various decisions affecting a given design element are attached to it as layered properties.

Code Generation

Actual implementation languages (programming and databases) do not have this decision-based structure. Their elements depend on internal language features and are not necessarily well-matched to development decisions. Changing decisions can require extensive modifications to the code. For example, the decision to change the name of a variable may require changes to many statements within a complicated scope. Making the change is tedious in a text editor, although it can be done easily by an incremental compiler, which uses an internal parse form better matched to the actual decisions than source code.

The best way to match decisions to results is to generate major portions of the code from the model. This requires a code generator parameterized by the design decisions.

Choices within the programming domain become design decisions in the model. This requires some judgment about what the important language-level decisions are, because they may transcend many lines of code. If decisions are changed, the code can be regenerated. This is practical for declarative structure as well as many stereotypical operations, such as access methods and constructors. However, algorithmic programming must still be done using actual code; generating the code would require inventing a new programming language, which is unlikely to be successful. Therefore programmers must be able to work simultaneously in the model domain and the language domain, although it may not be necessary to use both domains for the same element. Code regeneration must not destroy any previous work in the language domain, even though the two domains are mixed together in the actual code. This will require some disentanglement mechanism, such as marking generated regions or having a smart editor.

Architecture

In this approach the architecture is built into the model as it evolves. The architecture *is* the large-scale organization and strategies of the design. Some authors have argued that logical structure and architecture can be developed independently. I disagree. It is not possible to separate the architecture from the model of the application. The architecture is not a separate independent thing that can be applied arbitrarily to any logical model. The architecture and detailed design are the enfolding of the model.

Development Pace

From a development point of view, it is desirable to spread out the decisions across the development lifecycle, as decisions represent the result of work. Of course, the nature and scope of decisions are not uniform: early decisions may have a vast scope and may require more forethought, late decisions must take account of the many previous decisions and so may require more examination. In any case, it is unreasonable to expect linear progress; mistakes will be made and will have to be corrected, with consequent subordinate effects. Ideally, each decision will be orthogonal to others, but this is not totally feasible. Design and implementation decisions depend on the previous analysis decisions. At best, a change in an early stage can be automatically propagated forward; at worst, we expect that the dependents of an early decision will be known within the model and can be automatically flagged for human inspection and modification.

Example

This example shows a series of decisions that can be separated and modeled as distinct elements in the Unified Modeling Language model.

1. Identify classes A and B. Model them as separate classes.

2. Recognize that instances of A and B are semantically linked. Make an association between A and B.

3. Decide the role that each class plays with respect to the other. Assign role names to the ends of the association.

4. Decide how many instances of A go with a particular B, and vice versa. Assign multiplicity to the ends of the association.

5. Decide if the ordering of the instances in an association direction conveys information. Set the *ordering* property on each end.

At this point the semantic information is complete (analysis). Further decisions affect the implementation.

6. Decide whether the association must be traversed in both directions during the execution of the planned program. Set the navigation property on the roles.

7. Decide whether the association must be indexed (in either direction). Add qualifiers where indexes are needed.

Further decisions get close to the language.

8. Pick a default family of data structure classes to implement associations. This is a global decision that is based on the class library used.

9. Decide whether to override the implementation of the A-B association. If so, give an alternate data structure family that has been loaded into the code generator.

At this point the data structure for the association can be generated automatically.

Changes

Now let's consider changes to the model and how they apply to each decision. I also show what would be needed to work directly in C++ without an additive model.

1. Elimination of a class destroys the association and every decision tied to it, because they are now meaningless. The code generator doesn't generate them any more. No manual update is needed. In C++, a lot of data structures and code would have to be tracked down and killed.

2. If the association is eliminated, all the remaining decisions become moot and disappear. If the association is instead moved up or down the class hierarchy, all the remaining decisions still make sense and can be preserved. It is possible that the code in the source class may not even have to change. In C++, all of the pointers would have to be changed individually, together with all the access operations.

3. If the names are changed, the attribute name containing the pointer is changed. In this case it is the same as working in C++. The code text must still be modified.

4. Making A singular will moot point 6 but is orthogonal to the remaining decisions. The code generator will generate a scalar or a container class depending on the multiplicity. Changing the multiplicity in C++ is a lot of work and involves changes to data structure and access methods.

5. Changing ordering is orthogonal to most downstream decisions. It affects the generated classes.

6. Changing the navigation affects a lot of the code. The code generator can make code to keep both ends consistent. Treating the two halves of the association as distinct makes changing the code much more difficult.

7. A lot of code can be generated automatically from this decision.

8. The code for the entire model (or a portion of it) can be changed quickly by changing the default class assignments, for example, to use a different class library. This would be an enormous work by hand.

9. Overriding can be on an individual case. If it is removed, the code reverts to the default case.

By factoring into separate decisions, changes are much easier and more consistent than by hand.

Looking at the code to use an association, it might have to be written by hand. A smart editor could potentially modify it automatically, however.

Models and Methods

A layered additive model supports a seamless development process that avoids the need for translation between formats. Any translation loses information, so it is better to avoid introducing rigid boundaries that require translation into a method.

A Private Workspace
Why a Shared Repository is Bad for Large Projects
September 1995

The Myth of the Shared Repository

A popular approach to parallel development by multiple developers is the *shared repository*, in which each developer sees the latest version of each model element (classes and methods) in the entire project. Several development tools support this approach. This is bad for anything but a small project. Different developers get in each other's way because their temporary changes are visible to everybody immediately. Each developer or development team needs a private workspace in which the developer can work with a stable version of the system until his or her changes are ready to be shared with everybody. This article explains the problem and the right way to handle projects.

A shared repository is a central database that contains a single version of the entire system. As developers make changes to elements, the changes are visible to the entire project. This *seems* like a good approach. Everybody sees the latest changes quickly so there is less chance of inconsistency. What is wrong with this approach?

A shared repository is good for a command-and-control system, such as a "war room." A war room is a command center for managing a complex, messy, real-time parallel operation, such as a battle. Non-military examples include air traffic control, a city firefighting dispatch center, an overnight shipping company, and the registration desk for a conference. In all of these examples, lots of things are changing concurrently in real time. The goal of a command-and-control system is to bring together the rapidly changing information as well as possible in real time. A shared repository is useful for a command-and-control system. It allows the latest information to be absorbed and organized in a real-time system that needs fast response to a confusing collection of concurrent activity. Because there are delays and noise in gathering information, the system must not demand absolute internal consistency of information, but must expect and deal with various kinds of information errors without crashing.

We accept the inconsistencies of the war room because we have no choice if we are to react to rapidly changing real-world situations. The information is unstable because the real-world situation is unstable. This is not a good model for engineering design (unless we are trying to fix an acute problem, such as a crippled spacecraft). We would prefer to produce engineering designs in a stable environment without inherent inconsistencies caused by continual uncontrolled changes. Of course, requirements change during the development process, but we want to organize the design process so that changes are accepted at well-defined points with controlled consequences.

On anything but a tiny project, the work must be divided into parts and done in parallel by different developers. Each developer designs part of the system and uses the rest of it. But if the rest of the system is constantly changing, then the poor developer is constantly bombarded by outside changes.

The problem is that each part of a system depends on many other parts of a system. Changes to a supplier component require changes to its clients. If a developer is changing the interface to one part of the system, many other developers may have to change their work. This applies at all stages of the development life cycle, but it is particularly acute during programming, because programs are notoriously intolerant of small errors and inconsistencies that might possibly be ignored during earlier stages (but not always). It is true that all changes must be integrated into a single system before the entire system is released. But it may be inconvenient to force all developers to see all changes immediately. To force the entire system to be up-to-date at all times would force development to be sequential, destroying the value of parallel development. This is unacceptable on a medium- or large-sized project. Developers must be able to work with mature, stable parts of a system that are being extended by others so that they can get their own work done. Eventually the work must be merged together, but if the merge process is small compared to the development time of the parallel pieces, things will get done more quickly in parallel.

Even if changes to a part of the system do not involve its public interface, it is an unfortunate fact of life that developers are not perfect. They make bugs. (What, *you* don't make bugs? Quick, send me your resume.) Other developers do not want to see a "work in progress" with all its bugs. They want to see other people's changes only at appropriate points of their own choosing after the changes have been validated by their developers.

For these reasons, the concept of a single shared repository is bad for engineering, such as software development. To permit parallel development with order and stability, each developer needs a private workspace whose contents are not affected by anybody else's work. Each developer needs explicit control on seeing changes by others.

Why is this different from the command-and-control system? In the real-time system, there is only one real world and it imposes its reality on us. But during a creative process, such as engineering design, different people can construct different virtual worlds. At well-defined milestones the different work must all be integrated together, but between milestones we want to have both parallel development and some stability.

Parallel Iterative Development

Iterative development is a style of work in which a system is developed in a number of *iterations* each culminating in a new *release* of the system to customers. Each release defines a new version of the product with improved capabilities for the users. Iterative development is used within a project to reduce the risk and difficulty of integrating all the changes to the release at once. Features to be added to a product are allocated to a series of internal development releases that force smaller-scale integration on a more frequent basis. Smaller integrations are easier to complete and debug and design problems show up earlier in the development cycle. Slips to the schedule are much harder to disguise because they show up as delayed or missing releases or missing functionality. Even if a project slips behind schedule, a system with reduced functionality will be available and may be usable (which is usually not the case with a "grand implosion" model of system integration).

How do developers work in parallel? In all but the smallest one-person projects, a normal approach to system development is for two or more developers to work in parallel as part of an overall team. Each developer is assigned part of the problem. The developers cannot afford to wait for each other; they must work in parallel. This means that each developer must make modifications to the system under development but does not want to see the intermediate work of other developers, because the intermediate states of each developer's work may be inconsistent. In addition, a developer may not want to see even a consistent result from some other developer, as those changes may be inconsistent with the current state of his/her own work.

There needs to be some way to assign responsibility for parts of the system to individual developers, so that their work does not overlap and create incompatibilities that are difficult to resolve. A *category* is a user-defined subset of a model that is (by definition) a unit of access control for making changes. (I had previously used the term *subsystem*. In UML we have adopted the word *package* to represent any grouping of model elements. There is unfortunately no consistency in terminology across different crafts and domains.) The definition of categories is a developer responsibility. They can be drawn as broadly or narrowly as desired, down to a single class or method and up to the entire system. A category should be tightly bound internally and loosely bound to the rest of the model. (In other words, there should be many internal dependencies among components of a category and fewer dependencies among categories.) Categories can be nested. The entire system model is the top-level category. The developer must draw the boundary lines correctly or unnecessary dependencies will be introduced among categories, which will complicate parallel development.

Categories are the basic units of configuration control. Each category undergoes a sequence of *versions* during its development (branching versions are also possible but I won't discuss them now). At any point during an iteration, some of the categories are undergoing modification by various developers.

A *baseline* is a version of the entire system that is globally consistent and one on which every developer can build. A baseline consists of a specified version of each category in the system. The baseline is well tested and satisfies a set of objective requirements. A baseline represents a well-defined starting point for extensions to the system. Baselines corresponding to releases need to be archived so that software releases can be reconstructed if necessary in the future.

Iterative Development Process

On a new project, an initial project configuration is defined with a number of categories in it. This creates the initial system baseline. Each project team is assigned one or more categories. During the initial development iteration the categories must be developed individually and integrated gradually. On subsequent iterations integration of new category versions can be done by replacing previous versions within the context of an existing system baseline. Having a full system context permits testing of modifications as part of an operational system.

A project team using iterative development produces a series of baselines between each release, starting from the baseline of the previous release. Each baseline represents a consistent view of the system. However, an internal development baseline may omit functionality needed in an external release. For now I assume a linear sequence of baselines, that is, we ignore the possibility of variant branches to the development process; these deserve consideration but represent a more complicated possibility that I will not cover now.

During a system iteration each developer extends part of the system working from the previous baseline. Each developer checks out one or more categories, modifies them, and builds a private version of the system in the context of the baseline versions of all the other categories. Each developer gets a stable view of the entire system, including public and private categories, that is unaffected by changes made by other developers. Each developer sees a different version of the full system containing his/her own changes. Conceptually the developer makes a snapshot of the baseline into a private *workspace* and makes changes to the workspace without impacting other developers. Developers *check out* categories that they want to modify. Typically a configuration management system (such as Unix SCCS or some more robust commercial product) prevents, or at least discourages, two developers from checking out the same category simultaneously.

Category versions, baselines, and private workspaces can be stored in a configuration management system, which can be implemented in various ways, using files, databases, or third-party configuration control systems. The private workspaces can also be stored separately from the baselines. In practice, only categories that are modified by a developer must be copied into a private workspace; others could be accessed by reference from the configuration management system. The storage mechanism does not affect the semantics.

When the developer is satisfied that his/her work is correct and consistent, then a new version of each modified category is created and added to the system. However, other developers do not automatically use the latest new versions, as the new versions may be inconsistent with their own work or require additional changes that the other developers do not want to perform immediately. Developers may be notified about changes by other people but they continue to work with their own existing view of the system. They can accept new versions from other developers whenever they want, however. Creation of new category versions does not create a new baseline, as the changes may be incomplete across the entire system. Often two developers share new versions of interdependent categories before the categories are ready for general use.

A developer does not see changes by other developers until new versions of modified categories are created and stored in the configuration management system. (Of course a tool could permit looking at in-progress work by other developers, but nobody is forced to accept external changes until ready. Whether people can see other people's incomplete work is a political question and not part of the methodology.)

Typically a developer needs to work privately for periods ranging from part of a day to several weeks. This precludes working out of a single shared workspace in which all developers see the same version of each category. Changes during that period must go into the developer's private workspace. Both public and private versions of categories can be stored under configuration control, but they must contain enough information to keep them distinct.

Developers of interdependent categories must ensure that changes to them are compatible before a new baseline can be created. If other categories do not depend on the modified categories, new versions of the modified categories can simply be created. Otherwise other affected categories must be updated to be consistent with the modifications before the baseline is complete. In simple tools, reconciliation would be manual (the developer would have to examine the consequences of modifications and make appropriate changes to his/her categories). A more advanced tool would support some form of automatic checking and/or update. This is more difficult and involves considerable involvement with programming language semantic analysis.

Adding new categories does not create problems for other categories, but adding a new category to the system updates the configuration of the system itself. This can be handled by treating the system configuration as a module with versions of its own that is a part of the baseline. Deleting a category from the system requires moving or deleting all the information from it first.

This is a high-level statement of the process and raises many issues. In particular, it can be difficult to merge arbitrary changes to a system into a single consistent picture, because changes to different categories often interact. Modularity is an attempt to allow creation of independent categories that can be easily reconciled without the need for manual intervention (which remains a possibility of last resort in any design process). Merging of independent changes is possible if we can separate the effects of the changes so they do not interfere.

A new baseline must specify particular versions of each of the categories (usually but not necessarily the latest version of each category). Creating a baseline is a statement that the various category versions in it are compatible and consistent. This is an assertion by the developers; there is no magic way to prove it. Syntactic and semantic checks can identify many kinds of inconsistencies, but they cannot identify all logical inconsistencies.

A Sample Scenario

Figure 1 shows a sample project at several stages. The diagram is highly schematic and is grossly simplified compared to a real project so you can see what is going on. Categories are drawn as tabbed boxes containing classes (in earlier OMT writings I used a dashed-line box

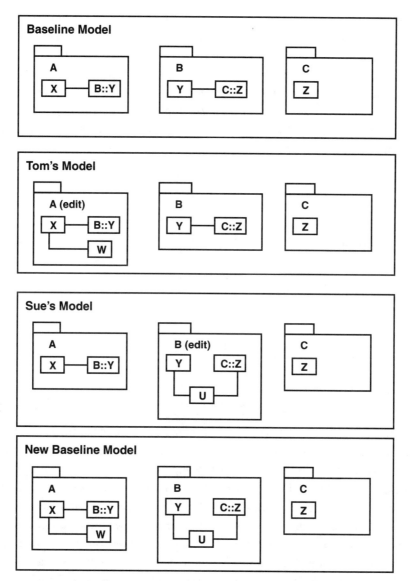

Figure 1. Sample project showing baselines and private workspaces

for a category). The notation **B::Y** within category A means that category A contains a reference to class Y that is defined within category B.

The initial baseline of the system is shown in the diagram. Tom checks out category A and adds a new class W. Sue checks out category B and adds a new class U between classes

Y and Z. Nobody modifies category C. Tom builds his system with the old version of B and tests his new code until it works. Then he puts a new version of category A back into the system configuration management. Sue continues working with the old version of category A until her code works, then she checks a new version of B back into the system configuration management. Categories A and B are independent so no reconciliation is needed when Sue checks her category back in. After both developers have updated their categories, the project administrator declares a new baseline using the two updated categories. The new baseline is shown at the bottom of the figure.

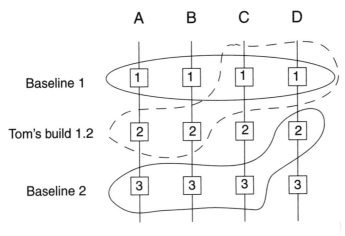

Figure 2. Two baselines and a private build

It is not necessary for updated versions to enter a new baseline immediately. Developers who are working together can exchange updated versions of categories without forcing everyone else to accept the changes immediately. Figure 2 shows two baselines as solid outlines. Baseline 1 includes version 1 of each category. Baseline 2 includes version 3 of categories A, B, and C and version 2 of category D. (Note that category version numbers are completely distinct from baseline version numbers.) During the second iteration, Tom accepted some of Sue's changes to category B after they had been stored as version 2 of B but before they had been incorporated into a new baseline. Sue had made some changes that Tom needs for his work. Tom made his own internal build 1.2 of the system (dotted outline) consisting of his new version 2 of A, Sue's updated version 2 of B, and the baseline versions of categories C and D. Everybody else continued to use the baseline version 1 of category A because Tom's work is incomplete. Eventually Tom updates his final changes as version 3 of category A. No one else ever uses version 2 of category A.

It is useful to keep both baseline versions and intermediate working versions of categories under configuration control. If a developer encounters a dead end and has to back off from a design approach, a set of intermediate versions can provide a clean place to restart the effort.

Metamodel of Projects

Figure 3 shows an OMT metamodel for the structure of a project-based model. A development design tool needs to implement the concept of projects, categories, and model elements. Projects are the top-level binders of information shared across a team and across development time. A project encapsulates one or more related applications that share models and code. A category is a user-defined unit of access control during the development of a project. Categories contain model elements, such as class definitions, class imports, associations, and code bodies. Every element must be owned by one category, although it can be referenced by other categories.

Each category is owned by one project. A project can also reference categories from other projects, but cannot modify them. I call these imported categories *library categories,* because they generally come from stable libraries, but even libraries change from time to time. Each modeling element (such as classes, associations, and generalizations) is owned by one category, but each one can be referenced by other categories as well. A developer must have checked out the "owner" category of an element in order to modify it. The categories in a project partition the contents of the project.

A project consists of a series of public and private baselines, each of which defines a complete build of an entire system at a moment in time. In the simple nonbranching case, a project is a linear series of baselines, each derived from the previous baseline.

Changes to categories are eventually stored as new versions. Additions of new elements pose no problems and can just be merged in. Implementation changes to classes or code bodies are invisible outside the category, so merging them is no problem. Specification changes to elements are visible elsewhere and must be propagated. Normally the developer will have to modify uses of an element (such as method calls) to make them consistent with specification changes. One special case is a name change, which should be supported by a tool. Name changes can be automatically propagated to client references if the references are clearly identified (straightforward within models, much more difficult inside code, which must be parsed within name scopes).

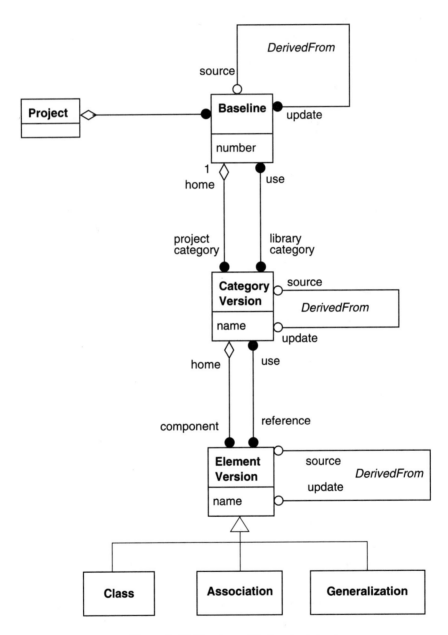

Figure 3. OMT metamodel of project structure

Choosing Categories

Categories have several connotations that should be observed in defining their boundaries:

A change to part of a category is likely to involve changing the rest of the category. A category represents an atomic unit of change to the model. There should be fewer dependencies across category boundaries than within a category.

A change to a category is less likely to involve changing another category. A category represents the smallest practical unit of change to the model. It is usually not necessary to place each class in a separate category, although this is possible.

It is often possible to merge changes from two or more separate categories by simply updating each category independently, if the public interfaces of the categories have not changed. Categories should be more or less independent with well-defined interfaces and dependencies.

Model elements in categories may use elements from other categories, inducing a client-supplier dependency between the categories. The dependency can be specified in terms of the public interface of the supplier. Changing the public interface of a supplier category requires the client categories to be updated to be consistent. A change to the implementation of a supplier category is encapsulated and invisible to other categories. Because most changes are to internal implementations, the amount of forced updates to a well-structured system is limited.

Two categories may be interdependent. This results from mutual client-supplier dependencies between the categories. Such cycles of dependent categories are most difficult to extend, because no single category can be modified separately.

Avoiding Conflicts

Different developers can make changes that are not independent. This can arise in two ways:

1. Different developers modify the same category; or

2. Different developers modify different categories, but the changes affect each other.

To prevent developers from accidentally making inconsistent changes to the same category, categories can be *locked*. Only one developer has permission to modify a locked category. A developer *checks out* a category by locking it and later *checks in* the modified category to return it to the mainline. Another developer can then check it out, modify it (consistent with the changes made by the first developer), and then check it back in. Locking serializes access to a category to prevent inconsistencies. Each category has a series of versions that might or might not be archived.

This process breaks down if two developers need to simultaneously modify the same category. In that case, the changes to the category have to be manually reconciled before the second developer creates an updated version of the category. There are several approaches:

- Subdivide the category so that the changes occur in different subcategories. If a category is large this should usually be the first approach.

- Forbid parallel changes to the same category. This is the normal intent of locking categories. This avoids the problem, but may introduce an unacceptable delay into the development process. Applying this approach rigidly is not practical.

- Allow branching of versions of a single category. The first developer gets the mainline version of the category, subsequent developers get branched versions that must be manually merged into the mainline version. For pragmatic reasons this possibility must usually be supported, although the goal should be to avoid it as much as possible.

Some developers have reported that rigid predefined categories may not be convenient for many kinds of development. It may be useful to allow developers to define *virtual categories* dynamically. Each dynamic category would contain a subset of model elements, but the dynamic categories could cut across the permanent logical categories. The dynamic categories would be used to control access to model elements on an ad hoc basis and would be abandoned when a given development task is complete. The same effect could be obtained by moving elements among categories but dynamic categories would be more convenient. (It is equivalent to making temporary changes to the category organization.)

Why Hasn't the Problem Been Seen?

Many tools support the concept of a shared repository in which all users see the latest work of all other users. Why hasn't the problem with this approach been reported yet? Well, it has been reported, but awareness of the problem depends on the phase of development and the size of the model.

During high-level analysis having everybody work out of a single shared repository that anyone can update concurrently may work acceptably for small systems. Because the model is under development and tentative in many respects, it is not critical for one developer to have a stable view of the whole system. Small inconsistencies in an analysis model do not have the same devastating consequences that small inconsistencies cause for compiled code.

This approach does not work so well for a large project. Perhaps a high-level analysis model can be created by a single small group for a small or medium project, but a large project requires work by separate teams and therefore multiple categories even during analysis. Building the design model for an entire project usually takes the effort of several developers on even a medium-size project. Unless there is some way to divide up the system they may interfere with each other. But until the model is built there are no elements to partition! The concept of category provides a high-level partitioning before the system is populated with model elements, so that different developers can work in separate regions. However, this lack of modularity would not be apparent unless a large project were modeled to full detail. It would not show up in a quick prototype. But many early OO developers have built small prototypes to get started.

During detailed design and implementation, the lack of private workspaces would be more apparent. When working with code, even a small change to an imported category can prevent a program from running or even compiling, so stability of the developer's view is more critical when programming. I suspect that most users of shared-repository systems have not reached (or used the tool for) the implementation stage for a large system, so the impact of these issues will not have been seen yet.

Modeling Concepts

O NE OF the advantages of writing a column is the opportunity it affords to devote more attention to certain topics than a textbook permits. This section contains a selection of articles covering various important modeling concepts in some detail.

The most important thing about an object is the fact that it exists and is different from all other objects; this quality is called *identity*. Failure to recognize and capture the separate identity of different objects is a frequent cause of modeling failure. *A National Identity Crisis* explores the meaning of identity with a real-world anecdote.

Objects in isolation aren't very useful. To build a system, the objects have to be connected to each other so they can share the job of forming an application. *Associations* are the glue that holds a model together. From the very beginning I have stressed the importance of associations as the right abstraction for modeling system connections. In *Horsing Around with Associations* we learn more about using associations by taking a trip to the race track.

One of the most common computing operations is selecting an object from a set of objects based on a unique index value. To make this possible, the association between a source object and its set of target objects must attach a unique selector value to each target object. This frequently occurring situation can be modeled as a *qualified association*, in which the *qualifier value* serves as the unique index value. If we look carefully, we discover that many kinds of names are really qualifier values rather than attributes of objects. *What's in a Name? A Qualified Answer* explores qualifiers as constructs that are important for both modeling and programming reasons.

When constructing an analysis model you should strive to capture everything important about a problem, but you should try to avoid redundancy in the model, because redundant models appear to have more degrees of freedom than they actually contain. Minimalist models are the cleanest and easiest to maintain. However, sometimes it is desirable to represent several alternative views within a single model. *Derived Information* shows how to identify and mark redundant information so that it can be included in a model without misleading the reader about its information content.

Good models are useful for small systems but they are essential for large systems. When modeling large systems, however, simply capturing the semantic properties of the system is not enough. The system model itself must be organized into coherent packages so that it can be understood, worked on in parallel, and stored. The modeling technique must provide constructs for organizing models and for building large model pieces out of smaller ones. The original OMT book was weak in describing model packaging and organization constructs, and providing system-building constructs was an important goal of my subsequent work. The articles *Building Boxes: Subsystems* and *Taking Things in Context: Using Composites to Build Models* describe two complementary ways of constructing hierarchical systems. The latter article on composites combines two original articles that I wrote over a period of a year.

A National Identity Crisis

October 1992

WHAT is an *object*? What does *object-oriented* mean? Peter Wegner made a commonly-accepted definition of an object-oriented language: objects + classes + inheritance[1]. But what is an object? There are many definitions of this intuitive concept, such as a conceptual entity that combines state and behavior into a single package. Objects have a number of characteristics, some quite fundamental and others no more than quibbles among followers of different OO sects. To me, however, the most fundamental, irreducible characteristic of objects (and the source from which everything else flows) is their *identity*.

According to a very-frequently-referenced paper, "identity is that property of an object that distinguishes each object from all others."[2] In other words, each object is inherently unique, independent of its attribute values, state, or relationships to other objects. Real-world objects all have this property. Two chairs in a matched set are still independent and distinct objects, even if they are all the same size, shape, and color. Two persons with the same name and birthdate are nevertheless unique individuals. Of course, at some level of detail the objects do differ; two chairs cannot be at the same location, and two persons with the same name born at the same moment will have different parents. However, in modeling things the distinguishing properties are often of secondary importance for a particular application, and it is more convenient to think of identity as an inherent characteristic that adheres to each object.

It is not always easy to establish identity in practice. In a previous column I described a problem in which one goal was to avoid sending duplicate mailings to any individual. It is difficult to eliminate all duplicates. How do we determine that a mailing is a duplicate? Personal names are inadequate; two persons can have the same name, and persons can write their names in various ways. An address is not sufficient; people move, and occasionally two persons with the same name live at the same address (and usually have a devil of a time sorting our their mail).

There is a real and frequent danger of confusing an object's identity with its attributes and thereby compromising the identity of an object. Unless an attribute is an intentionally-created identification number, there is a big risk in treating it as providing identity. None of the attributes of a person, such as name, address, or birthdate, by themselves constitute an unambiguous identifier of a person.

In the United States, the Social Security number has become a de facto universal identity code. Originally Social Security numbers were assigned only to workers in certain designated industries. As the amount of record keeping in American society grew enormously the difficulty of matching personal identity across different databases became apparent. The Social Security number was already a national identifier of fairly wide distribution and its use expanded gradually, first to cover all workers and eventually to cover all citizens for tax, banking, employment, and other purposes. Much to the dismay of civil libertarians, universal identity numbers, such as U.S. Social Security numbers, are used for many purposes precisely because they serve (by intent) as surrogates for personal identity.

One way of handling identity is to treat one object as a surrogate for another. A *surrogate* is an object that stands for another in one-to-one correspondence. For example, a computer system treats someone who knows the password for an account as a surrogate for the person authorized to use the account. This is a convenience, because the account owner can extend access by telling others the password to the account, but the identity is broken if someone guesses the password maliciously.

A common mistake is to mistakenly consider one objects as a surrogate for another when they don't have the same identity. This mistake occurs frequently in everyday systems. For example, a computer user ID or a credit card number are not really surrogates for persons, but for computer accounts and credit card accounts. Let me illustrate by an actual anecdote of mine.

Preferring Privileges

Recently I made a trip to Philadelphia during which I rented a car from National Car Rental. They have a promotion called "Privilege Preferred" for frequent travelers. Customers with Privilege Preferred accounts can check in more rapidly because their name, address, driver's license number, and car rental preferences are already present in an individual customer

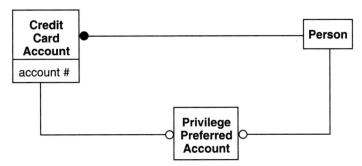

Figure 1. Flawed model

profile. Instead of giving the customer a special card with a rental-company-specific customer number, as with some other car rental agencies, National allows the customer to use an existing credit card, which must be preregistered in National's database. The idea is presumably to reduce the number of cards a customer must carry and to tie the car rental account to a card that a customer is likely to always carry.

The clerk took my VISA card and read it through the card reader. I peeked at the screen as my account information appeared on the screen. The home address looked right, but my work phone number and address looked wrong. I stared a little more (I had to read it upside down, of course) and realized that my wife's profile was on the machine. At that moment I realized that the credit card scheme for identifying rental car customers was fundamentally flawed. The system developers had made a fundamental modeling error: they had incorrectly used one object (the credit card) as a surrogate for another object (a customer) that did not stand in one-to-one correspondence (Figure 1). If two persons share a credit card then they can't both access distinct Privilege Preferred accounts using the credit card (Figure 2). This is not a fault of poor implementation, but a fundamental logical flaw built into the system concept itself.

How have they managed to live with a flawed system so long? The same way that we live with most systems, of course, because the problems are infrequent and not catastrophic. This problem will not occur unless a husband and wife both share a credit card, both travel, both have a National account, and insist that the transaction printout distinguish among them. Even if the wrong profile comes up, the customer can object and have it fixed. This does not mean that the design is correct, but simply that you can often live with an incorrect design using work-arounds.

Actually half the blame for this particular flaw lies with the credit card company. Although my wife and I have two physically distinct credit cards, they have the same number,

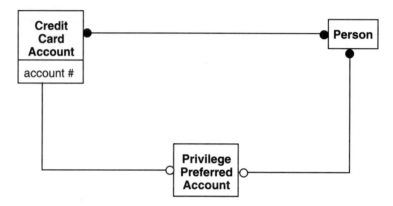

Figure 2. Correct model

so charges to each card cannot be distinguished. This is a loss of identity of the individual physical cards acting as surrogates for different persons sharing a single account. It would make plenty of sense for the credit cards to contain distinguishing information. Then each card would have identity. If one card were lost or stolen, then the other cards in the account would not have to be canceled. Also, charges to each card (and by implication, by each authorized user) could be separately listed.

In fact, I am told by an owner of the Discover card that the Discover card does have this property and customers receive bills listing charges by each user separately. All of the cards for one Discover account have the same account number, however, so the card must contain additional information in its magnetic stripe that is available only when a card is "swiped" through a card reader. So the full internal serial number on the Discover card provides identity to the individual user level. Because this information is not part of the serial number printed on the card, it would not be available to a manual transaction, however. It is also likely that the National system would not take advantage of the internal information, as I suspect that the Privilege Preferred account is tied to a numerical credit card number.

Why not simply use several different credit card numbers yet allow them to be part of a single account for billing purposes? Well, I suspect it is probably because banks just don't think that way (why should they go to trouble just for *your* convenience?), but maybe they also think it would be confusing to the customers (which it probably would be). Also, the whole analysis is much simpler and more obvious if you think in terms of object identity in the first place, so the implications of the policy may not have been obvious originally.

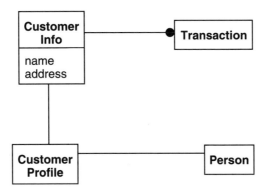

Figure 3. Bad model of transaction

Transactions are Objects Too

Unfortunately (for National) this is not the end of the story. After I noticed that the rental profile was my wife's and not mine, I asked the clerk to modify the information for the current transaction so I would have a receipt with my name on it. We quickly discovered, however, that a change to the information on the screen modified the entire permanent profile. This was Identity Violation #2, a failure to distinguish a particular transaction from the permanent profile. Each of these has distinct user information, such as name, address, and phone number. The purpose of the profile should be to initialize the user information for a new transaction, not to be identical with it.

To add insult to injury, when the clerk tried to cancel the changes she had made, she was forced to reenter the entire profile from the beginning, including information that was the same for me and my wife. This was Identity Violation #3, a failure to distinguish the transient information on the screen from the information associated with the transaction or the permanent profile. Figure 3 and Figure 4 show the incorrect and correct models.

This little episode was only a minor inconvenience, but it illustrates the need to keep straight the identity of different objects. Identity is the guide to finding objects and particularly the guide to untangling a set of related but distinct objects. Failure to keep the distinct objects separate results in the inability of the system to represent certain reasonable situations. In database modeling, such breakdowns appear as normalization failures.

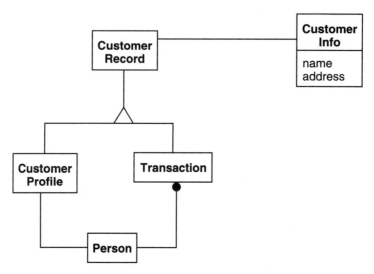

Figure 4. Correct model of transaction

Numbers are not Objects

In our book *Object-Oriented Modeling and Design*, we have consistently distinguished between objects and pure values. This is a distinction that many people do not make, particularly within programming languages, but I think it is sound. An object is something with identity, something that you can (conceptually) point to and say "that object" about, something that can be distinguished from other objects inherently. Under this viewpoint, even attributes and operations take a secondary position to identity in establishing the objectness of an object. You can attach properties to an object and remove them during the course of designing a system, without affecting the inherent existence of an object.

By this standard, a number is not an object, because it does not refer to any individual. All copies of a number are the same. They represent the elements of a value domain. You can't very well add properties to a number or delete them. A number has certain mathematical properties and that's that. It is an element of a type (an abstract data type, to be more precise), not an object. You can *use* a number, you can compute new numbers from old numbers, but you can't do anything *to* a number. You never actually *create* a new number;

they already exist conceptually within mathematical sets. By contrast, objects can be created and destroyed as individuals and can assume values as their states.

The most usual kinds of primitive values are numbers, text strings, and user-definable enumerated values, such as Color or SwitchSetting.

A value need not be atomic. Values can be structured from other values. For example, an address might consist of a street address and a city address, where the street address consists of a street number, street name, and an optional apartment number.

An object is an individual that has a value as its state. For example, a building is an object that has an address as value. Even if the address is changed or the building has no address at all, the building keeps its identity. On the other hand, it makes no sense to talk about changing the address itself; an address is simply a structured string of numbers and text.

The advantage of a value is that it can be exported from a system (in text, for example) and later reimported into a system or another system without loss of information. A value and its text representation can be put into one-to-one correspondence. An object, however, cannot be represented outside of a system without some kind of plain-text surrogate.

My remarks refer primarily to modeling and not to implementation. Yes, I know that everything in Smalltalk is an "object," numbers and other values included. That's fine, and the uniformity of reference makes life simpler than in a hybrid language such as C++, in which some things are objects and others are not. In a language, we are concerned a lot with representation, but in modeling we are concerned primarily with semantics and it is useful to acknowledge a big difference between things that *have* values (objects) from things that are *values*. In practice, it is difficult or impossible to distinguish an immutable object with a value from the value itself, but immutable objects are not very interesting anyway. It is the mutable objects, the ones subject to side effects, that make computing interesting and challenging.

Qualifiers

I have mentioned using an object as a surrogate for another, but frequently we want to use a value as a surrogate for an object, because values can be communicated freely and unambiguously. In fact, a Social Security number or a credit card number is an *identifier* for an object, that is, a globally unique surrogate value (Figure 5). However, as I mentioned in a previous column, few if any identifiers are truly unique in the whole world. Social Security numbers are unique within the United States, but other countries may have their own citizen identity numbers that overlap in value. Credit card numbers are unique for a given kind

Figure 5. Qualifier

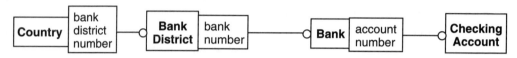

Figure 6. Chain of qualifiers

of card, but they are not likely to be unique across banks unless the banks have gotten together and divided up the set of numbers. (Actually they have done this to avoid getting each others' charges by mistake. But in any case it takes conscious action to make things unique.)

Generally each kind of identifier is unique within some predefined context. Automobile license numbers are unique with respect to a particular state or country. Bank account numbers are unique with respect to a particular bank. In the United States, each bank has a unique number with respect to its designated Federal Reserve regions, so that a combination of Federal Reserve Bank number (1-12), bank number, and account number uniquely defines a particular checking account, for example (Figure 6).

A value that is unique with respect to a particular context is a *qualifier* on a link between the context object and the object identified by the value. Within the context, the qualifier value is a surrogate for the target object. The identifier can be exported from and reimported into a system. It can be used for communication between systems. But keep in mind that a qualifier is not the same as its target object. If the linkage among objects can change, then a given value may identify different objects (or no object) over time. Only if a qualified association is immutable (and therefore somewhat uninteresting) do the qualifier and the target object share identity within the context.

Avoiding Identity Crises

In building a model, pay attention to the separate existence, that is, the identity of the various objects. In particular, be alert for two (or more) objects that are closely connected and are often, but not always, in one-to-one correspondence, such as the credit card and the rental car account. In building an initial model, first identify objects before worrying about identifier values. When an identifier value is needed, make it a qualifier and consider carefully the context that it qualifiers. If necessary, make up a class to define the context objects for identifiers.

To summarize, find the identity and the objects will follow.

References

1. Peter Wegner. Dimensions of object-based language design. In *ACM OOPSLA'87*.

2. Setrag N. Khoshafian and George P. Copeland. Object identity. In *ACM OOPSLA'86 Conference Proceedings*.

Horsing Around with Associations

February 1992

I HAVE been pushing the concept of associations in the object-oriented community for a long time. I believe that for modeling systems they are even more important than inheritance but have been neglected in the O-O programming community. I am not alone in stressing the importance of associations. Shlaer & Mellor and Coad & Yourdon have similar models of associations, and the concept of associations has been explored for a long time in the information-modeling community.

In this column I will illustrate some aspects of the use of associations by modeling a day at the racetrack. (Any confirmed railbirds must forgive any simplifications I make.) I will start with a simple model and gradually add details.

Let us start with the OMT class model in Figure 1, which shows the horses entered in races at a track. Each race is run at a single track; each track hosts many races. Each race contains many horses; each horse runs in many races (on different days, anyway). To review OMT notation: A box indicates a class, with its name in the top part and its attributes in the second part of the box. We omit operations for now; they would be shown in the third part. A line connecting two boxes indicates a binary association between the classes. In the original OMT notation, a black dot indicates a multiplicity of many; the absence of a black dot indicates one; an open dot indicates optional one. In the UML notation, the string "*" indicates a multiplicity of many, the string "1" indicates a multiplicity of exactly one, and the string "0..1" indicates a multiplicity of optional one. Multiplicity indicates how many instances of one class *may* be associated with any one instance of the other class.

An *association* is a pattern defined over a list of classes whose value is a set of *links*, in which a *link* is a list (*tuple*) containing one object from each corresponding class. Each link

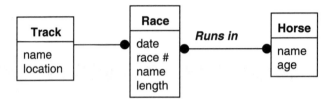

Figure 1. Class model of horse race

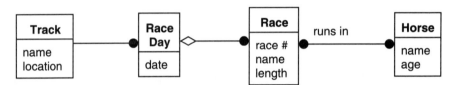

Figure 2. Modified class model

represents a semantic relationship among object instances. Each position within the list is called a *role*; roles are not interchangeable. In lieu of using position, each role can be given a *rolename* to distinguish it from the other roles in the association. The same class can appear more than once in the list and each occurrence must be distinguished by its position or rolename. The number of classes in the list is called the *arity* of the association. In modeling we most often use associations of arity 2, called *binary associations*, which have the useful property of defining paths among classes that can be mapped into access operations.

We now make some changes to the initial model. It is convenient to add a class **RaceDay** that groups together all the races at the track on a single day. Figure 2 shows the modified class model: Each race is part of a single race day, which contains all the races run at a single track on a given day. The diamond next to **RaceDay** shows that the association is an *aggregation*: a **RaceDay** is composed of **Race** objects; they are inherently part of it. We have removed attribute **date** from **Race** because it is found in the **RaceDay** object uniquely determined by the many-to-one association from **Race** to **RaceDay**.

Qualifiers

Let's take a closer look at **Race**. Its attributes include the race number and the name of the race (if any), such as "Travers." We can make a couple of improvements. First, there can be

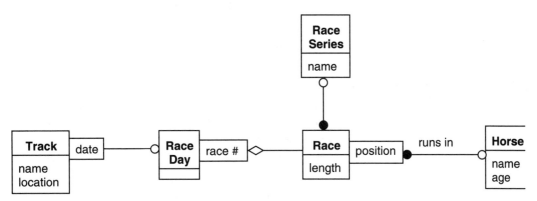

Figure 3. Qualified associations

only one first or fifth race at a given track on a given day. The race number serves to select a unique race out of all the races run at a track on a given day. An attribute that picks a unique object from an association is called a *qualifier;* it is drawn as a small box on the end of the association near the class that it qualifies. Race day plus race number selects a unique race, as shown by the *qualified association* in Figure 3. The qualifier reduces the multiplicity of the association from one-to-many down to one-to-one. A qualifier is an attribute of the association itself (a *link attribute*) that is unique with respect to an instance of a given class, in this case RaceDay. (Nonunique qualifiers can be defined but they are less useful.) We do the same thing with the Track-RaceDay association: date is a qualifier of Track that selects a unique RaceDay. (Normally, anyway. The Boston Red Sox used to pull the trick of charging two separate admissions for a doubleheader with the Yankees on Patriot's Day, and race-tracks have done stranger things, so you have to be careful what assumptions you make.)

We also create a class called **RaceSeries** to group together all the (usually annual) races with names, such as the Travers or the Kentucky Derby. This gives us a place to attach information about the race series as a whole by giving it identity. For example, we may want to know the founder of a race series. This class may be unnecessary, however, if we have no use for it in an application, in which case it might well be omitted. In any case, we show a many-to-optional-one association between **Race** and **RaceSeries**, because most races are not part of a series and are unnamed.

Note that in ordinary English the word "race" could mean either an individual event on a particular day or a named race series, such as the Travers. In building models, you have to watch out for this kind of name overloading and make up new names if necessary to distinguish all the uses. The phrase "race series" is not very pretty but at least it gets the right idea across. Coming up with good names can be one of the most difficult arts required in build-ing models.

We have now removed many of the attributes from **Race** and moved them into unique associated objects. The _horizon_ is all of the objects that can be uniquely reached from a given object by following association roles of multiplicity one or zero-one. The attributes of ob-jects within the horizon are unique and may be regarded as (possibly optional) pseudoat-tributes of the object itself. For example, **date** can be obtained from **Race** by following the associations to **RaceDay** and then to **Track**. During modeling, you may navigate freely through the association network to obtain attribute values. It is sometimes arbitrary where some of the attributes go.

We have also added the qualifier **post position** to qualify the horses in a particular race, because only one horse may start in a given gate. In the reverse direction, the multiplicity is many: a given horse may start in many different (race, post position) pairs. Note that **finish position** as a qualifier would not guarantee a unique selection, because two horses some-times finish in a dead heat.

Recursion

Figure 4 shows some additional information about a horse. Each horse has one trainer and one main owner (who could be a syndicate—an owner is not necessarily a person). These are many-to-one associations. We have also added associations to show the sire and dam (father and mother) of a horse. In doing so, we have specialized **Horse** into 3 subclasses: **Stallion** (full male), **Gelding** (neutered male), and **Mare** (female—nobody neuters female horses). The subclasses inherit the attributes of **Horse**, such as **name** and **age**. They also in-herit the associations of **Horse**, such as **owner** and **trainer**. Associations are inherited by subclasses just as attributes are. Note that the subclasses also inherit the two parentage as-sociations, because a stallion, gelding, or mare _is_ a horse. A stallion has a sire and a dam. The two parentage associations are prototypical recursive associations: an abstract super-class (**Horse**) is specialized by two or more subclasses, one (or more) of which (**Mare**) has a one-to-many association with its superclass (**Horse**). This same kind of pattern occurs with parts hierarchies. Note that the recursion in Figure 4 never terminates. As a practical matter, at least one horse would have to be represented without its parents.

A binary association can be viewed as an operator on an object that returns a set of re-lated objects. We use the syntax _x.r_ to indicate the object or set of objects obtained by start-ing with object _x_ and traversing across the association to rolename _r_. For example, Aly-

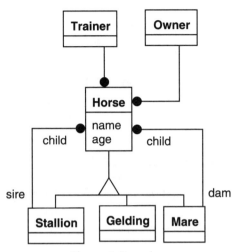

Figure 4. Recursion

dar.*child* is the set of children of Alydar and Alydar.*dam.sire* is his maternal grandfather. This convention requires that no two associations leaving a given class (including any inherited associations) have a common destination rolename. The incident rolenames can be the same; both the **sire** and **dam** associations lead to **Horse** through rolename **child**. You can string together chains of rolenames to indicate a path through the object diagram. For example, Alydar.*child.race* would indicate all the races by children of Alydar. This operational syntax is convenient for writing operations for the functional model as well as conditions for the dynamic model.

We could define the association **Horse-parentOf-Horse** as the union of the associations **Stallion-sireOf-Horse** and **Mare-damOf-Horse**. The links of the new association are the union of the links in the two original associations. This new association is a *derived association*, that is, one that is defined in terms of other values. A derived association does not add any new information to the model so it should be clearly distinguished from the *base associations*, whose values must be determined by enumeration of links. Derived associations can be useful in writing functions compactly and also in understanding a model. Figure 5 shows the new derived association **Parentage** with a slash before its name to suggest that it is less "real" than the base associations. The figure shows a possible notational convention to connect the derived union "superassociation" to its component "subassociations."

Incidentally, naming associations can be a bit awkward, because you have to indicate in which direction to read the name. You can place a direction arrow on the name, but I have

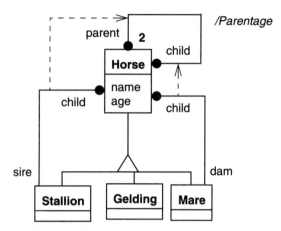

Figure 5. Derived association

tended to use rolenames rather than giving a name to the association itself. You can even omit names entirely when there is a unique association between two classes, although you should clarify the meaning of the association by a paragraph in the data dictionary (as you should for any entity, including classes, attributes, and operations).

Associations as Classes

There is a fine line between a class and an association. Both describe patterns of data and behavior. Both have instances, objects and links respectively. Can they be made even more similar?

It is possible to attach attribute values to an association. Each link in the association has a distinct instance value. Such an attribute is called a *link attribute*. Link attributes are useful for representing information that is part of an association and not of any single class in it. For example, the finish position of a horse in a race is not an attribute of either the horse or the race alone; it is an attribute of the association between them. The link attribute **finish** and **weight** are shown in Figure 6 on the **Race-Horse** association. A link attribute is listed within a degenerate class box attached to the association line.

Qualification is a special case of a link attribute that is unique within the links of a given association attached to a single object. We have already seen it several times. We use the operator syntax *x.r[q]* to indicate the related object on association *r* selected by qualifier *q*. For

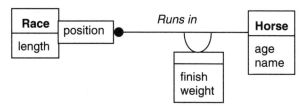

Figure 6. Link attributes

example, Travers.*entrant[2]* indicates the horse in post position 2 in the Travers. The expression Travers.*weight[2]* indicates the weight assigned to the entrant in post position 2.

(Actually we allow qualification to return a set of values, in which case it is merely a way to group links on some index value. In that case, the multiplicity of the qualified association remains *many*. I have discussed qualifiers as if they always select unique values because that is their main use.)

It is possible to go even further and make an association into a class. This is an example of *reification*, the making of an abstract concept into a concrete object (from the Latin *res* for thing). We call such a class an *association class*. Figure 7 shows such a class, *Entry*, for the entry of a horse in a race. Note that a link attribute is an attribute in an association class. In addition to the attributes listed in the class box, each link has a pair of implicit object references to the classes in the association.

You can define associations between association classes and other classes or association classes. These are second-order associations. For example, we need to represent the jockey riding a horse in a race. The jockey is not associated with either the race or the horse alone, but with both of them together, that is, with the link between them. Figure 7 shows this association between class **Jockey** and the link class **Entry.**

Another way to represent this relationship would be to use a ternary association among **Race, Horse,** and **Jockey** (Figure 8). Ternary and higher degree associations are drawn as diamonds with a line to each participating class. Using a ternary association is less precise than using a binary association between a class and an association class, however, because the concept of multiplicity is not meaningful for an association of more than two objects. Taken in pairs, we have three many-to-many associations (Figure 9), but the situation is not symmetric. Given a (race, horse) pair, there is a unique jockey, and (race, jockey) corresponds to a unique horse, but the same (horse, jockey) pair may run in many races. The correct way to characterize multiplicity for n-ary associations is to specify the *candidate keys* of the association. A *candidate key* is a minimal set of roles that selects a unique link. For the

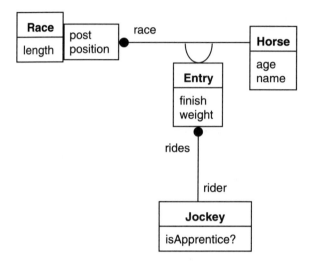

Figure 7. Association class

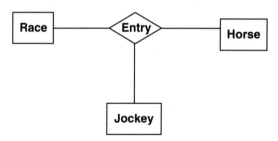

Figure 8. Ternary association

situation in Figure 8, the candidate keys are (race, horse) and (race, jockey), because specifying either of these pairs uniquely determines the third value in the association. Specifying (horse, jockey) does not uniquely determine the race, so it is not a candidate key.

Generally it is better to use binary associations and association classes as shown in Figure 7 rather than ternary associations because binary associations permit the use of traversal operation notation and also new relationships can be added to the model without modifying existing associations.

You can even define operations on link classes. These would manipulate the link attributes. For example, *computeFee* might be an operation on an *Entry* link that computes the jockey's fee.

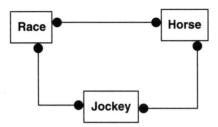

Figure 9. A ternary is not three binaries

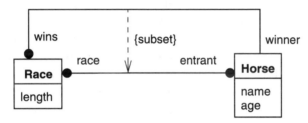

Figure 10. Subset constraint

Constraints

Suppose we want to keep track of the winners of each race. This is another kind of derived association—it is just the subset of the links in the **Horse runs in Race** association for which the **finish** position is first. **Horse wins Race** is a one-to-many association because each race has a single winner but each horse can win many races. (Actually in practice there could be ties but we will ignore that messy possibility for now.) If we did not store the finish position, then this association would supply new information and would not be derived, but it would not be entirely free either, because the winner of the race must run in the race. The links of the **wins** association are constrained to be a subset of the links in the **runs in** association. Figure 10 shows the constraint as a dotted line between the associations: the line labeled **subset** indicates that the **wins** association is a subset of the **runs in** association. More complex constraints can be expressed in natural language.

Subassociations

I will finish modeling with a complicated example (Figure 11). There are several different kinds of horse races that have different kinds of entrance requirements. Kinds of races are sweepstakes, handicaps, allowance races, and claiming races. These can all be subclasses of **Race** with appropriate attributes (which I have not all listed). I want to focus on claiming races. Each claiming race has a specified claiming price, such as $5000. After a horse is entered in a race and before the race is run, any registered owner can put in a bid, called a claim, to buy the horse at the conclusion of the race. The original owner gets the winnings (if any) of the horse in the race and the claimer gets the horse afterwards in exchange for the claiming price.

How should we model a claim? Certainly it should be an association between an owner and something, but what? Putting the association on **Horse** misses the point that a possible claim is part of running in a claiming race. It is better to make **Claim** an association between **Owner** and the link class **Entry**. But this overstates the case: claims may only be made during claiming races, not during other races. We should define an association class **Claiming Entry** between **Horse** and **Claiming Race** and attach **Claim** to it. But this is a redundancy, because **Claiming Entry** is just a special case of **Entry**. The correct way to show special cases is to use generalization: **Claiming Entry** must be a subclass of **Entry**, as shown in Figure 11. **Claiming Entry** inherits the attributes of **Entry**, as well as its association to **Jockey**, and it adds the association **Claim** to class **Owner.**

This notation works but it is pretty ugly.

Implementation

Keep in mind that an association is a logical modeling construct that does not imply any particular implementation. (On the other hand, modeling object connections by object attributes does restrict the implementation.) During analysis, you should avoid making unnecessary implementation decisions.

Use of associations in a model does *not* imply that you have to implement them as association objects, although you could do so in a programming language and probably would do so in a database. Normally programmers in C++ or Smalltalk would use pointers within the associated classes. You can automate the generation of the pointers and access methods to read and write them. In my Object Modeling Tool, I provided the ability to select among various optimizations so that no efficiency is lost even though the design is ex-

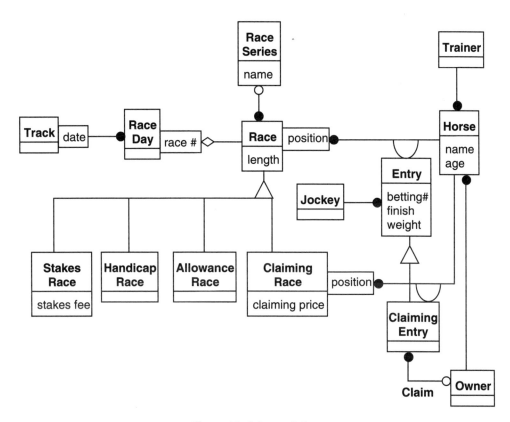

Figure 11. Subassociations

pressed entirely using associations. I discuss implementation techniques at greater depth elsewhere.

One point deserves mention. Associations represent a limited breakdown in encapsulation of classes. During modeling this is not a fault because the information in an association is truly shared among several classes. During implementation, update methods need access to both classes in an association, however. In C++, the *friend* construct is useful to permit the kind of limited breakdown of class encapsulation needed to implement associations cleanly.

Use associations rather than pointers in modeling a system. They are intuitive, logical constructs that make minimal assumptions about implementation yet can be mechanically converted into as efficient an implementation as you choose.

What's in a Name?

A Qualified Answer

July 1993

Does an Object Own its Name?

What is a name? Most people might say that it is an attribute of an object of type *String*. This seems to be true of persons' names. A name is an inherent property of a person. Each person has one name (in some cases, such as entertainers, maybe more than one) but many persons can share the same name. Personal names do not have to be unique.

Is a name always an attribute of an object? Consider a Unix file. In a Unix file system, a file may have more than one name in more than one directory. Which name is the true name of the file? All of them! So how can we model the situation? The right approach is to use a *qualified association* (Figure 1). The file name is a *qualifier* of the directory on the **Contains** association. The interpretation is: directory plus file name yields a unique file; a file corresponds to many possible (directory, file name) pairs.

A qualifier is an attribute value of an association with a special property: an object from one class (the *source class*) plus a qualifier value determine a unique object from the other class (the *target class*). In other words, a qualifier is a value that is unique within a context, namely, the set of attribute values associated with a given source object. It is not an attribute

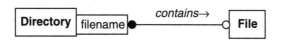

Figure 1. Filename as a qualifier of directory

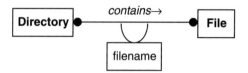

Figure 2. Filename as link attribute

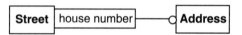

Figure 3. House number as qualifier of street

of either object. Is the file name an attribute of the directory? Hardly. Then is it an attribute of a file? No, because a file need not have a single unique name. It is a link attribute of the association between a directory and a file; it represents the name of the file within the directory (Figure 2). However, a qualified association is more precise than a link attribute, because the qualifier shows that the attribute is unique with respect to the source class. Also, there can be only one link attribute for a given pair of objects, but there can be more than one qualifier value for a pair of objects, provided the qualifier value itself is unique for the source object (i.e., a file could have more than one name even within the same directory).

Qualifiers are very useful and common modeling constructs. In some of our models over half of the associations are qualified. Qualifiers add precision to modeling and permit a more efficient implementation.

Can Attributes Be Unique?

In modeling objects some people pay a lot of attention to whether an attribute value is unique among all objects. I think this usually indicates a restricted viewpoint based on the limitations of the current problem. Values are seldom if ever unique in the entire universe. Most values are unique within some limited context. For example, a house number identifies an address with respect to a particular street. In other words, the house number is a qualifier of the street on the street-address association (Figure 3).

What about an employee ID number? Wouldn't this be unique within a payroll program? Perhaps, but would it remain unique under a change of circumstances, the acquisition of a new subsidiary, for example? It is better to think of an employee ID number as a qualifier on the employer-employee association: company plus employee ID gives a unique

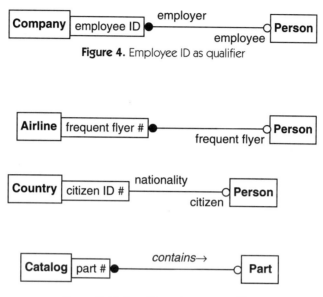

Figure 4. Employee ID as qualifier

Figure 5. Various ID numbers as qualifiers

person as employee. A person might have more than one job and therefore more than one employee ID number with more than one company (Figure 4). Even if the payroll program only involves a single company, include the company in the model as context.

Don't build assumptions about your current problem into your model. State the context of the problem as well as possible. The best way to do this is often to introduce an object to represent the context (such as the current company whose payroll is being run) and to make the "unique" attributes (such as employee ID) be qualifiers of it.

Use a qualifier when the following conditions are satisfied: there is an attribute that applies to an association rather than either of the classes involved; there may be many links from the source class to the target class; and the attribute value is unique within the set of links associated with each source class.

ID numbers and other forms of code numbers are almost always qualifiers. Don't think of them as attributes of objects, instead try to find the context object that they qualify (Figure 5). For example, think of a driver's license number as qualifying the state on a state-is-sues-driver's license association. Similar qualifiers include Social Security number (qualifies country as citizen ID number), part number (qualifies parts catalog or manufacturer), engine number (qualifies engine model), or frequent-flyer number (qualifies airline to identify person).

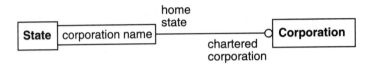

Figure 6. Corporation names are unique in their home state

Figure 7. ISBN number as qualifier of a singleton class

Names as Qualifiers

Are names qualifiers? Some are and some aren't. If the name is unique in some context, then it is a qualifier. The name of a corporation is unique by law within the state where it is chartered. The name of the corporation is its only legal identifier; it qualifies the state in the *state-charters-corporation* association (Figure 6). Similarly, one may regard the name of a state or province as a qualifier within its country.

On the other hand, names of persons are not unique. Names of books cannot be copyrighted, and they need not be unique either (Figure 7). The book name is not a qualifier; it is a nonunique attribute of class **Book**. The ISBN number of a book uniquely identifies it. But what does an ISBN number qualify? There is only one ISBN system. Nevertheless it is a good idea to make up a class to hold it, say **BookIdentificationSystem**, and let ISBN number qualify its only instance. This class is a *singleton class,* that is, a class with only a single instance (shown by the little number in the right-hand corner). Singleton classes define the global context of a model.

Aggregation Chains

Frequently an object can be decomposed into parts using several layers of aggregation. The name of a university department is a qualifier of the university (Figure 8). The name of a company division is a qualifier on the company. Any time the purpose of a name is to uniquely identify some object within a context, then the name is a qualifier.

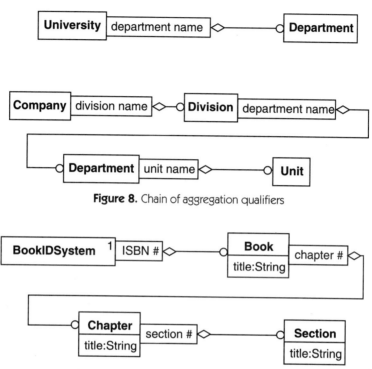

Figure 8. Chain of aggregation qualifiers

Figure 9. Chain of qualifiers to find a book section

Books contain chapters, which contain sections (Figure 9). Each of the aggregations can be qualified, using ISBN number, chapter number, and section number. Starting from the singleton class **BookIdentificationSystem**, the sequence of ISBN number, chapter number, and section number describe a particular section in a particular book. This sequence is a *path name* that describes a way to walk a path in the object model, starting at some initial object, possibly a singleton object. In a pure relational database, the entire path name would have to be propagated into the table for the bottom-level element, such as **Section** (Figure 10). This inefficient process is avoided in an object-oriented model. In an object model, an object has inherent identity, regardless of its attribute values, unlike a row in a relational database. (You can do the same thing in a database by assigning IDs to rows of tables, but that violates the pure relational principle that all tables should contain only real-world values.)

Recursion results in a second kind of aggregation chain. A directory contains many nodes, where a node is either a directory or a file (Figure 11). In other words, directories can contain other directories recursively, eventually ending in simple files. The chain of filena-

Section

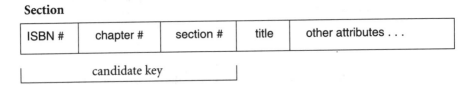

ISBN #	chapter #	section #	title	other attributes . . .

candidate key

Figure 10. Pure relational database table for Section

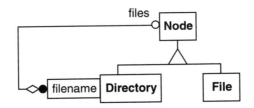

Figure 11. Recursive definition of File with qualifiers for pathname

mes encountered on the path from the root directory to a file is the *pathname* of the file; it is a sequence of qualifiers in the recursive structure. Qualifiers are used for navigation in an object model.

Navigation

The most important reason to use qualifiers is to facilitate navigation through the object model. Many associations in an object model are one-to-many. It is no problem to navigate in the *one* direction, but the introduction of qualifiers makes it possible to navigate in the *many* direction and still obtain a single value. A qualifier reduces the unqualified *many* multiplicity to a qualified *one* multiplicity by selecting a single object out of a set.

Qualifiers generally come from the problem domain and are usually meaningful in the user interface. Qualifiers generally represent pure values, such as integers or strings, and so are directly mappable to an external representation. Object identity, on the other hand, is not externally representable and must be mapped onto some arbitrary coding, such as arti-

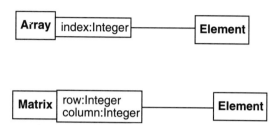

Figure 12. Array and matrix as qualified associations

ficial identifiers or code numbers of some kind. Qualifier chains provide an alternate way to identify objects suitable for external representation.

Navigation Syntax

It is convenient to have a pseudocode language for expressing navigation in an object diagram. We let a dot (.) represent navigation across an association or an attribute. We place an expression in square brackets after the association rolename (**.rolename[expression]**) to represent selection by a qualifier value. For example, a file would be **directory.files[filename]** (Figure 11) and an address would be *c*ountry.states[statename].cities[cityname].streets[streetname].addresses[house-number]** (Figure 19).

Arrays

An array is a qualified association in which the qualifier is an ordered enumerable type. The array index is a qualifier: the array plus the index gives a unique element of the array (Figure 12). In a two-dimensional matrix the qualifier is simply a structured value with two integer values. In general, it is not necessary to model an array as an object in a model; instead use a qualified association between the owner of the array and the elements of the array.

Avoid including data structure objects in your models; instead model the relationships between objects directly using various kinds of associations (Figure 13). For example, a chessboard qualified by rank and file (both integers from 1 to 8) yields a square on the

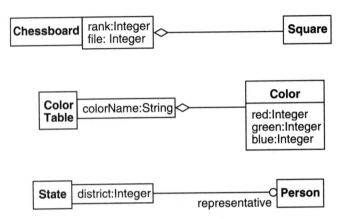

Figure 13. Some qualified associations instead of explicit arrays

board. There is no need to introduce explicit array or matrix objects; the qualified association contains them implicitly.

Tables can be indexed by enumerated constants as well as by integers. A color table for a graphics system is a qualified association between a workstation and a triplet of intensities, one each for red, green, and blue. The qualifier is the color name (such as pink, turquoise, or sea shell). The color names could be drawn from a predefined enumerated set, or they could be represented by strings with no limitation.

Similarly, the congressional representatives for a state are numbered, but there is no need to introduce an explicit array. Simply use the district number as a qualifier.

Qualifiers with Multiplicity Many

I said before that qualifier values must be unique within the links from a given source object. This was a lie to get the main idea across. Although the most important use of qualifiers is to reduce the multiplicity of an association from *many* to *one*, they have a meaning even when the multiplicity is *many*. A qualifier with multiplicity *many* selects a set of target objects associated with a given source object. In effect, qualifying a given source object partitions the set of target objects into subsets each sharing a single qualifier value. For example, consider the association between an organization and its officeholders as qualified by the name of the office (Figure 14). If the office is "President" then there is usually only a single

Figure 14. Officeholders in an organization

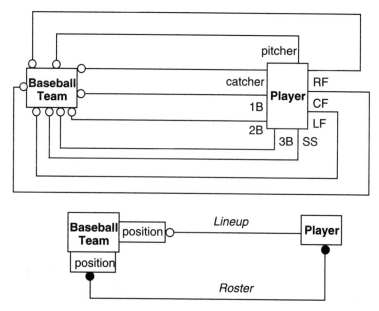

Position = {pitcher, catcher, 1B, 2B, 3B, SS, LF, CF, RF}

Figure 15. Baseball team lineup as individual associations and qualified association

officeholder. But if the office is "Vice President" there may be several, and for "Trustee" there are always several.

Finite types

Qualifiers of finite types are interchangeable with multiple explicit associations. In the top of Figure 15 we see a baseball team represented as a set of nine individual associations, one

SalesRole = {buyer, seller, broker, lender, ...}

Figure 16. Transactions and roles

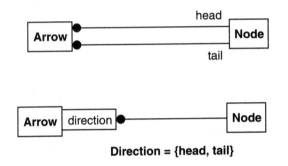

Direction = {head, tail}

Figure 17. Two views of a graph

for each position. By inventing an enumerated type called **Position** we can replace the nine individual associations with a single qualified association **Lineup** in the bottom diagram. This qualified association is optional-to-one, because each position must be filled by exactly one player, whereas a given player may or may not be playing in a certain game. At the same time, we can add another association, **Roster,** that indicates which players can play which positions, a many-to-many qualified association.

Figure 16 shows a commercial transaction, such as a real estate sale. Again we replace individual associations by a qualified association whose qualifier indicates the role of the participant in the transaction. In this case, the multiplicity is optional-to-optional, as certain roles (such as broker or lender) might be absent in any given transaction.

Figure 17 shows two views of a directed graph. The top view assigns two roles to each arrow, **head** and **tail** classes on individual associations. The bottom view introduces an enumerated type **Direction** to represent the two ends of the arrow. As with the other examples of finite sets as qualifiers, the qualified form is more compact and permits a more uniform implementation as well.

Notation Syntax

At this point I will summarize the full syntax for qualifiers. A qualifier is drawn as a small box at the point where an association line meets the source class. Inside the box are the name and optionally the type of the qualifier. It is possible to have multiple attributes on a single qualifier; simply list all of them inside the box. The full qualifier is the Cartesian product of all the attribute values.

The multiplicity of the target class indicates the number of target values for a given (source class, qualifier) value pair. In most cases, this is one or optional one, because the purpose of the qualifier is usually to reduce the multiplicity from *many* to *one*. Note that a qualified association without the qualifier is always *many*, as the association can take on many different qualifier values. If the target multiplicity is *many*, then each qualifier value selects a set of target values rather than a single value.

The multiplicity of the source end of the association indicates how many (*source class, qualifier*) pairs are associated with a given target object. Multiplicities of either one or many are both common.

To be completely precise we should distinguish between a multiplicity of one and a multiplicity of zero-one for the target class. A multiplicity of exactly one indicates that a link exists for every possible value of the qualifier for each source object. This makes sense only if the qualifier type is a finite set. The baseball lineup shown in Figure 15 is a good example in which every position must be filled by exactly one player. The transaction in Figure 16 is an example in which every role need not be filled. For any infinite set, such as a string type, the qualified association would always be partial, so the multiplicity should be optional one.

Indexes

During analysis use qualifiers to indicate values that are unique in some context. During design you can also use them to *index* attributes for faster access. An index is a qualified association in which the qualifier is an attribute of the target class. A *unique index* has multiplicity one and might well already be represented by a qualified association. More generally an index is a one-to-many qualified association: the context object plus the index value gives many target objects. The purpose of an index is not to reduce the multiplicity of the association to one, but merely to partition the set of associated values by the index value. Adding an index to a model is an example of designing by gradual transformation. A transformation is a single incremental change that does not change the semantics of a model but that

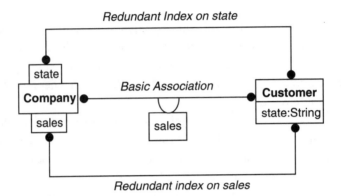

Figure 18. Index of customers by state

permits more efficient access to it. An index is a redundant association that permits a more efficient way of finding objects containing the index value.

For example, consider a company with customers in many states. An index by state allows direct access to the customers of each state, but the index does not add any information to the model (Figure 18). The set of customers in a state could be obtained by scanning the entire set of customers of the company and selecting those in the given state. An index can also be constructed on a link attribute of the association. The example shows an index on the sales amount for a company-customer pair. This index would best be implemented by sorting the qualifier values numerically.

Are Names Really Qualifiers?

I have said that names usually qualify something, for example, the name of a city qualifies the state or country it is located in (Figure 19). I confess that I am less comfortable with this example than the filename that is unique within its directory, because a filename is created with the intention that it distinguish files, while the name of a city or other geographical feature was usually invented on a local basis. Probably we should consider these names to be proper attributes of their entities. After all, I know of several West Mountains in New York State, and their are at least two Frankfurts in Germany, distinguished by the rivers they are on (Frankfurt am Main and Frankfurt an der Oder).

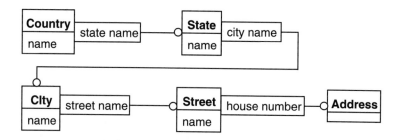

Figure 19. Names turned into qualifiers

Most natural names may arise as attributes of their objects, whereas many invented names, such as filenames, paint colors ("Dusty Road" and "Anenome Blue"), and college building names, are intended to be unique within their context. Nevertheless it is often useful to find qualifiers even where they were not intended because sequences of qualifiers are so useful for representing identity. Even if the names in Figure 19 were not originally unique, usage has made them unique so that they can be used for addressing letters. So even in those cases where we might question whether a name really goes with the object or the association, we may nevertheless be able to use the name as a qualifier for design and access purposes.

Implementation

Qualified associations are easy to implement. In fact, one reason for including them is to permit a more efficient implementation than would otherwise be possible. Typically a qualified association can be represented as a lookup table (a Smalltalk **Dictionary** class) in the context object. The selector values in the lookup table are the qualifiers, and the target values are the objects in the other class. If a lookup table is implemented using hashing, then access times are constant on average.

If the qualifier values must be accessed in order, then the qualifiers can be arranged into a sorted array or a B-tree. In this case, access time will be proportional to $log N$, where N is the number of qualifier values.

If the qualifiers are drawn from a compact finite set, then the qualifier values can be mapped into an integer range and the association can be efficiently implemented as an array. This approach is more attractive if the association is mostly full rather than being sparsely populated and is ideal for fully populated finite sets (such as the baseball team lineup).

Use of Qualifiers

We have found that qualifiers are one of the most useful and most common modeling constructs. They express greater precision in modeling, permit navigation and propagation of object identity, and indicate the opportunity for a more efficient implementation. At present, they are unique to the OMT notation, but we would encourage other methodologists to adopt them, as the gain in precision and expressiveness is substantial in many practical situations.

Derived Information

March 1992

WHEN building an object model you should separate its contents into two parts: fundamental *base* information that must be explicitly enumerated and *derived* information that can be computed from the base information. Base information is information whose form is specified but whose instances must be explicitly enumerated or populated. Derived information is information that can be computed from other information according to some fixed rule. For example, the derived attribute *area* of a rectangle is the product of its base attributes *width* and *height*.

This does not mean that derived information is unimportant in designing a system; the main job of the system builder is to find meaningful ways to organize complex information. However, in building models you should separate base information from derived information. You can change derived information freely without changing the information content of a model. For the same reason, you should avoid any redundancy in the base information. Usually the exact choice of base attributes is arbitrary but their dimensionality is determined by the problem domain. The base model should define a minimal spanning set of the information in a system.

For example, *age* is a derived value obtained by subtracting base value *birth date* from the environment variable *current date*. To treat birth date and age as independent would be misleading, because they only contain one independent value between them. Birth date is a better choice as a base value because it does not change, whereas age does change. Similarly, *grandparent* is a derived association obtained by composing the *parent* association with itself. The *parent* association can be defined directly in real-world terms, whereas the *grandparent* association must be defined indirectly.

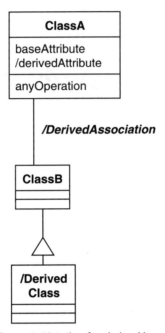

Figure 1. Notation for derived items

Derived entities are specified by rules used to compute them from base entities (or other derived entities, provided there are no circular definitions). Mathematical formulas are useful for geometry and other complicated situations, but you don't always have to be highly formal as long as the rule is expressed clearly in natural language.

We propose a simple pictorial notation to indicate derived entities of various kinds, including attributes, associations, and classes: Draw a small slash in front of the name of the derived entity (Figure 1). Note that there are no derived operations, because operations are invariant anyway.

Derived Attributes

When building a model you often have more attributes than are required to represent the base information; you must arbitrarily choose some subset of values for the base model. For example, a 2-dimensional point can be characterized by its Cartesian (x,y) values or by its polar $(r,angle)$ values (Figure 2). Either will do, but not both. The remaining values may be

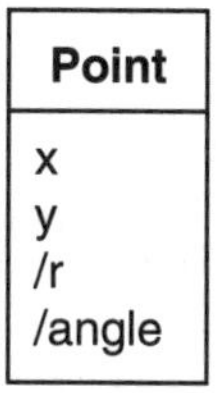

Point

x
y
/r
/angle

Figure 2. Derived attributes

considered derived values. It is important to recognize the number of degrees of freedom within an object and choose the correct number of base attributes accordingly. Confusion occurs because often it doesn't matter which subset of the values you pick. But watch out for singularities for certain combinations of attributes: Representing a point by its (*x,angle*) values fails when *x=0*

You can think of base attributes as specifying the internal description of an object and derived attributes as specifying the external description. Externally *x, y, r,* and *angle* all are perfectly valid attributes of a point. Internally, however, only two coordinates can be set independently. Either (*x,y*) or (*r,angle*) can be called base attributes; it doesn't matter which, because the other two attributes can be derived from them. In a program, all external access to attributes (base or derived) would pass through access methods, so the distinction between base and derived attributes is not externally visible.

Derived attributes are usually straightforward enough and can be analyzed using the concept of degrees of freedom. For example, a rectangle has 5 degrees of freedom; base attributes might be a corner point (2 coordinates), width, length, and the angle between the "length" side and the axis. Another representation would be two points on one side and the rectangle height, understood to be perpendicular to the left of the baseline defined by the two points. Choosing two opposite corner points and another value would also work, but would make for awkward geometrical calculations and is best avoided.

During analysis don't worry too much about *which* attributes you choose for base attributes, but do choose them to establish the degrees of freedom in the problem. During design, you will want to select the base attributes that are most convenient for computation. Within a program, all access to attributes (base or derived) should be encapsulated within access methods so that their representation is hidden.

Derived attributes can also be obtained by traversing associations to the attributes of related objects. The *horizon* is the boundary of objects uniquely determined by associations from a given object. Any attribute of an object within the horizon is uniquely determined

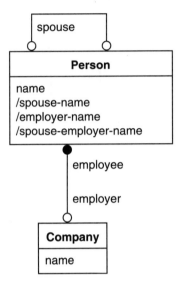

Figure 3. Derived attributes on the horizon

and can be regarded as a derived attribute of the original object. For example, the name of a person's spouse is a derived attribute of Person (Figure 3). Because a person may be unmarried, this derived attribute may have a null value. You can traverse a chain of something-to-one associations to obtain a derived value, such as the name of the spouse's employer. Of course, if a person may have two jobs (or two spouses) then the value is not unique and does not constitute a good derived attribute. (A derived attribute could be a set of values but in general there is little to be gained by doing so.)

A default value that may be overridden is a more complicated kind of derived value. For example, suppose that within a document the font of a character is the font of the paragraph containing it unless an explicit font is given for the character. We need to distinguish three attributes: the base attributes **Paragraph::explicitFont** and **Character::explicitFont**, which can be null, and the derived attribute **Character::effectiveFont** defined in terms of the base attributes (Figure 4). Changing the explicit font of the paragraph or the character implicitly changes the effective font of the character. Of course longer chains of dependency are possible, such as default values for chapters and documents.

So far we have considered derived attributes that are copied from other attributes or are computed as functions of a fixed number of attributes. Another useful kind of derived attribute is a *summary value* computed over a set of values obtained by traversing associations

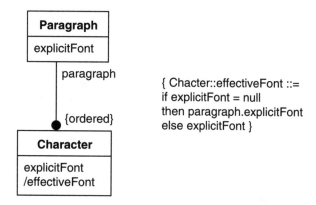

Figure 4. Deriving an overridden default value

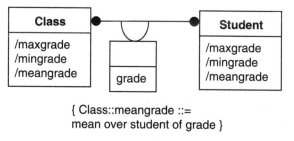

{ Class::meangrade ::=
mean over student of grade }

Figure 5. Summary value

with multiplicity *many*. For example, the maximum, minimum, and mean grades of the students in a class are summary attributes over the **Class-Student** many-to-many association (Figure 5). This association can also be traversed in the other direction to derive the maximum, minimum, and mean grades for a particular student among all of the student's classes.

Summary attributes are particularly useful with aggregation trees and other transitive associations, for which they can be defined recursively. For example, the weight of an aggregate is the sum of the weights of all its parts, applied recursively. Other summary functions, such as minimum, maximum, and mean, can be defined recursively.

In another column I described replacing a one-to-many association between **Cell** and **Bacteria** by the number of bacteria in a cell. The number of bacteria is a derived summation attribute. It is the sum of the value 1 over all associated bacteria.

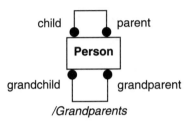

Figure 6. Derived association

Derived Associations

Derived associations are perhaps more interesting to show on an object diagram than derived attributes. The simplest form of derived association is the composition of several base associations. For example, **grandparent ::= parent.parent** (Figure 6). Such a chain of base associations is a kind of shortcut in the object diagram.

More interesting derived associations involve constraints on objects or their attributes. For example, we could define **sibling ::= x such that x.parent = self.parent and not x = self.** We could write this in a more operational way as **sibling ::= parent.child - self.** Similarly, we have **second-cousin ::= grandparent.sibling.grandchild.** All of these derived associations have multiplicity many-to-many.

Associations can also be derived from other associations subject to attribute constraints on the associated objects. For example, we define **son ::= child where gender = male** (Figure 7). We can also define **uncle ::= parent.sibling where gender = male.** From another column, we also have the derived association **winner-of-race ::= entrant-in-race where finish = 1** (Figure 8). The dotted lines show the subset dependencies between the derived associations and the base associations.

Another kind of derived association is the union of several other associations. We have **sister-in-law ::= spouse.sister or sibling.wife,** in which one person may serve different roles. We could define the derived association **immediate-family-of** from a whole set of simpler associations.

A very useful kind of derived association is the transitive closure of a transitive association. (The transitive closure is the set of all chains of links of the association of any length.) For example, **ancestor** is the transitive closure of **parent.** Following extended BNF (Backus Naur Form) notation, we may write "+" to indicate transitive closure and "*" to indicate reflexive transitive closure (those that include chains of length 0, i.e., the original object): **an-**

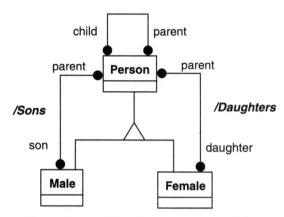

Figure 7. Association derived using a constraint

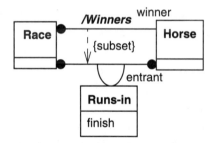

{winner ::= runs-in where finish = 1}

Figure 8. Derived association subject to constraint

cestor ::= parent+. Note that not all associations are transitive. For example, **half-sibling-of** is not transitive, as two persons may share a half-brother or half-sister without being related.

Transitive closures frequently cause naming confusion, because it is usually necessary to distinguish the explicit direct association (such as **parent**) from the derived indirect association (such as **ancestor**). Family relationships have distinct names, but consider a stack of cards or workstation windows; we must distinguish **directly-on-top-of** (the base association) from **indirectly-on-top-of** (the transitive closure association derived from it). Unfortunately, many programmers simply use a name such as **on-top-of** without distinguishing which meaning is intended (or without realizing there is a difference). Other examples in which this confusion is possible include **connected-to** and **variable-in-scope-of-block**.

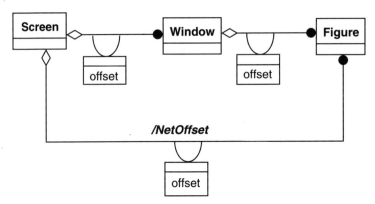

Figure 9. Composition of two transformations

A derived association can be defined in terms of a boolean function applied to all instances of a class. For example, we could define the association **overlaps ::= x where intersects (self.boundary, x.boundary)**. The boolean function **intersects** takes two boundaries and returns whether they intersect. This is actually a generic form that could be used to define an association between any two classes for which the function **intersects** may be applied to their respective boundaries. It generates a whole family of distinguishable **overlaps** associations for various pairs of base classes.

Consider a transformation matrix for a geometric figure in a window. The figure has an offset with respect to its enclosing window, which in turn has an offset from the screen coordinates (Figure 9). The offsets are matrix-valued link attributes. We can derive the resultant offset of the figure from the screen coordinates. The resultant matrix is the product of the two offset matrices. Because the resultant transformation matrix is defined in terms of other attributes, it is a derived attribute of a derived association. The resultant matrix is dependent on the others and cannot be updated in isolation. Again, it is somewhat arbitrary which is the base entity and which is the derived entity; the resultant matrix could be the base entity and the offset matrix could be derived from it. What really counts is the degrees of freedom in the problem, so the designation of certain objects as base entities does not mean that they are more important than other views of the system. Nevertheless it is important to pick something as base information so you can clearly define the state of the system.

Derived associations are very useful in defining functions and constraints, but if you do not distinguish them when building a model you will overspecify the base information. One source of confusion is that derived associations often have names within the problem domain and it can be difficult to extract a minimal set of base associations. Your goal should be to define the fundamental base associations whose links must be explicitly enumerated, separating them from derived associations whose links can be calculated.

Derived Classes

Derived objects are almost a contradiction in terms. A derived entity is a computable value, whereas an object is an entity with identity. During implementation you may choose to program derived structured values using classes in an O-O language, but you must make sure that their values remain consistent with the derivation rules after updates. During analysis you should not represent such values as objects.

A derived class does make sense. One kind of derived class is a class subject to a constraint on its attribute values. The objects of the class have identity; their assignment to classes is not fixed but instead depends on a rule. For example, a square is a special case of a rectangle in which all the sides are equal (Figure 10). **Square** can be considered a derived subclass of class **Rectangle**. We can think of a constrained subclass as being a particular state of the superclass, provided the object is free to change its value and thereby no longer satisfy the constraint. However, you would not actually program a state as a subclass in a conventional O-O language because programmed objects cannot change class at run time. It would be a useful extension to O-O languages to permit method dispatch to depend on state and to allow objects to change state even within a type-safe language.

Beware, however, because the implicit assumption in most O-O languages and models is that objects may not change their classes at run time. If a square must always remain a square, then it is *not* a subclass of a mutable rectangle, because it does not support all of the operations on a rectangle, such as changing its aspect ratio (Figure 11). There is a difference between a rectangle object that happens to be a square at a given moment and a square object that must always be a square. In general, constrained classes should *not* be modeled as subclasses if objects may not change their classes. Failure to understand this point has caused untold confusion among O-O writers who (incorrectly) cite rectangles and triangles as subclasses of polygons. Although there is no reason in principle why objects should not be allowed to change class, few object-oriented languages permit it.

You must therefore think of a derived subclass, including a substate, as different in kind from ordinary unrestricted generalization. Most of the time a derived subclass would not be implemented by an actual class in an O-O language. If a derived subclass is implemented as an actual subclass, then you must take care to make sure the implementation has the correct update semantics.

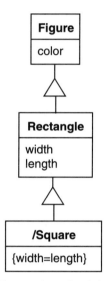

Figure 10. Derived class

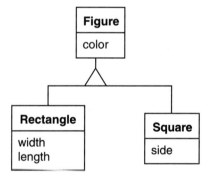

Figure 11. Square is not a subclass of Rectangle

Figure 12 shows a possible notation for states of a phone line. Use of state subclasses permits a tighter specification of attributes and associations that are meaningful only in certain states. In many cases, however, the gain in precision is minimal. I would recommend this kind of notation only in rare circumstances.

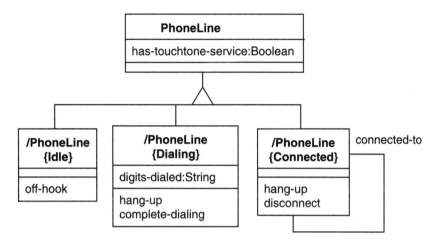

Figure 12. State as a derived subclass

Analysis and Design

During analysis derived entities do not add any information to a model but they provide additional names for concepts that are meaningful in the problem domain. In particular, they may make it simpler to specify operations. For example, it is simpler to say "take one deduction for each member of your immediate family" than to have to repeatedly expand "immediate family" into its definition in terms of the base concepts *child* and *spouse*. Derived entities are a kind of declarative "data subroutine." Keep in mind, however, that the purpose of analysis is to understand a problem without specifying its implementation, so avoid the unnecessary use of derived entities. A base model with no derived entities shows the information contained in a system clearly.

During design derived entities are often implemented as actual entities. If a concept is important enough to have a name in an application domain, it is frequently useful to make it manifest in the design. Every derived entity that is implemented as an actual entity represents a design optimization gaining information access speed at the increased cost of maintaining redundant information. The alternative is to leave a derived entity as a virtual entity and simply write an access method that computes its value dynamically. Of course, you should write access methods to hide *all* of your attributes and associations anyway, so that you are protected against changes in representation. Clients of a class should be unaware of which entities are actually implemented as base entities.

Operations

A *query* is an operation that returns a value without causing any side effects. An *action* is an operation that performs a side-effect without returning a value. Some programming languages distinguish clearly between these two kinds of operations. The concepts of derived attributes and derived associations are interchangeable with queries and with navigational paths in the object diagram, because they all imply values computed by rule. Declarative specifications are easier to work with than procedural specifications. During analysis it is useful to ignore queries entirely as they do not affect the state of the system. Do not bother to include them in an object diagram, except to the extent they are needed to define other operations.

During design you must decide which queries need to be implemented. Keep a rigid distinction between queries and actions. Because queries do not affect the state of the system, they can be added or removed freely as need arises, whereas the effect of an action may propagate a long way through the system and be difficult to untangle.

Queries may be written freely in terms of any other queries, using base or derived information. Actions may use any queries and may update base entities. Update operations on derived entities may or may not make sense. If you can reduce them to operations on base entities, then the meaning is clear.

Constraints

Derived information is really a special case of *constraints* within a model. A *constraint* is a condition limiting the legal values that a set of related entities can have. A derived entity is constrained by a formula that entirely specifies its value; derived entities therefore do not add any information to a model. In a more general constraint, each entity supplies information, but the values are not totally independent. For example, an arbitrary polygon with *n* vertices has *2n* degrees of freedom. A convex polygon still has *2n* degrees of freedom, but not all combinations of *2n* coordinate values are possible. Inequalities and other constraints can be very difficult to analyze mathematically.

The database concept of *views* is a form of derived information. A *view* is a subset of the whole model that includes derived entities and projections from base entities. A view is a derived model. Querying views is easy but updating them is not always meaningful. The problem is that a derived entity may not have enough information to reconstruct the base entity, so updating it can cause ambiguities. If you can reduce all of the operations to operations on base entities, then you will not have any update anomalies.

Generalization of Associations

Generalization (the inheritance relationship) is a key relationship useful for organizing classes and reducing redundant specification. Can we apply the concept of generalization to associations as well? To the extent that they can be reified (made into objects), we would expect to be able to. But what does the concept mean for associations?

By analogy to class generalization, we would expect that a link of a subassociation must be a link of the superassociation. In addition, any link attributes (values associated with a particular link) or link operations on the superassociation must also be inherited by all subassociations. A union of associations clearly meets these requirements. For example, **parent** is clearly a general case of **mother** and **father**, and **immediateFamily** is a general case of the various relationships that make it up. Associations subject to constraints may also be considered as derived subassociations, with the same caveats that I mentioned under derived objects. For example, **son** is a subassociation of **child** and **winner-of-race** is a subassociation of **runs-in-race**. However, unless the superassociations have link attributes or operations, use of association generalization is probably not worth the bother.

Conclusion

I have presented the specialized topic of derived information fairly informally. To some extent the concept of derived information is useful as a thinking point while building a model rather than a formal concept. The main lesson to take away is the importance of understanding the constraints within a model so as to avoid overspecifying a system. An analysis model should be a minimal model sufficient to define the problem domain. Thinking about derived entities can help to prevent redundancies from creeping in. During design, derived entities become manifest when redundancy is used for optimization. In general, derived entities are more useful during design than during analysis.

Building Boxes

Subsystems
October 1994

Organizing Large Systems

Small flat one-page models (of the kind found in textbooks, magazine columns, and toy programs) are simple to understand, but large real-world systems have large models that must be structured in some hierarchical way. Classification and inheritance are OO contributions to organizing models, but they are not sufficient for most kinds of large systems. Scaling constructs are needed to build large models out of smaller pieces. Existing computing terms for generic scaling constructs include *package, subsystem, module, component, leveling, abstraction, aggregation, CSCI, CSC, ensemble,* and *subassembly.* There is considerable overlap in these terms, so I will try to show how to structure large OMT models.

What is the underlying idea in all of these structuring constructs? They provide a way of relating a higher level, more abstract view of a model to a lower level, more detailed view. There are several reasons for doing this.

Abstraction

Abstraction helps us understand a large model by suppressing detail and providing an overall look at how it fits together. At a lower level each part can be understood by itself as a smaller entity.

This requires two views of the same model, a high-level view and a low-level view. Both views must be maintained and the relation between the two views must be clear. To be un-

derstandable, each component from the top-level model must map into a set of components in the lower level model, more or less independently of the rest of the model.

Experience has shown that it is difficult to synchronize changes to multiple models of
the same thing. The most practical way to maintain two views is therefore to generate the
high-level view from the low-level view by projection, in which low-level elements are either
suppressed or subsumed by high-level elements in the high-level view. Finding the projection is usually *not* automatic, but must be specified as part of the model itself.

Decomposition

Decomposition provides a top-down path for decomposing a system into parts that can be
developed by parallel work teams. The developers first build a high-level model that shows
the overall system structure, then decompose it into subsystems and assign a work team to
each subsystem. Each team builds a separate submodel of its subsystem.

This requires development of several successive models of the system with increasing
detail. The requirements are much the same as in the previous case. It is essential that the
dependencies between the different subsystems be clearly stated and minimized as much as
possible.

Understandability of the entire system is almost always an issue on a large project, so as
a practical matter it is necessary to have both high-level and detailed views of the same system. This does not mean that we need to preserve the original high-level views developed
at the start of the top-down development process, because flaws will be discovered in any
initial high-level view of a system as development proceeds. Rather, it is necessary to develop a system model containing both high-level views and detailed views, both of which
evolve together. The obvious approach is to start with an initial high-level view of a system
and then to expand it into a more detailed view, preserving the relationship between the two
and regenerating the high-level view as changes are made to the detailed view.

Reuse

Reuse permits separate components of the overall system to be reused independently in different contexts (such as class libraries, frameworks, subsystems, etc.). The best situation is
when a component can be used in any context whatsoever, provided its client follows the
rules specified in its "contract"; such a component is a *supplier* and its users are called *clients*.

This requires that the relationships and dependencies between the components must be clearly and explicitly defined, reasonably simple and straightforward; their *interfaces* must be specified. It also requires that the separate components be *useful* by themselves or in reasonable combinations with other components.

These are more severe requirements than for the previous case, as a reusable component must be packaged *before* its use, whereas components of a system under development can evolve together. However, they are excellent goals to strive for during system development.

Concurrency

Concurrency permits the executable system to be constructed out of discrete parts whose internal structure and behavior are hidden (*black boxes*). The implementation of the parts can be changed not only during design but also at run time (by substituting different black boxes). In many cases the discrete parts will execute concurrently.

The requirements are similar to those for reusability, with the addition that each component is a kind of object: it has identity, state, concurrency, and behavior. However, the behavior of these subsystem objects can be complex. They will not be implemented as monolithic objects; instead each subsystem object will have an implementation that may include a large number of object classes and object instances. We need a way to relate the high-level view of the subsystem object to its implementation in terms of simple objects.

Abstraction Dimensions

There are two orthogonal dimensions for abstracting detailed views into abstract views, or conversely, expanding abstract views into detailed ones:

1. Aggregation. A set of objects taken together is viewed as a single high-level object. Any relationships (association, generalization) to the constituents are subsumed by the aggregate object in the high-level view. The cells in a spreadsheet compose an aggregation.

2. Subsystems. A set of modeling elements (classes, relationships, code, etc.) taken together is regarded as a subsystem, a high-level subset of the entire model. Any relationships to the constituent elements are subsumed by the subsystem. The classes in a spreadsheet program that deal with cells compose a subsystem.

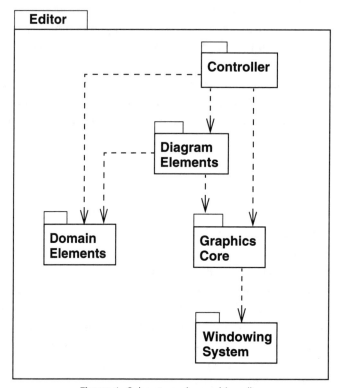

Figure 1. Subsystems in graphic editor

Note the subtle but crucial difference between these two forms of abstraction. Aggregates group objects, links, and other *instances*; subsystems group classes, associations, and other *types* (modeling elements that *describe* other elements).

The two dimensions coincide for subsystems that are implemented as discrete, possibly concurrent, objects, such as window managers or data base servers. Such *subsystem objects* combine both logical and physical abstraction and are suitable when functionality is to be implemented in physically distinct packages.

Subsystems

A *subsystem* is a part of a model, that is, it is a grouping of model elements. Each modeling element (class, association, generalization) belongs to one subsystem. Subsystems can also contain other subsystems, so subsystems are recursive and form a tree. An entire model is a top-level subsystem. A class could also be thought of as a degenerate subsystem. It is the intermediate levels that are interesting. Figure 1 shows a sample graphic editor decomposed into top-level subsystems.

A subsystem has several properties as described in the following sections.

Ownership.

The constituents of a subsystem are classes, relationships among classes (such as association and generation), and other subsystems. We can talk of the subsystem that "owns" each class and association. Ownership provides a mechanism for change control: changes to class structure or behavior must come within the owning subsystem; locking and check-out mechanisms are easily implemented. Other subsystems can "use" the definitions by subclassing from, associating to, or using instances of a class. Such a use does not require update access to the subsystem that owns the definition.

Figure 2 shows the ownership of classes by subsystems of an audio workshop application. Classes **AudioDevice, AudioFile,** and **AudioRecordFile** belong to subsystem **Physical-Format.** Classes **AudioChapter, AudioClip,** and subsystem **Phrases** belong to subsystem **LogicalFormat.** Nested subsystem **Phrases** contains classes **AudioPhrase** nd **PhraseMarker.** Class **File** is not defined at all within the application but is imported from some outside library. Class **AppnController** is not part of a subsystem but is part of the top-level system.

Public view

The public view is a set of publicly-visible classes and their public relationships, attributes, and operations. These are the elements that can be used freely outside the subsystem.

Figure 3 shows the public classes for the graphic core subsystem of a graphic editor. A fuller view would show the public operations of these classes also.

Private view

The private view consists of the private classes and also the private parts of the public classes that form the implementation of the elements in the subsystem. The public view is a subset of the private view.

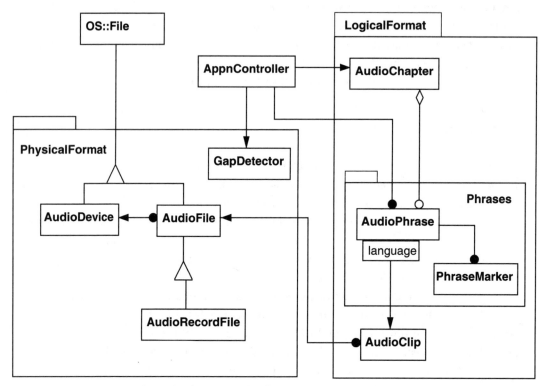

Figure 2. Class ownership for audio workshop subsystems

Figure 4 shows the public and private classes for the graphic editor subsystem. Here we see that graphic elements are actually organized into a quadtree for efficient spacial access, but this implementation detail is not part of the public interface.

Constraints

There may be constraints on the way the subsystem is connected to or used by other subsystems. However, subsystem constraints limit flexibility and should be avoided if possible. A pure supplier has no constraints on its usage; any subsystem can have associations to it, hold variables referencing classes in it, and call operations on classes in it.

Frameworks are not simple library packages; they usually have constraints on the connection of their subsystems. For example, in the model-view-controller framework the view classes have full knowledge of the model classes, but the model classes may not update view

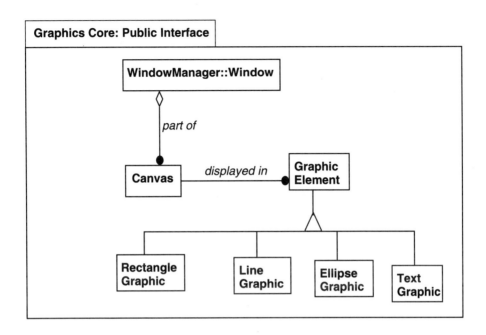

Figure 3. Public interface classes for graphic core subsystem

classes directly. However, each model class is required to notify all of its view classes when it changes; this is a constraint on the way the two subsystems are related.

Subsystem Notation

A subsystem is drawn as a box with a *graphic marker* indicating a *subsystem*. I will draw the subsystem graphic marker as a tabbed rectangle, but other graphic markers are possible, such as dashed lines, double lines, light gray lines, thick lines, colored lines, shaded interior, and so on. Although many people get overly concerned about shapes and symbols, these are really minor issues in modeling and depend a lot on the medium used (such as print, hand written diagrams, or interactive tools), so feel free to make substitutions for convenience. The concepts are more important than the symbols.

There are two views of a subsystem, the *high-level (abstract) view* and the *low-level (detailed) view*. Normally the two views would not be shown at once, except to give a condensed presentation of a reasonably small system.

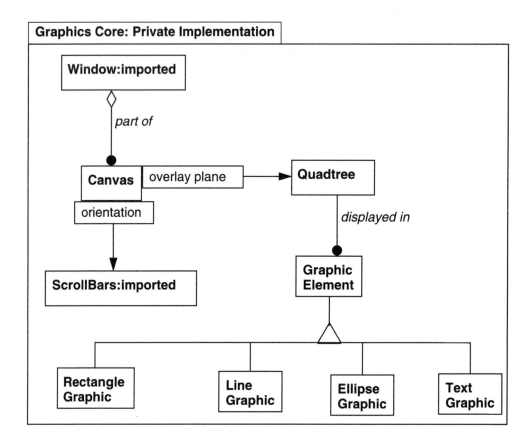

Figure 4. Private implementation classes for graphic core subsystem

In the abstract view, the subsystem is drawn as a simple box with a dotted outline containing the subsystem name. Figure 5 shows the high-level view of the **GraphicsCore** subsystem.

The detailed view shows the contents of the subsystem. There are two parts of the detailed view, the public part and the private part. These could be shown simultaneously using different colors or some other graphic marker, or they can be shown as two different pictures. In a tool, the private part could be toggled on and off dynamically.

Figures 3 and 4 show the public and private view of the **GraphicsCore** subsystem. A complete view would include the attributes and operations of each class with public/private

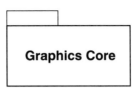

Figure 5. Subsystem notation

markers for each member. We have used the convention of prepending a plus ('+') or minus ('-') sign to the member name to indicate public or private access; for C++ we also use a pound sign ('#') for protected access.

The public part shows the publicly visible classes and their publicly visible attributes, associations, and operations. (Many designers prefer to keep all attributes and associations private, so the public view would show only public operations.) The private part shows the private classes plus the private attributes, associations, and operations of the public classes. These constitute the implementation of the subsystem and are not directly accessible outside the subsystem, therefore no outside relationships to them from other subsystems are allowed, but relationships from them to other subsystems are allowed. In other words, dependencies to a subsystem can only arise from its public information, but dependencies from a subsystem to other subsystems can arise from its private information.

Normally one subsystem at a time will be shown on a diagram. The diagram shows classes and associations defined in the subsystem. Each modeling element (class, association, etc.) must belong to one subsystem.

Classes of other subsystems that form associations with internal classes are indicated as *imported classes* and annotated accordingly with the name of their home subsystem. An imported class would normally not show its attributes or operations (although it may sometimes be useful to show the operations used by the importing subsystem).

In Figure 2 class **File** is imported from the operating system. In Figure 3 class **Window** is imported from the window manager subsystem.

In the general case, there may be constraints on the way subsystems can be connected together. These can be specified as ordinary OMT constraints by writing them as text inside braces. For example, a framework may require the presence of several subsystems with specified roles. However, it is better to avoid constraints on usage and have pure supplier subsystems when possible.

Structural Dependencies

Subsystems depend on other subsystems because their components depend on each other. Components can have structural and behavioral dependencies. The structural dependencies are association and generalization.

Association

A class has an association to another class. I have emphasized that associations should be thought of as being bidirectional during analysis, but during design we have many classes whose purpose is to be used by other classes. The relationship is not really equal; one class is subordinate to another. The subordinate supplier class has no knowledge of its clients and cannot initiate any actions on them, but instead is acted upon. We can represent this kind of asymmetric knowledge by a unidirectional association with an arrow from the client class to the supplier class. The arrowhead (supplier end) can have a multiplicity symbol, indicating the number of instances known to the client. The arrow tail (client end) *may* have a multiplicity indicator, but normally it will be omitted and will imply indefinite multiplicity, usually because it doesn't matter and doesn't affect the implementation. If there is no arrowhead or arrowheads on both ends, then the association is a joint responsibility of both subsystems (and introduces a mutual dependency between the subsystems). An one-way association to an imported class is shown in the subsystem that defines the association

For example, in Figure 2 an **AudioClip** knows that it is part of an **AudioFile,** but the **AudioFile** doesn't know what is in it; all the control comes from the **AudioClip** telling the **AudioFile** what to do. In a similar fashion, the **AudioClip** is known by an **AudioPhrase** which tells it what to do.

Subclassing

A class is a subclass of another class. The subsystem containing the subclass depends on the subsystem containing the superclass. For example, in Figure 2 the **PhysicalFormat** subsystem depends on the external subsystem containing the definition of class **File.**

Usage Dependencies

Implementation or *usage dependencies* arise from the operations and their code. Usage dependencies are inherently language-dependent, because different languages have different kinds of code dependencies, but some common ones include the following:

1. *Holds reference.* The implementation (i.e., the code for a method) of a class holds a variable containing a reference to objects of another class, either as an input argument or as a result of calling another method.

2. *Calls.* The implementation of a class calls (sends a message to) an operation on another class. This can occur only if the caller has a link to an object of the class or holds a variable of the class, so *calls* implies *holds.*

3. *Sends.* The implementation of a class sends an event to another class. Again, this can only occur if the caller has a reference to an instance of the class, so *sends* implies *holds.*

4. *Instantiates.* The implementation of a class instantiates an instance of another class. After the instantiation the caller holds a reference to the class, so this dependency also implies *holds.*

Because these dependencies are so tightly related, we group them together as *uses* dependencies. To show a *holds, calls, sends,* or *instantiates* dependency between a class and another class, use a dotted arrow for *dependency (uses).* An annotation may be added to precisely specify the dependency, such as the operation called or the event sent, but this is usually too fussy for a model intended for understanding. For implementation, the information is usually directly available from the low-level model, so there is no need to show it explicitly on a high-level view.

Figure 6 shows a sample class diagram with various dependencies between classes. Class **A** has a structural link to a set of objects of class **D**. Classes **B** and **C** are subclasses of class **A** and are therefore dependent on its definition. Class **C** holds a variable of class **D**, possibly obtained as an argument of a method on itself, which it uses to call some operation on class **D**. The specific operations called by each class could be listed in a table but it is usually too messy to try to show them in diagrams. Class **C** also sends an event to class **E**, which is a global server with an implicit reference from everywhere.

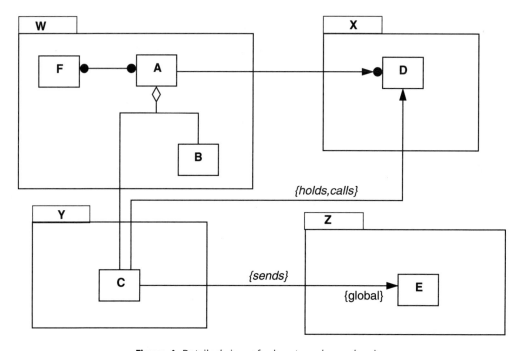

Figure 6. Detailed view of subsystem dependencies

Subsystem Dependencies

It usually takes too much detail to show the dependencies of each class on all other classes. By abstracting to the subsystem level we can get a better understanding of the dependencies present in a design.

When abstracting from classes to subsystems, we abstract the class-to-class dependencies to subsystem level also. A dependency between two classes is abstracted to a dependency between their subsystems, shown as a dotted arrow between them. A single dotted arrow represents any number of underlying structural or usage dependencies between classes. The dependency arrows can be labeled, if desired, to show the exact nature of the dependency.

We can show the dependencies between subsystems on a subsystem-dependency diagram. The dependencies are shown as dotted arrows. Note that this is not really a new kind of diagram; it is just a class diagram whose only elements shown are subsystems.

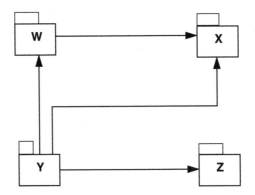

Figure 7. Abstract view of subsystem dependencies

For example, Figure 7 is an abstracted view of Figure 6. Subsystem **W** depends on subsystem **X** because of the association from **A** to **D**. Subsystem **Y** depends on subsystem **Z** because of the event sent from **C** to **E**. Subsystem **Y** depends on subsystem **W** because **C** is a subclass of **A**. Subsystem **Y** depends on subsystem **X** because **C** calls **D**. The diagram might suggest a way to simplify the dependencies. Perhaps subsystem **Y** can call subsystem **W** and let it call subsystem **X,** as **W** already depends on **X.** Although this adds an indirection at run time, it may simplify modifying the system in the future.

It is possible to have mutual dependencies between subsystems. This means that classes in each subsystem use classes in the other subsystem. (Note that this does *not* necessarily imply compile-time dependencies such as Ada *uses* or C++ *includes,* although these are among the dependencies.) Mutual dependency is not an ideal architecture, because neither subsystem is reusable without the other, but it does arise in many real systems. However, it can often be avoided by introducing a third subsystem as a mediator and controller.

Subsystem Nesting

Subsystems can contain other subsystems. This corresponds to several levels of abstraction during development. We can show this decomposition by embedding subsystems in other subsystems. This is the *leveling* or *abstraction relationship.* It is a kind of aggregation, but unlike an ordinary aggregation, which relates instances, it relates the model elements themselves (rather than instances of them). In Figure 2 subsystem **LogicalFormat** contains the embedded subsystem **Phrases.**

The subsystem decomposition must be a strict tree, not a partial order, as each subsystem can only be defined in one place (recall that we are decomposing the model itself, including code, not the clustering of the objects in the run-time system generated by it).

If several subsystems are shown on the same diagram with their contents, then associations between classes in different subsystems can be shown directly without the need for imported classes. Figure 2 shows such an example. A unidirectional association belongs to the referencing subsystem. The association from **AudioClip** to **AudioFile** belongs to subsystem **LogicalFormat.** If there is ambiguity about which subsystem owns an association, the association can be drawn as a diamond symbol and located within the correct subsystem box.

As an alternate notation, we can show the overall decomposition of the system as an aggregation tree of subsystems. The aggregation lines are solid because they represent the actual aggregation of the subsystems themselves, not an abstraction of their contents. Figure 8 shows an alternate view of the graphic editor subsystems first shown in Figure . The entire system is shown as **Editor,** which contains the various top-level subsystems.

A diagram containing only subsystems is a *subsystem diagram.* It is really just a class diagram showing only subsystems (their contents are suppressed), but it is useful for understanding the overall structure of a system. A subsystem diagram shows aggregation of subsystems, dependencies between subsystems, and inheritance of subsystems.

Subsystem Specialization

Because a subsystem has a specification (public part) and implementation (private part), it can be implemented in different ways. It makes sense to define different implementations of the same specification as *specialization* of the same generic specification subsystem by different implementation subsystems. The normal OMT generalization symbol can be used to show this. In this case, the symbol is *not* dotted, as it represents an actual relationship between the two entities (in this case the subsystems themselves) and not an abstracted summary of relationships between the contents. A client of the generic subsystem would use only information in the specification part and would have no direct knowledge of the different implementations.

Figure 8 shows two implementations of the **WindowingSystem** subsystem of the graphic editor, one for Motif and one for Microsoft Windows. These represent two distinct off-the-shelf windowing libraries. There may actually be little in common between them.

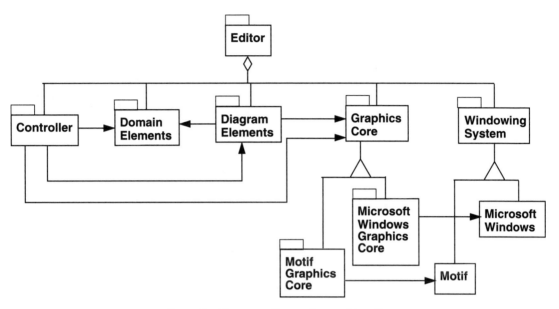

Figure 8. Subsystem diagram for graphic editor

Subsystem **GraphicsCore** is the responsibility of the application developer. To achieve portability, this subsystem defines a set of virtual graphics operations that the application uses to draw diagram elements. The rest of the application is not allowed direct access to the windowing subsystem.

There are two implementations of **GraphicsCore,** one for Motif and one for Microsoft Windows. Each implementation depends heavily on its corresponding windowing system and must be updated if the windowing system changes. However, because the bulk of the application code does not depend directly on the window systems, it need not be changed when the window system changes. A new implementation of **GraphicsCore** could be added at any time to port the application to a new platform, such as Macintosh, for example.

Taking Things in Context
Using Composites to Build Models
November 1994, November 1995

I have discussed the need for scaling constructs for building large models for real-world problems. I argued that there are two dimensions of scaling: the model elements and the execution elements. I defined a *subsystem* (called a *package* in the UML) as a part of the model itself, including classes, associations, and the code for methods. At a high level the model is partitioned into subsystems. These are descriptive elements.

On the other hand, the actual run-time objects in a system can be organized into groups by aggregation relationships. We want to abstract the aggregation tree at various levels. I call an abstraction by object aggregation a *composite*. In this column I will explore composites.

Composites

A *composite* is an aggregation that can be viewed from two levels, either in detail or as a single abstract object subsuming relationships to its parts. It is really not a new concept, but rather a slight extension of the aggregation concept and notation in the original OMT book [1].

For example, at a high level we might think of a traffic light as an object connected to other traffic lights and a central computer (Figure 1). If we look a bit deeper, we find that each traffic light is really a composite, comprising a controller, many lamps, and many sensors. It is the controllers that are connected to other controllers and the central computer. The traffic light itself is a higher-level abstraction (Figure 2).

Figure 1. High-level view of traffic light

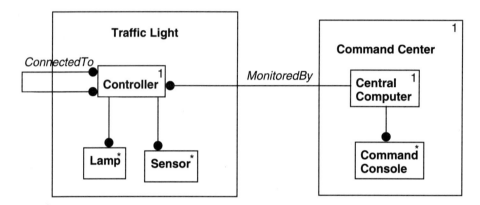

Figure 2. Low-level view of traffic light as a composite

A composite is drawn as a rectangle containing classes and associations. All of the contained object instances and links are *part of the* composite instance. Note that both objects and links are included in the aggregation. This is an improvement on the simple OMT notation for aggregation as a tree, in which there is no convenient way to include associations as part of the aggregation.

A *composite* is a class that defines a particular configuration of objects and links within it. It is a class because it defines a general type that can be instantiated to produce individual instances. It contains references to classes and associations that have individual identity with specific roles within the composite. When the composite is instantiated, the internal objects and links form part of the instantiation.

A composite object imposes identity on its parts. For each composite object, there is a corresponding set of constituent object instances and links. An association between two classes inside the composite indicates that both objects and the link must belong to the same composite object. To show an association between a component of one composite and a component of another, the association line must break the contour of the composite object. For example, in Figure 2, the links between traffic light controllers connect different traffic lights, because they cross the composite boundary, whereas the links between controllers, lamps, and sensors must all stay within individual traffic lights, because they are drawn within the boundary.

Composites can be nested. Aggregation relationships are transitive to any level. Catalog aggregation (sharing of subtrees) is *not* allowed; composites represent physical aggregation and must be pure trees.

Note that composite objects are *not* subsystems and therefore do not encapsulate class definitions. The same class can appear inside more than one composite object, but a given instance would never be part of more than one composite, of course.

Multiplicity in Composites

The aggregation relationship can have multiplicity. In a composite the multiplicity of the composite end is always *one* (or *optional one* if the component class may appear elsewhere); each part belongs to one composite. If multiple objects of the same class, all play the same role within a composite, they can be represented by a single class icon with a *class multiplicity indicator* in the upper right corner of the icon; the multiplicity of the component within the composite can be fixed or unbounded (this notation is taken from Embley, Kurtz, and Woodfield [2]). The indicator specifies how many instances of the component class can appear in one instance of the composite.

Following Embley, we have previously noted that a multiplicity indicator can be used in an ordinary model to show a *singleton class,* i.e., a class with a single run-time instance. This notation can now be regarded as a special case in which there is an implicit "system" or "application" or "universe" composite object at the top level of the model and class multiplicity is defined relative to it. Since the default multiplicity is *many,* ordinary classes are unchanged under this interpretation.

For example, in Figure 2 each traffic light has one controller and each command center has one central computer. There is only one command center in the system. If the scope of the system is changed to include several traffic systems, then the singleton indication on **CommandCenter** can be removed.

Another Example

Figure 3 illustrates these points with a model of a security system. The security system may contain many sensors and alarms. The individual sensors and alarms do not play distinct

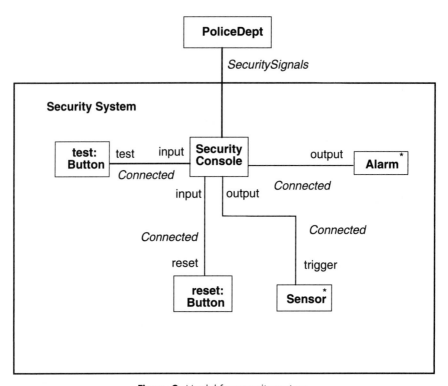

Figure 3. Model for security system

roles. To indicate that many instances of the alarm and sensor classes may occur within one security system object, the multiplicity symbol "*" for many has been placed in the upper right corner of the class icons.

There are also two instances of class *Button.* However, the occurrences are distinguishable and have different purposes within the security system, therefore each has been given a unique name within the security system composite. The name of a class icon is equivalent to the rolename of the (implicit) aggregation relationship between the composite and the component class.

The security console object is connected to a *PoliceDept* object which is outside of the security system. This is shown by an association between the *securityConsole* object and a *PoliceDept* class drawn outside the composite.

We can use instances of composites inside larger composites. Figure 4 shows an *EmergencySystem* composite that contains many instances of the *SecuritySystem* composite. A

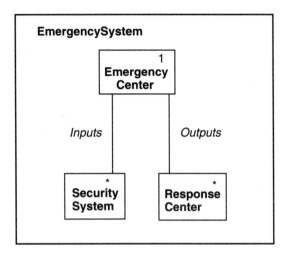

Figure 4. Nested composites

composite is a class and can therefore be used whenever a class is meaningful; instances of it can be used inside of other composites.

High Level View

In understanding a large system we do not always want to see everything. It is important to be able to step back and get the big picture by ignoring a lot of low-level details. Composites provide a vehicle for suppressing detail. Since the components of a composite are enclosed by it and share its identity, they can be suppressed in a high-level view without losing high-level information. Both internal objects and internal links can be suppressed. Links from internal objects to external classes can be elided to the composite itself; usually all links from internal objects to an external class can be subsumed by a single high-level association from the composite to the external class. In Figure 4 the internal details of the *SecuritySystem* object have been suppressed and the links within it elided directly to the *SecuritySystem* icon.

Composites can be used as part a top down elaboration process of constructing a model. At first the high-level view of the system is developed. Then the high-level classes are refined into several low-level parts. In many cases a high-level class becomes a composite. Associations to the high-level class will be assigned to individual components as part of the refinement. By keeping the composite as part of the final model, the low-level detail can be

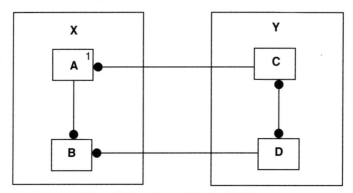

Figure 5. Sample model (detailed view)

easily suppressed to obtain a high-level view. For example, in Figure 3 it is highly likely that class *SecurityConsole* will be refined as a composite to provide additional detail.

In many cases there is an object in the full expansion that corresponds to the composite itself, an object that contains attributes and operations common to the entire composite and not to any single piece. Embley et al call this a *dominant* class, since it dominates the other classes in the composite (we have since recognized that this is a class reference, i.e., an object). Any association to the composite as a whole goes to the dominant object by default. Often the dominant class has the same name as the composite or a similar one. However, I am not sure that any special notation is required, since normally the developer is refining the model in a top down fashion, rather than trying to push a button and expand the definition. In Figure 4 the object *EmergencyCenter* is a dominant object for composite *EmergencySystem*.

It would be possible to always require a dominant object within a composite, and perhaps this might be a good design rule to keep designs simple with clean interfaces. De Champeaux describes a similar concept that he calls an *ensemble* [3]. He requires that all interactions between an ensemble and its constituents pass through the dominant object of the ensemble.

Figure 5 shows a sample model containing two composites with multiple associations between their constituents. The abstract view of this model is shown in Figure 6. The association in Figure 6 subsumes both of the concrete associations in Figure 5. The overall multiplicity is many-to-one.

Note that an ordinary class can be regarded as a composite of its attributes. The attribute names are the role names of the attribute types within the class. Attributes are nor-

Figure 6. Sample model (abstract view)

mally used for simple pure-value types with no explicit interrelationships except for their mutual containment by the class.

Application System as Composite

When a computer application is modeled it eventually results in an executable system. We can treat "the system" as an object. The "system object" is the eventual root of identity in the program: global variables, resources, and all the nested program context is contained within it and reachable from it. We can think of "the system" as a composite that contains the entire model.

It is generally necessary to have a root of identity in almost any model. This root defines the starting place for name paths, for example. It is convenient to assume that any model has an implicit composite surrounding it; we might call this composite the system, the world, the environment, etc.

Assuming an implicit universal composite around any model facilitates understanding of *singleton* classes that are often found in models. Embley, et al, define a singleton as a class that contains one and only one object [2]. For example, a model might contain a single company with a single president. But these objects (company and president) are singular because they are implicitly part of a given configuration, such as the organization of a particular company. They are not inherent properties of the world, but they may be *accidental* properties (philosophical usage) of a particular application model, which then corresponds to a composite. Different objects of the same class may play different roles. A singleton is simply an object that appears once within a composite, rather than an inherent constraint on the existence of members of the class, which is rarely meaningful.

If we take this viewpoint, then any multiplicity for a class (such as a singleton object) is really a specification that the implicit system object contains some number of predefined objects. Constraints on instantiation must always be within some context, i.e., within a composite.

Subsystem Objects

A *subsystem object* is a subsystem that can be instantiated as a composite object. It combines a subset of the design space with a subset of the execution space. It permits the substitution of different subsystems even at run time without recompilation, because all of its functionality is encapsulated in distinct objects. Subsystem composites are normally applicable to physically-distinct processors and devices, but they can also be used for tightly encapsulated servers within a single operating system or network.

In a subsystem object, all services provided and all objects created are part of the composite object. Initial access is usually mediated by the dominant object of the subsystem. The caller must have a handle to a subsystem object, which may or may not be a singleton. Calls to the subsystem object may create internal objects whose handles are returned to the caller. Such internal objects are visible to the caller and can be sent messages, but they are part of the subsystem object and cannot be removed from it. The subsystem object may add its own internal objects, links, and messages.

Since a subsystem object is a physically discrete object and not simply a compiler construct (as an ordinary class is), different subsystem objects can be substituted at run time without affecting their clients, provided their public interfaces are the same.

No new notation is needed for a subsystem object. It is drawn as a subsystem box (with a tabbed rectangle) surrounding a single composite rectangle. In the high-level view only the public operations are shown. In the detailed view, the private classes, attributes, and operations may be shown in a subdiagram. Subsystem objects can be singletons or they can be multiple. Figure 7 shows the notation for a subsystem object.

Examples of executable subsystem objects include an XWindow server, a database engine, an operating system, or a spooler. The components of many real-time systems are also subsystem objects, such as the concurrent objects in the printer system shown in Figure 8.

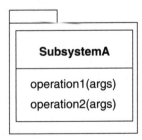

Figure 7. Subsystem object

Concurrent Objects

All objects are conceptually concurrent. Sequential execution is an artifact of computer limitations and therefore mostly a concern of the design phase. During analysis get the semantics right under the real-world assumption that all objects are concurrent. However, during design we must indicate which objects are really implemented as concurrent and which are sequential.

Composite objects are good vehicles for indicating concurrency. We can annotate composites (and other classes) with a *active* property. An *active object* has its own thread of control. It can execute in parallel with other concurrent objects. Messages between active objects are real-world signals. Messages within active objects are just internal subroutine calls to methods.

We can indicate an active composite object with the *active* keyword. If composite objects are nested inside other composite objects, then the containers are also active (whether or not someone has shown it). Higher-level active objects would have multiple threads of control possible.

Figure 8 shows the high-level model of a high-performance PostScript laser printer (somewhat simplified). In this device, input processing, PostScript interpretation, and output processing occur concurrently. These tasks are three of the concurrent objects shown on the model. Input is stored in a text buffer until it can be processed by the interpreter. The input buffer subsystem object contains the text buffer and also the job buffer, listing details of the jobs queued in the buffer. The input buffer does not contain a controller, but it does exist concurrently with the input processor and the interpreter must synchronize concurrent requests from them. On the other hand, the page image built by the interpreter is not a separate concurrent object, because it need not be shared by the interpreter and the output processor. Both interpreter and output processor subsystems have their own private copies of a page image; when interpretation of a page is complete and the output processor is ready to print another page, then they "swap" page images (most likely logically rather than by copying) and proceed.

The control panel also operates in parallel with the other concurrent objects. The operator can query the printer while it is operating. However, if the operator stops or cancels a job or takes the printer out of service, the control panel component sends appropriate messages to the other subsystem components.

Note that this system contains both hardware and software components. An unfortunate distinction is often made, within both the hardware and software communities, between hardware-software systems and software-only systems. In reality, the issues of man-

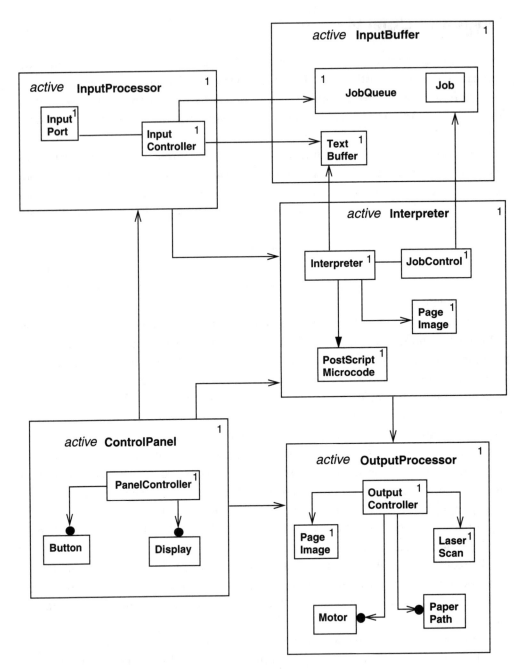

Figure 8. Concurrent objects in PostScript printer

aging complexity, ensuring interchangeability, and understanding designs are the same for all kinds of systems, so it is time to put the ancient hardware-software biases to rest.

Versioning

Composite objects provide a basis for versioning, locking, clustering, etc. The essential basis for any of these operations is identity and partitioning of the system into discrete parts, preferably with a multilevel hierarchy. Composite objects provide these properties.

Other Work

There has been a moderate amount of work on subsystems and composite objects, but many approaches ignore one or the other of the concepts or mix them together inextricably.

Ada packages are similar to subsystems. Ada tasks are somewhat similar to concurrent composite objects. The correspondence is not exact.

Wirfs-Brock [4], among others, describes subsystems as groups of related classes without much additional semantics. Embley describes semantics for high-level views in some detail (compare to composite objects), but he does not have a concept for subsystems that are not objects. De Champeaux [3] describes ensembles, which correspond to subsystem objects; he does not allow the two structuring concepts to be used separately. Kim [5] and others have described ways of modeling composite objects, but these were concerned more with data aggregation and clustering and not with information hiding and modularity. Firesmith [6] has extensive notation for subsystems (which he calls *subassemblies*, recently changed to *clusters*). Shlaer-Mellor [7] have a well-developed concept of subsystem with notation to show three kinds of relationships (static relationships, interactions, object access).

The concepts and notation described in this column and the previous one are not brand-new additions to the original OMT work, but rather slight extensions of the OMT concepts of *module* and *aggregate*. Keep in mind that its main use is design, not analysis, so don't use it when it is unnecessary. Also take care not to specify high-level models in excessive detail. It is usually better to undermodel than to overmodel.

References

1. James Rumbaugh, Michael Blaha, William Premerlani, Frederick Eddy, William Lorensen. *Object-Oriented Modeling and Design.* Prentice Hall, Englewood Cliffs, N.J., 1992.

2. David Embley, Barry D. Kurtz, Scott N. Woodfield. *Object-Oriented Systems Analysis: A Model-Driven Approach.* Yourdon Press, Englewood Cliffs, N.J., 1992.

3. Dennis De Champeaux. *Object-Oriented Systems Development.* Addison-Wesley, 1993.

4. Rebecca Wirfs-Brock, Brian Wilkerson, Lauren Wiener. *Designing Object-Oriented Software.* Prentice Hall, Englewood Cliffs, N.J., 1990.

5. Won Kim, et al. Composite object support in an object-oriented database system. *OOPSLA'87 Proceedings, SIGPLAN 22,* 12 (Dec. 1987) 118-125.

6. Donald Firesmith. *Object-Oriented Requirements, Analysis, and Logical Design.* Wiley, 1993.

7. Sally Shlaer, Stephen Mellor. *Object Lifecycles.* Yourdon Press, Englewood Cliffs, N.J., 1992.

Acknowledgments

The basic inspiration for composites came from the high-level views and singletons of Embley, et al, but they have been distorted by me probably beyond recognition by the original authors.

Modeling Conundrums

I HAVE taught a number of people to use OMT for modeling systems. Like any coach or teacher, I notice that certain kinds of errors are particularly common in new students' models. In some cases this is because students bring certain preconceived notions with them from previous experience, in others because the concepts are inherently somewhat tricky and confusing. This series of articles explores various "conundrums" that come up frequently.

Trouble with Twins: Warning Signs of Mixed-Up Classes discusses perhaps the number one source of serious logical errors with models and system designs: the mixing together into a single class of classes that are really different but that frequently appear together. Splitting up these misguided fusions can often rescue a model that appears hopelessly contradictory.

Some situations can be modeled in more than one way. Sometimes all alternatives are equally good, but sometimes one viewpoint works better in a given situation. *On the Horns of the Modeling Dilemma: Choosing Among Alternate Modeling Constructs* describes some of these choices.

Inheritance is the feature most associated with object orientation in many people's minds, and it is one of the most abused of modeling constructs. In the early years of object-orientation there was a certain kind of pride to see who could construct the deepest inheritance hierarchy, but in recent years the pendulum has swung back to a more moderate use of inheritance and the understanding that other constructs are often preferable. *Disinherited! Examples of Misuse of Inheritance* describes some of the wrong kinds of inheritance and how to avoid them.

Trouble with Twins
Warning Signs of Mixed-Up Classes
July 1994

Suspicious Signs

I have repeatedly urged readers to build models of systems before building the systems themselves, because the smaller size and greater simplicity of a good model make it easier to understand the essentials of a system without getting bogged down in minor details. Although building good models is something of an art, most people can learn to do a reasonably good job at it, given some training and experience. There will always be an element of judgment in building a good model, but there are a number of warning signs that indicate the possibility of questionable constructs.

Perhaps the most troublesome common modeling problem, even for experienced modelers, is mixing together two distinct concepts in a single class. The solution is to break up one class into two or more classes, but the problem is not always obvious. One difficulty is that two distinct concepts often have the same natural-language name, so they tend to get confused. Look in any dictionary: you will find a sequence of numbered definitions, each describing a slightly different concept.

In this column I will describe some incarnations of the two-in-one problem with their respective warning signs. This list is not necessarily complete, but it may provide some help in avoiding modeling mistakes.

One-to-One Associations

A one-to-one association is often problematic: are there two distinct classes or is one class simply being described in two pieces? It is acceptable to break up a class for organizational reasons, as long as you realize that the pieces aren't really independent; on the other hand, combining two independent pieces into a single class can lead to disaster. But what difference does it make? It would seem that if objects are in a one-to-one association they are equivalent.

The answer depends on whether the association between objects is *mutable*, whether it can change after the objects are created. If a one-to-one association is mutable, then one object may be associated with a sequence of other objects over time, so each object preserves its identity. If the association is immutable, then an object is always associated with the same other object, and it becomes difficult or meaningless to distinguish them in any fundamental way.

For example, consider a gymnastic team competition. During each round, several teams perform simultaneously in several events (Figure 1). Each team performs one event at a time, but during the round the teams change events. A team is clearly distinct from the event that it is performing at a given moment.

Things are less obvious if one object is or appears to be part of another object. Should a part be considered a distinct object? Mutability can be a guide. The tires on a car can easily be changed, so it makes sense to distinguish a car from its tires, even though they are related by aggregation. What about the arm on a person? Probably not worth distinguishing.

Figure 2 shows a more troublesome case. Several different shapes are modeled as subclasses of a *Shape* class. Associated with each shape object is a *Transform* object that specifies an offset, scale, and rotation for the object, implemented by a multidimensional matrix. Each shape object has its own transform. Should *Transform* be distinct from *Shape,* or is it just a container for attribute values that might just as well be in *Shape*? Since *Transform* never exists by itself in this problem, it does not appear to have separate identity. However, it

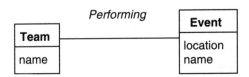

Figure 1. Gymnastic competition

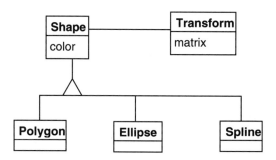

Figure 2. Transform

often pays to think ahead. It makes mathematical sense to apply transforms to other transforms, and it might be handy at some point to have a set of free-standing transforms that could be applied to anything. For these reasons, it is probably better to separate *Transform* from *Shape,* even though it does not have separate identity in this problem.

Temporal and Eternal Objects

One of the key dichotomies in modeling is between an object-at-a-point-in-time and an object-through-time. Typically objects have values that change over time; usually we care about the current values at some moment. Operations on the object query and change its state. For some purposes, however, we care about an entire history of values that an object has had. We need a concept of an object that transcends the current moment, an "eternal" object, whose attributes do not change. This concept is actually implicit in the concept of object *identity* anyway. Operations on the eternal object could append new values to the history but it doesn't make sense to change past values, so the eternal object doesn't have a state. The two views are obviously related: the object in time is just the last value in the history of the object through time; changing the value of the object in time corresponds to appending another value to the history object.

It is easy to mix up these dual viewpoints. *When was the modern Olympics founded* and *who won the decathlon in the 1992 Olympics* are about *Olympics* objects from two different classes (Figure 3), one of which might be called *SportsEvent* (the "eternal" event with all-time records, a founder, etc.) and the other that might be called *SportsEventOccurrence* (one particular "moment-in-time" occurrence with a date, city, etc.).

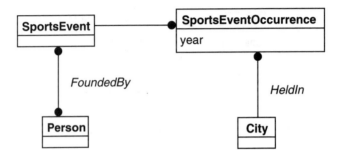

Figure 3. Object-through-time and object-in-time

The same observations apply to associations. The association *MarriedTo* (Figure 4) is optional-one-to-one (at a point in time) or many-to-many (over time). In going from an association in time to an association over time, we need to add link attributes for **date terminated** and **reason terminated** (such as divorce, annulment, death), because we are no longer concerned just with an existing state but also how it may have terminated. We also note that both ends of the association-through-time are ordered; the last link in each direction is the link for the **Now-married-to** association, provided it has not yet been terminated, otherwise the current state is **unmarried.**

In many cases, all you need is the object in time. The object through time is needed if you are logging information or trying to summarize things over time. If you don't need them both, then there is usually no problem. If you really need both viewpoints in the same program, then model them as two distinct but related classes.

Actors and Surrogates

One kind of confusion arises when modeling real-world objects that must also be represented within a program. What should we model, the real-world object or its representation inside the system? The answer is that there are two classes involved, a real-world domain object, often an *actor,* and a *surrogate* that represents the real-world object within the system. An *actor* is an object that spontaneously initiates behavior. For example, consider an air traffic control system. Airplanes and flight plans are both real world objects, but they are subtly different. A real-world airplane has values for position, altitude, and velocity, among other things. The air traffic control system represents the airplane internally by a *surrogate*—an internal representation that stands for the real thing. The values of the surrogate,

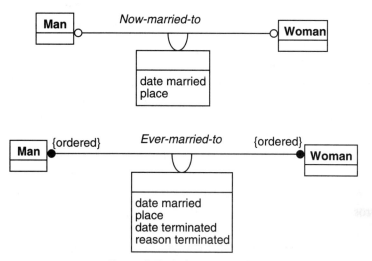

Figure 4. Two views on marriage

however, are only a guess at the values of the actual airplane—they may have errors due to time delays, sensor inaccuracy, distortion, or other causes. The job of the air traffic control system is to *try* to keep the surrogates in alignment with the real planes, but we must always keep in mind that they are not the same objects. (The problem would be even more acute in a defense radar system, in which the enemy planes are trying very hard not to be where the system thinks they are.)

Do we need to model both objects? The real airplane is part of the environment, so we might want to model it during early analysis. However, it is not really part of the computer system—it is outside the system boundary, so in fact it is not a necessary part of the class model. (It is of course part of the entire real-world hardware-software system. Here we see a two-in-one confusion about the use of *system,* which has many different layers of meaning.) The real airplane is outside the physical control system but is part of the environment in which the system operates. The real airplane interacts with the system by sending radio transmissions and by reflecting radar beams. Although the real airplane need not appear in the class model for a system, it would appear in the dynamic model as an external actor— an object that is outside a system but which interacts with it.

Although real world objects are usually active (they initiate action on their own) their surrogates are usually passive—they don't initiate any action within the system. Instead, external events (such as radio messages and radar scans) are used to update the state of the surrogates to match the perceived state of the real-world objects.

This dichotomy between real-world objects and their surrogates within a system causes a lot of trouble for modelers. Most of the time you need the surrogate, and the real-world object may be modeled simply to decide what values to track. The real-world object appears as an actor in the dynamic model.

In simulations, this distinction is not valid. The purpose of a simulation is to create a virtual world, so the simulated object is active within its simulated world. In creating simulations, model the real-world objects, including both their state and their operations, to the level desired by the simulation.

How is a flight plan different? Flight plans must be filed with the appropriate authorities to be valid, so the filed flight plan is part of the system. In this case, there is no discrepancy between a physical object about which our knowledge may be incomplete and an internal surrogate; the internal flight plan *is* the real thing. A flight plan is an *application object*, an object that makes sense only in an application context. In this example, I am using the phrase *application object* more broadly than I normally do, because a flight plan is certainly meaningful beyond a single computer system, but it is similar to other classes such as ticket reservations, meal orders, and so on, in that they are directly known as logical entities within some system, rather than having to be estimated based on physical parameters of the real world.

Confusing an Object with Its Name

Be careful not to confuse an object with its name. An object has identity; it can be distinguished from other objects with the same value. A name is simply a string indistinguishable from other strings with the same value. For example, I have seen someone propose the model of house addresses shown in Figure 5. There are two problems here. First, it is redundant to include more than one object from the same aggregation tree, because the lower-level object (such as **House**) implies all of its enclosing containers (such as **State** and **City**). Second, an **Address** is not an aggregation of objects; it is a composite value containing all of the names found on the aggregation path. The correct model is shown in Figure 6. You can obtain a **House** by using an **Address** value as a search path of qualifiers in the aggregation tree. Note that **Address** is not an object at all; it is merely a composite value, a record structure. (I make a distinction that many modelers ignore between objects—things with identity that can be manipulated—and values—mathematical constructs, possibly structured, out of some mathematical domain, that are fundamentally immutable and have no identity.)

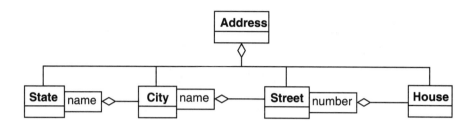

Figure 5. Bad model of address

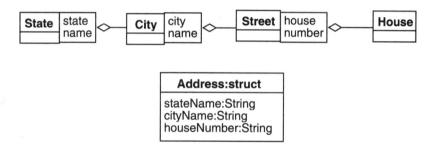

Figure 6. Good model of address

In a nested hierarchy names are often qualifiers within the hierarchy. A *path name* is a sequence of qualifiers, one from each aggregation level starting at the root of the aggregation tree. A path name maps the root object into the leaf object found by traversing the aggregation tree. Each leaf object has a path name that can be found by navigating toward the root object. A house address and a file path name are two examples. Although there is a one-to-one correspondence between path names and leaf objects, they are not the same; one is a composite value, the other a genuine object. Use them both but don't confuse them.

Patterns and Instances

Another situation in which an object appears at two different levels is the case of a pattern and an instance of the pattern. Suppose we want to keep track of telephone services, such as voice messaging and call waiting, which must be subscribed in advance and that have a charge for each use. Figure 7 shows a possible model. Here we see three distinct semantic levels of service:

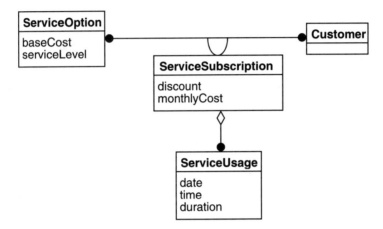

Figure 7. Phone services

1. The phone company has a set of services (such as voice messaging and call waiting) available to each category of customer (such as residential or business). Each **ServiceOption** object has a set of properties, such as cost, availability, and so on.

2. Each customer may subscribe to a set of services. This is an association between **Customer** and **ServiceOption.** We can treat this association as a link class, for example, **Service-Subscription,** and attach properties to it, such as **discount** and **cost** (maybe some customers get a better deal than others).

3. Some services need to be tracked each time they are used. For example, each use of voice messaging may carry an incremental charge in addition to the monthly charge for the availability of the service. I have modeled this as **ServiceUsage** which has a many-to-one association with **ServiceSubscription.**

There is a tendency to model variations as subclasses, for example, one subclass per service type, and let the subclass distinguish the variation, for example, the subscriptions. Although this is not wrong, I have found that it can be restrictive; there is a danger of modeling too much as well as too little. I recommend avoiding subclasses when qualifiers, attributes, or pattern objects will do. Use subclasses when the form of each subclass is different—different attributes, associations, or operations. In this example, we want to avoid making up a new subclass for each new kind of service; instead try to represent the individual differences as different attribute values. Make up subclasses when the attributes themselves are different.

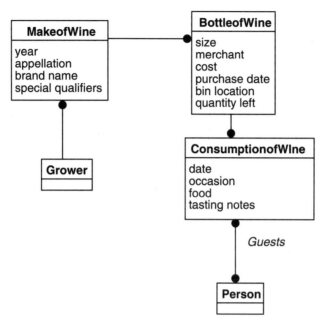

Figure 8. Wine cellar

Wine Cellar

Here is an example that combines a path name with several levels of pattern objects. I want to keep track of my wine cellar. Figure 8 shows a possible model. Here we see three distinct semantic levels:

1. *MakeofWine* is a particular kind of wine from a grower in a particular year—name and year and any other necessary qualifiers to identify the specific batch of wine, for example, *1961 Chateau Lafite* (only in my dreams, folks, not in my cellar). The scheme that I use in a wine database consists of style (e.g., red), year (1989), country (Italy), appellation (Chianti Classico), maker (Rufino), and variety (Riserva Ducale). As there are several ways to organize the qualification, the *MakeofWine* is useful as a well-defined end point.

2. I may own multiple bottles of each make of wine. Each one is a **BottleofWine**, with attributes such as **size, merchant, cost, purchase date, bin location,** and the all-important **quantity left.** There is a one-to-many association between **MakeofWine** and **BottleofWine**.

3. Using a nitrogen gas system, wine can be drunk on several occasions over several days. Each occasion is a **ConsumptionofWine** with attributes such as **date, guests, occasion, food,** and **tasting notes.** There is a one-to-many association between **BottleofWine** and **ConsumptionofWine.**

In a relational database (which is the sensible way to do this) each of these three semantic levels requires its own table. If you try to combine two tables (such as **BottleofWine** and **ConsumptionofWine**) then there are things that you can't show, such as tasting notes over several days. In a relational database the problem of getting the levels distinct is known as *normalization*; in an object model, it corresponds to not confusing two objects that are inherently distinct.

Fat Objects

A final case of two-in-one objects is simply the case in which the modeler has combined two distinct objects into one "fat" object. This is really the general case of merging classes together, so the warning signs are more general too. The main warning sign is a lack of cohesion about the class, a tendency to break up into two or more parts that feel different somehow, a feeling of "discord" about the attributes or operations within the class. This is a somewhat subjective measure, of course, but recognizing discord is a skill that develops over time as someone practices object-oriented modeling. For example, if a class seems to contain several well-defined subsets of attributes, see if the operations partition the same way; if so, the class should be broken up into smaller classes. See if the operations on one part are independent or nearly independent of the other parts. Does the object have two or more concurrent states that can change independently? If so, break it up.

The idea is to avoid unnecessary dependencies between things that can be used independently. A class should be coherent and "single-minded." Of course, it is possible to carry this too far by breaking things into minuscule pieces; you have to strive for a balance between simplicity and precision. Too much detail, too much independence, too much "object-orientedness" can be just as bad as too little.

There are probably many other special cases in which two or more objects get mixed together. Watch for them and try to avoid them and your models will be much cleaner.

On the Horns of the Modeling Dilemma
Choosing among Alternate Modeling Constructs
November 1993

Modeling Choices

I frequently receive inquiries from readers asking for guidance in situations that seem to permit more than one way of modeling. Sometimes there is a clear preference between the choices, sometimes the choice is arbitrary, and sometimes it is necessary include both viewpoints in the model. In this column I will try to show how to resolve some of these conflicts.

Attributes or Subclasses?

There is often a choice between including an enumerated-value attribute in a class or making a separate subclass for each enumeration value of the attribute. For example, we could distinguish three subclasses of books: leatherbound, cloth cover (hardcover), and paperbacks (Figure 1). Alternately, we could make **cover** an attribute of **Book** with the enumerated values of **leather, cloth,** or **paper** (Figure 2). Which one is preferred?

Use generalization when each subclass has a different form: different attributes, operations, or associations. Also use generalization if the subclasses have the same form but different behavior, that is, if they have different methods for the same operations. Use an attribute when the objects can be partitioned into different subsets but all have the same form and behavior. Generalization divides a superclass into subclasses, but so do attribute values; don't use generalization just to partition a set of instance objects. For the **Book** class, we would normally prefer attributes to special subclasses.

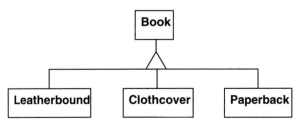

Figure 1. Book subclasses

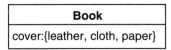

Figure 2. Books distinguished by attribute

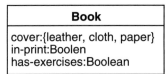

Figure 3. Book with Boolean attributes

A common special case is an attribute that represents a Boolean value. For example, whether a book is in print and whether it has exercises might be Boolean attributes of **Book** (Figure 3). It is unnecessary and messy to make subclasses for special cases that are simply Boolean choices.

Use generalization when the different sets of objects have different forms. For example, a publication is a book or a periodical (Figure 4). Each of these has different characteristics so generalization is most appropriate. Some magazines are numbered consecutively throughout an entire volume of several issues, for example. I have further divided books into simple books and anthologies. Each subclass has different attributes and different associations to other classes.

In some cases, an unnecessary subclass can be eliminated by treating it as a special case. For example, we could distinguish full-fare tickets from discount tickets, but a simpler ap-

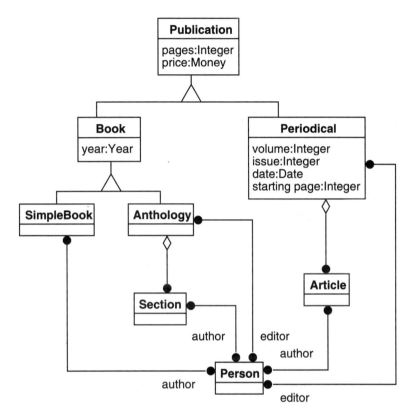

Figure 4. Publication subclasses have distinct forms

proach is to recognize that the difference between full-fare and discount tickets is simply in the nature of the restrictions, such as discount tickets being nonrefundable (Figure 5).

If the values under consideration can change during run time, then you should almost always use attributes rather than making up subclasses, because we don't usually want objects to change class (dynamic classification). For example, if we are keeping track of products in a store, we should make **in stock** a Boolean attribute, rather than having separate classes for **InStockItem** and **OutOfStockItem.**

Novice modelers tend to overuse generalization simply to distinguish sets of objects. Don't introduce a subclass simply to represent a subset of the values a class can hold.

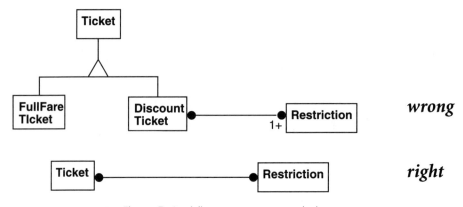

Figure 5. Avoiding an unnecessary subclass

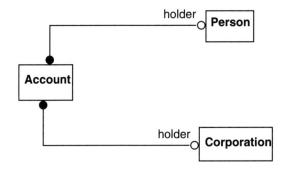

Figure 6. Needs or-associations

Or-Associations

Frequently an association from a class can go to two or more other classes. For example, a bank account can be held by a person or a corporation (Figure 6). The normal way to model an or-association is to use generalization. After all, generalization is the "or-relationship." Figure 7 shows an association between **Account** and **LegalEntity,** which is an abstract class that includes both **Person** and **Corporation.** This shows that an account must have exactly one owner, which can be a person or a corporation. Associations are inherited along with all other information in a superclass.

Although this technique works and captures the semantics correctly, it can be unpleasant to make up abstract classes *just* to share associations. Also, sometimes the various alter-

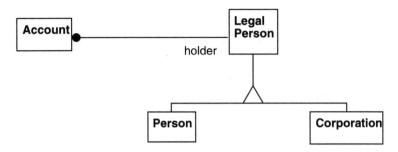

Figure 7. Generalization to model or-associations

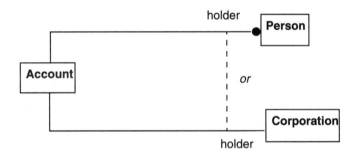

Figure 8. Constraint notation for or-association

nate classes have different multiplicities in the association. For example, perhaps an account could be shared jointly by several persons but a corporate account cannot be shared. One possible notation is shown in Figure 8, in which we allow multiple copies of the association between different classes, but indicate with a constraint that only one of them can exist at a time for a given **Account** object. This notation can be considered as a variation on existing OMT notation, except that we weaken the restriction that two associations must have distinct names and roles.

Figure 9 shows the parent-child relationship. Every person has a mother and a father and therefore participates in two associations as a child, but each person has children in only way, either as a mother or as a father. The or-constraint indicates that a person can have children as either a father or a mother, but not both; the constraint is drawn on the end with the multiple choice, in this case the end labeled "child." There is no constraint on the other ends of the associations, so a child has both a father and a mother association.

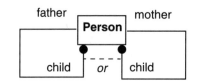

Figure 9. Or-association on a single class

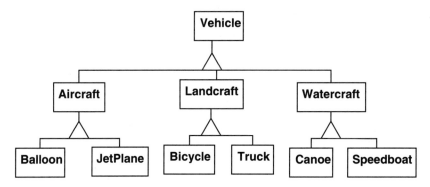

Figure 10. Two layers of generalization

Multiple Specialization

Sometimes a class can be specialized in more than one aspect. Consider vehicles (Figure 10). A vehicle can be specialized on where it travels, either the air, land, or water. Then we could specialize each subclass according to how the vehicle is powered—muscles, wind, motors, and so on. But this requires the duplication of the same kind of generalization for each second-level superclass.

The correct way to model a class with multiple dimensions of specialization is to use multiple specializations from the same superclass. For example, a vehicle can be specialized on its venue (where it goes) and its propulsion (Figure 11). Each distinct way of specializing is a *dimension* of specialization; the dimension name is written on the specialization leg. All the legs with the same aspect name represent different choices for that aspect. (The name can be written on the superclass leg, in which case it applies to all the subclass legs.) Any concrete vehicle must be a combination of each of the generalization aspects, that is, it must

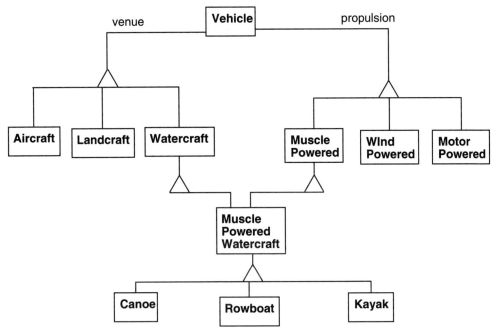

Figure 11. Multiple generalization and multiple inheritance

include both a venue subclass and a propulsion subclass. Class **MusclePoweredWatercraft** multiply inherits from both **Watercraft** and **MusclePowered.**

Multiple specialization implies that the Cartesian product *must* be taken to form concrete classes. You don't have to show all possible combinations in the class diagram. We have explicitly shown **MotorPoweredWatercraft,** but you can make up other combinations at run time, such as **MusclePowered** and **Aircraft,** even though they are not shown explicitly. Implicitly all combinations are valid unless excluded by a constraint.

None of the OO programming languages directly support multiple specialization—they all treat inheritance as a binary relationship between two classes. All of the subclasses of a superclass are equivalent—there is no way to say whether multiple inheritance from them is prohibited (the common case), allowed (overlapping generalization), or mandatory (multiple generalization). This doesn't mean that you can't implement multiple generalization, but you must mix all the subclasses together in one pot and manage the multiple inheritance yourself.

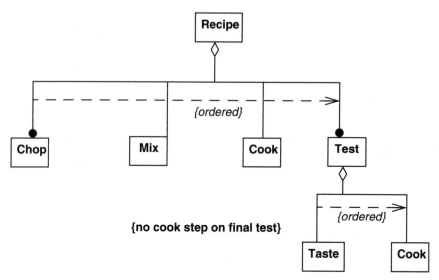

Figure 12. A recipe as an aggregation of steps

Aggregation and Generalization

Figure 12 shows a model for a manufacturing process, say making soup in a factory. We have represented manufacturing a batch of soup as an aggregation of steps, such as **Assemble** and **Mix,** some of which are themselves aggregations of steps. Each object captures the results of performing a step in the factory. I have indicated that the substeps are ordered with respect to one another by a constraint across them. Some of the steps can be applied more than once, as shown by multiplicity of *many.* I have also indicated that the *cook* step is omitted on the final test (that is, when the taste test succeeds, stop reacting). This diagram captures the recipe as a recursive aggregation of ordered parts that are explicitly specified.

At the same time, each step has its own internal description. Each kind of step is a subclass of class **Step** (Figure 13). **Step** holds values common to all steps, such as the start and stop time of each step and the sequence number of each step on its own kind of equipment. This diagram captures the internal form of each step, regardless of how the steps are put together. Together the aggregation hierarchy and the generalization hierarchy capture the external and internal structure of the lot and the steps in it. The classes in an aggregation hierarchy may also be part of a generalization hierarchy, and the two hierarchies need not correspond at all. The generalization hierarchy describes the relationship among classes that

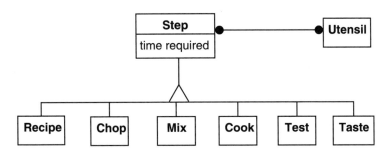

Figure 13. Description of steps

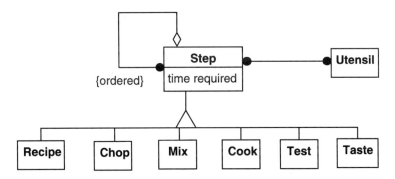

Figure 14. Metamodel of steps in a recipe

form the internal structure of individual object instances; the aggregation hierarchy describes the relationship among the object instances that populate a model. Both are needed in a complete model.

The aggregation hierarchy of Figure 12 is an attempt to capture the detailed semantics of the problem in the model. An alternate way of modeling the aggregation is shown in Figure 14. This is a metamodel for the first model. Here we have represented the entire process as a recursive aggregation of steps, each of which may be one of the steps listed previously (the generalization hierarchy is the same as before). The recursive high-level form of aggregation is simpler and more uniform, but it fails to capture all of the constraints shown in the low-level form. However, the high-level form may actually be preferable for implementation because of its simplicity. It is not always necessary to capture every semantic constraint in the object model; some of them can simply be run-time constraints. The first model is probably too restrictive, especially if we are trying to keep track of what was actu-

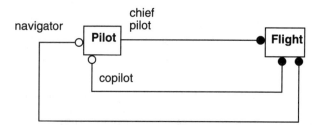

Figure 15. Flight crew as distinct associations

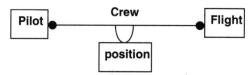

Figure 16. Flight crew as a single association

ally did, rather than what was supposed to be done. The first model is prescriptive and therefore inappropriate; we need to log what actually happened, including possible errors in sequencing. Don't feel that a model must always capture all the semantic restrictions of a situation. Usually it is better to be simple and more general, especially if the constraints may change. However, the first form is useful for communication about the legal process sequences (it is really a syntax diagram and a grammar might be a better way to show it).

Association Generalization

Figure 15 shows the cockpit crew of an airplane flight. There is always a chief pilot, there may be a copilot, and there may be a navigator. Figure 16 shows an alternate way of showing the same information at a higher level. In this case, we have a single association labeled **Crew** with a qualifier **position** to tell the various jobs apart. The higher level form has less information; it doesn't show that a chief pilot is required but that a copilot or a navigator are optional. This is understandable. Any higher level abstraction loses information; you are trading completeness for clarity.

I would argue that the chief pilot, copilot, and navigator associations are all special cases of the crew association. A chief pilot is a crew member, a copilot is a crew member, and a

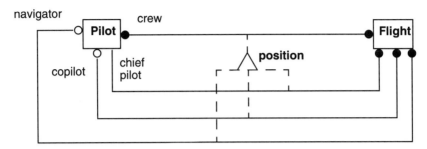

Figure 17. Association generalization

navigator is a crew member. But this is just the definition of generalization! I think that cases like this can be considered examples of *association generalizations.* Consider the notation shown in Figure 17 to represent association generalization; the crew association is the superassociation, and the other three are the subassociations that it covers. I have used the generalization symbol as in class generalization (the triangle with branching lines); the dotted lines are simply to reduce visual conflict with the solid association lines.

How would association generalization be implemented? The two levels of association are not independent; only one level needs to be implemented. Most of the time it is probably simpler and cleaner to implement the links as a top-level association and let the subassociations be thought of as run-time constraints on its contents. We could add a discriminator (an enumerated value that tells which subassociation it is) as a link attribute of the superassociation in the implementation, that is, we use the implementation of Figure 16. In other cases, the subassociations might be implemented directly as distinct associations, as in Figure 15.

Figure 18 shows two alternate ways of modeling the family relationships shown in Figure 9. We can model the relationship either as a single high-level association (**parent-child**) or we can use two associations with distinct roles **father** and **mother** connecting to distinct subclasses **Man** and **Woman.** In general, it is best not to make subclasses out of roles (such as copilot or navigator), but to use subclasses only to show inherent differences among objects. However, in this case the distinction between men and women is inherent and a legitimate use of subclassing.

Figure 20 shows the correspondence between the high-level and low-level views, using the proposed notation for association generalization. It is necessary to draw arrows on the association paths so the roles can be matched up correctly: role **parent** in the superassociation goes with role **mother** and role **father** in the subassociation. In this case we could figure out the correspondence from context, but in general the arrows help to clarify things.

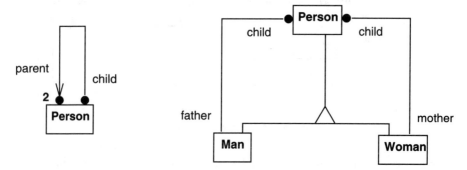

Figure 18. Alternate ways of expressing relationships

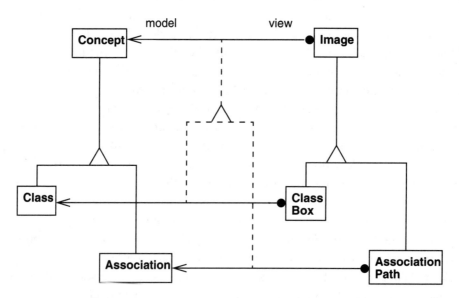

Figure 19. Association generalization with parallel hierarchies

Parallel Generalizations

Figure 19 shows the use of association generalization in the presence of parallel generalization hierarchies. This represents an object model of an OMT diagram editor using a model-

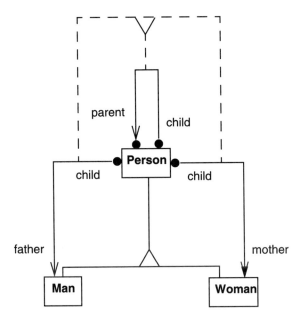

Figure 20. Association generalization with subclasses

view-controller type of architecture. There is a hierarchy of classes describing the objects representing semantic concepts, such as **Class** and **Association.** Collectively these are derived from class **Concept,** because they provide the semantics of the diagram but do not describe its appearance on the screen. There is another hierarchy of classes describing the graphical images on the screen, such as **ClassBox** and **AssociationPath.** These are all derived from class **Image** and they describe visual objects on the screen. Each view object describes one concept object; each concept object may have many image objects that provide different graphical views of it.

Any concept object cannot go with any image object. The match-up must correspond to the parallel generalization hierarchies: **Class** goes with **ClassBox, Association** goes with **AssociationPath**, and so on for other classes that I have omitted. I have shown this correspondence using the association generalization notation suggested above. If we use arrows on the associations to show directionality, then the role names on the subassociations can be omitted, because they can be inherited (although it is often a good idea to repeat them on the subassociations).

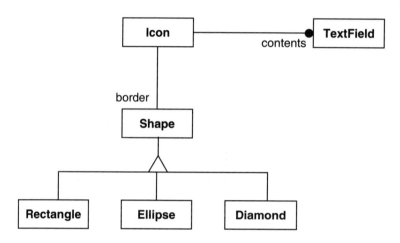

Figure 21. One-to-one association

One-to-One Associations

When there is a one-to-one association between two classes, there can be doubt as to whether the classes are actually distinct or whether they should be combined into a single class. If the association is optional in one or both directions, then the classes are distinct. Similarly, if the linkage between object instances can change at run time, then the classes are distinct. Figure 21 shows a graphic icon that has a border and text contents. Each icon has one border, which is a shape. If the border shape can change dynamically, then the distinction between the icon and its border shape is important.

Even if the classes are not semantically distinct, it can be useful to break a class into several parts that are in one-to-one correspondence so that each part will be simpler and smaller. Even if an icon has a fixed shape, it can be useful to break out the border as a separate object so that methods on shapes will be different from methods on text and methods that connect the icon to other icons. However, it is probably best not to break up classes arbitrarily unless there is a good semantic reason.

If another association connects to one of the one-to-one classes, you should determine which class in the pair it connects to semantically. If the one-to-one connection changes, which class should the other association remain attached to? In Figure 21, if we change the border shape, the text contents should not change, so the **TextField** association is correctly attached to the **Icon** class rather than the **Border** class. But suppose we add **Path** objects that

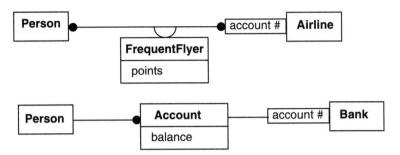

Figure 22. Link class versus ordinary class

connect icons together. Should the **Path** objects be connected to the **Icon** class or to the **Border** class? A good argument could be made for either alternative. When two alternatives seem equally good, then pick one and don't worry about it excessively.

Promoting Associations to Classes

Classes and associations are both kinds of entities, and associations can be treated as similar to classes. In the OMT notation we have the concept of an *association class,* that is, an association that is also treated as a class. An association class can have attributes, operations, and associations to other classes, but it is still an association and its elements take their identity from the objects that they connect. An alternative to using an association class is simply using an ordinary class connected to each of the classes in the original association by an association of multiplicity *one*. Which form should we use?

An association is a set of links. A link of an association or a link class (which is an association) represents a single unique relation between a pair of objects. You can't have more than one link between the same pair of objects; an association is a set, not a bag. If you can have more than one element connecting the same pair of objects, then you must promote the association to an ordinary class, otherwise you should use a link class.

Figure 22 illustrates this choice. Persons can sign up with the frequent flyer programs of various airlines, but the airlines require that each person may only have a single frequent flyer account with that airline, so frequent flyer membership should be modeled as a link class. On the other hand, a person can have several accounts with the same bank, so we cannot model a bank account as a link class; we must make it into an ordinary class. In both cases, the account number qualifies the organization issuing accounts (airline or bank).

Summary

Don't be concerned if you think of more than one way to model a situation. There are many correct models of any problem. Some modeling conflicts represent alternate ways to model a situation in which you would not pick both, such as the choice between subclasses and attributes to partition sets of objects. Other modeling conflicts represent different views of the same situation, such as the need for both aggregation and generalization or the choice between a high-level view and a low-level view. In such cases it is useful or even necessary to include both views in the model.

Disinherited!
Examples of Misuse of Inheritance
February 1993

Misusing Inheritance

Inheritance is probably the feature that most people think of first when the phrase "object-oriented" is mentioned. I have argued that other things are even more important, but there is no denying that inheritance is important both conceptually and pragmatically. Because of its high profile, inheritance gets misused a lot, even by people who ought to know better. In this column, I will cite some examples of misuse of inheritance that I have observed in published examples. I have disguised the examples to protect the guilty.

There is a simple rule that distinguishes most (mis)uses of inheritance: B is a subclass of A if you would say "B *is an* A." The *is-a* test is not infallible but it identifies most cases of inheritance misuse.

A distinction is often made in the object-oriented literature between a *type* and a *class*. A type is meant to be a logical black box specification of externally-visible behavior, whereas a class is meant to be an implementation description of internal form used for convenience without regard to logical typing. Later I argue that a class should always be a type. For the time being, you can interchange the words *type* and *class*.

Confusing the forest and the trees

The first misuse is shown in Figure 1. A apple orchard is alleged to be a subclass of both orchard and of apple tree. I have seen this kind of error in print several times. An apple or-

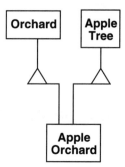

Figure 1. An apple orchard is not an apple tree

chard *is* an orchard. It should inherit all the properties of orchards. However, an apple orchard *is not* an apple tree. It *contains* apple trees, but containment has nothing to do with inheritance. Containment is an aggregation relationship, not a taxonomic relationship. Because an apple orchard contains apple trees, apple orchards may share some of the properties of apple trees, but the sharing must be deliberate and selective. For example, the harvest time of an orchard is the same as that of its trees, but the size of the orchard is much greater than the size of a tree. Only use inheritance when you want to inherit *all* of the properties of a superclass, not just some of them. Use aggregation when one object is made of other objects and *some* of the properties of the aggregate are shared by the parts. Figure 2 shows a correct model, in which there are two parallel subclass relationships: apple orchard is a subclass of orchard and apple tree is a subclass of fruit tree; orchards contain fruit trees and apple orchards contain apple trees. The second containment relationship is a refinement of the first; it is an example of *association inheritance.*

This confusion of a container class (such as an array or an orchard) with the things it contains (such as trees) usually involves the use of multiple inheritance when single inheritance and aggregation would have been correct. Multiple inheritance is absolutely necessary for correctly modeling many situations, but this is not one of them.

The Medium Is Not the Message

Don't confuse a class with the classes needed to implement it. Just because a class is implemented using other classes doesn't make it inherit from them. Suppose we want to represent a set of students taking a course, as shown in Figure 3. Logically we have a many-to-many

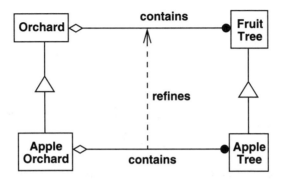

Figure 2. Parallel specialization as homomorphism

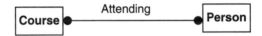

Figure 3. Logical model of students taking classes

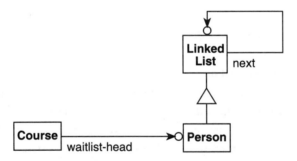

Figure 4. Bad model: A person is not a linked list

association between **Course** and **Person.** I have seen the implementation shown in Figure 4 suggested, in which the arrows show associations implemented in one direction as pointers. This implementation works (if you can call it that) only if each person can only take a single course. Can we honestly say that a person *is* a linked list? Hardly. This model has confused a construct used to implement a class (the linked list) with the class itself (the person).

If you *must* use a linked list (and there is hardly any reason to ever do so) then Figure 5 shows a better model of an implementation. First we have separated the linked list (the

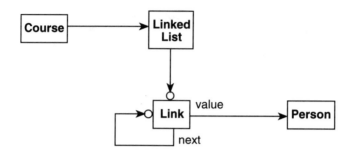

Figure 5. Good model: A linked list that references persons

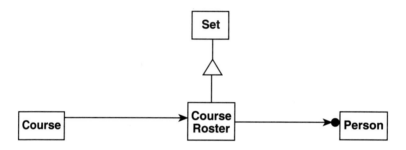

Figure 6. Use meaningful aggregates

whole thing) from its individual link elements. We have also externalized the link pointers from the **Person** objects, so that a person can be a member of many lists at once. In any case, we can see that a person and a linked list are two separate objects.

Even though this implementation works, it is not a good design model. For one thing, the students in the class are unordered, so a linked list is overly restrictive. Figure 5 is an example of premature implementation, which is usually accompanied by overspecification.

Person and **Link** are really at different levels of abstraction and should not be mixed in a model, because they don't relate. If you insist on modeling an aggregate for the set of persons in the course, then introduce a class that is meaningful in the application, such as **CourseRoster** as shown in Figure 6. I have shown this class as a subclass of **Set**. When you program this in a language, you could use a specific implementation of set. (Make sure your class library contains an implementation of Set using hash tables. If it builds sets out of linked lists, throw it away and find a decent class library.)

Most of the time I do not feel it is necessary to create classes to represent sets of objects in a model. Most sets are adequately represented by the *many* multiplicity on an association, as shown in Figure 3. Sure, these sets will be implemented using container classes, but there is no reason to put the container classes into the model. Only create a class to model a set (or array) if the class has operations of its own beyond simply adding or retrieving elements.

There Are Constraints on Inheritance

There are two ways to go about specifying a subclass. The first is to describe the incremental differences from the base class, in terms of new attributes or operations. All of the instances of the new class have to be explicitly identified. This is the normal kind of subclassing supported by object-oriented languages. I call this subclassing by augmentation.

The other way to form a subclass is to specify some constraint that instances of a base class must satisfy to be considered members of the new class. I call this subclassing by *restriction,* because the set of instances of the base class is restricted by the constraint to yield a set of instances of the new class. For example, a square is a polygon with four equal sides and four equal angles. This is the normal kind of type definition used in mathematics, but it does not match well the concepts in most object-oriented languages. The problem is that operations on the base class might modify an object so that it violates its constraints and ceases to be an instance of its restriction subclass. For example, a stretch operation might turn a square into a rectangle. Now there is nothing wrong mathematically with having objects change type. As I have stressed previously, it is object identity that is most fundamental, not inheritance or even classes. However, all major object-oriented languages expect objects not to change class during execution. This is an unnecessary limitation, of course, but for (supposed) efficiency reasons it is there, so we might as well accept it and go on.

But this means that you should not use subclassing by restriction. A square is *not* a subclass of rectangle, at least not in most object-oriented languages. Many authors have mistakenly used this kind of example to illustrate inheritance and subclassing, but they did not realize that there are two fundamentally different and opposed kinds of subclassing, one of which (restriction) is incompatible with most languages.

You can think of restrictions as defining different states of a class. An object can change states freely but cannot change class. It would be convenient if object-oriented languages would support state using the class descriptor mechanism, including method dispatching dependent on state. The existing typing and dynamic binding mechanism could be easily extended in C++ or Smalltalk, but I suppose it is too late to hope for this kind of change.

None of these problems arise if we have only pure functions as methods, that is, methods that do not have side effects, because the constraint cannot be violated if there are no changes in value. On the other hand, a functional object-oriented language is totally absurd—the purpose of identity (and therefore objects) is to preserve meaning over changes of value, and that inherently means side effects. Objects are all about side effects.

Implementation Inheritance

Implementation inheritance is the use of inheritance for programming convenience when instances of the subclass are not true instances of the superclass. Typically a programmer will find an existing class that is close to the desired target class, and will add, delete, or modify attributes or operations to make it come out right.

For example, suppose we have an **AsciiFile** class and want a **BinaryFile** class. A binary file is a lot like an ASCII file. Maybe we can just inherit **BinaryFile** from **AsciiFile** and make a few modifications. We could represent a binary word as a series of bytes.

Adding properties doesn't cause any trouble, but deleting or modifying them means that operations on the superclass might be invalid on the new subclass. This means that instances of the subclass cannot be used in all places where instances of the superclass are accepted, violating one of the main tenets of object-oriented programming.

Often the programmer will argue that the subclass is not supposed to be interchangeable with the superclass. After all, the subclassing was just for convenience, and who is to know? The subclass takes the operations it wants and suppresses the others. This reasoning may work well enough at first, but if operations are added to the superclass then the subclass will inherit them too, unless they are also suppressed. But this kind of dependency defeats the very modularity that object-oriented programming is meant to avoid.

We could be in for a nasty surprise with our binary file. Perhaps the ASCII file traps certain combinations, such as carriage return–newline, and maps them into something else, such as a simple newline. This could wreak havoc with our binary words.

A better principle is to make sure that a subclass is always fully compatible with its superclass in every respect. As some people put it, a class (considered as an implementation construct) should be a type (considered as a logical specification of behavior).

There is a growing backlash against the use of implementation inheritance. Several speakers at the recent OOPSLA'92 Conference denounced it. Avoid it on both theoretical and pragmatic grounds. Theoretically it spoils the principle that any subclass can be used where the superclass is accepted. Pragmatically you will eventually get tripped up by unexpectedly inheriting something you don't want if you use it. You will be sorry if you do.

How to Avoid Implementation Inheritance

Generally the use of implementation inheritance indicates a flawed object model that is easily repaired. There are two alternatives that usually work.

If class B is similar to class A but not a true subclass of it, a new abstract class C can often be constructed to hold the similarities of both A and B, with A and B each being subclasses of C. If the semantic relationships are correct, then class C can be extended with new operations that will be inherited by both A and B.

In our example, there is no reason to have one kind of file inherit from the other. Obviously both **AsciiFile** and **BinaryFile** should inherit from **File,** an abstract class that captures all the similarities between the two kinds of files. (Obvious? But have you ever tried to transmit binary data over an ASCII modem that treated certain characters as controls?)

Sometimes it is not possible to interpolate new abstract classes into the class library, which may be read–only, for example. In other cases the original and target classes don't share much other than a few operations or attributes. In these cases, it is best to simply use class A as a component in the implementation of B. There is no attempt to use inheritance. Any operations on A that are needed on B are simply implemented in B as calls to A. This has the added benefit that the operations on B can have different names that may be more appropriate for B. Sure, this means that you have to list the operations that you want to "inherit" and do the work yourself, rather than automatically inheriting them, but any time a subclass is not fully compatible with its superclass you have to specify what you want to keep one way or another, so you might as well be clean about it. If someone extends class A, then there is no impact on class B, because it only uses the operations on A that it needs and is unaffected by any new ones.

For example, it is possible to implement a stack using a variable-length array, but you should not use inheritance. Instead let the array be an attribute of the stack. You will have to redirect the **push** operation on the stack to the **append** operation on the array, for example, but this permits the proper names to be used on each class.

Avoiding Probate

You will have little trouble with incorrect use of inheritance if the following statement is always true when you use it: an instance of the subclass *is* in every respect an instance of the superclass.

Behavior Modeling

P ROGRAMS consist of structure and behavior, data and function, statics and dynamics. Most object-oriented methods have been good at modeling the static structure of systems. The modeling of dynamics has been more problematical. The original OMT book was strong on structural modeling but weak on behavioral modeling. The main behavioral modeling construct was data flow diagrams, which were familiar to many people from the non-object-oriented Structured Analysis method, but which many people felt were not truly object-oriented. Behavior within a single object could be shown by state machines, but I came to realize that the interesting thing was behavior that crossed objects and classes, which OMT originally could not show effectively. Eventually I decided that the essence of behavior was the flow of control among objects, and *collaboration diagrams (object message diagrams)* were the right way to show the flow of control between objects. I adopted Booch's object diagram notation with some additions from Fusion and some nuances of my own. *Going with the Flow: Flow Graphs in Their Various Manifestations* explains collaboration diagrams and their deep relationship to data flow diagrams. This evolution in thinking led me to the profound realization that object-orientation works because it fundamentally unifies data structure, control structure, and data flow structure. I no longer think it is useful to actually construct data flow diagrams; they are implicit in the other models anyway, which is why they are not needed in practice.

Many object-oriented techniques are essentially extensions of good practices that were invented in pre-object-oriented times. Not all, however; the concept of *reification* is about as object-oriented as you can get. Reification means taking something that is originally not considered an object and treating it as an object. It permits intractable things such as operations to be modeled in a flexible way that permits manipulation and modification. Reification is a tool that every object-oriented modeler and programmer should have in the conceptual tool kit. *Let There Be Objects: A Short Guide to Reification* introduces the concept of reification and gives some examples of its use. *Forceful Functions: How to do Computation* shows how to model a numerical computation problem, an area of programming practice that is often ignored by new computer science graduates. Reification is useful in such problems to permit variant algorithms within a single program framework. *DrivIng to a Solution: Reification and the Art of System Design* shows how to design a system architecture using reification to permit future extensions without having to redesign the program.

Going with the Flow
Flow Graphs in Their Various Manifestations
June 1994

Structures and Flows

To understand how a program works we must understand both its static structure and its behavior. Static structure is embodied in object classes and their relationships as shown in an object model. Behavior is implemented by messages, events, and methods as described in the dynamic and functional models. During analysis it is sufficient to describe a system operation nondeclaratively in terms of "before and after" conditions on the objects in the system. During design, however, we must specify how the transformations in the system state actually come about one step at a time, and this requires following the flow of control and data from object to object and operation to operation during the execution of the program. The flow of control and data cannot be adequately understood by looking at individual classes in isolation; instead we must understand how the objects in a system work together to make behavior happen. We can *describe* a system perfectly well in a reductionist manner, one class and one operation at a time; after all, that is what code is, and that is what is found in class library descriptions. But to *understand* complex behavior it is necessary to take a more holistic view to observe how all the pieces go together.

In this column I describe a major extension from our book [1] to OMT for design purposes: collaboration diagrams. Collaboration diagrams show the flow of control and data between and through objects in a system. I feel that this notation repairs one of the main complaints voiced against the original OMT, the lack of an adequate notation for describing procedural behavior during design. At the same time I want to show the intimate relationship between data flow and control flow. There has been a lot of nonsense written to the effect that data flow is not object oriented, and I want to dispel that misconception.

Flow Graphs

A flow graph is a directed graph that shows how something propagates through a network of nodes. The "something" can be materials, signals, data, or control; the nodes can be machine tools, signal processors, functions, or objects. Flow graphs have been around for a long time—at least 30 years as a formal computer science notation—and come in many different variations. A state transition diagram is a flow graph showing the flow of control among the states within a single object. A flow chart is a flow graph that shows the flow of control among the statements in a procedure.

The most interesting flow graphs show flows through an entire system rather than a single object or procedure. The two main varieties are *data flow diagrams* and *collaboration diagrams*. Data flow diagrams show the flow of data values through functions. Collaboration diagrams show the flow of control through methods on objects. I will show how the two are fundamentally related.

Before extending OMT I searched the literature, including both classic methodologies and object-oriented methodologies, for existing flow graph notations. There are more variations on object interaction notations than on any other kind of notation. This variety indicates that object interactions are an important concept that many people find useful, but that they have multiple purposes that are hard to combine in a single diagram. As I see it, there is a tension between trying to show everything relevant about a program and making the explanation understandable. To understand a complex program at a high level, we must omit details and tell "white lies" about its low level behavior. All modeling notations can be applied at different levels, but program execution can be approached at many different useful levels, probably more levels than most other concepts. So rather than trying to fix one level of detail as "best" I will show how to go from a high-level view of things to an extremely detailed view, a view that would be rarely used in practice.

The notation I use for object interaction graphs is adopted primarily from Booch's object diagrams [2] with the addition of Fusion's numbering scheme [3]. I add a few variations of my own when necessary. Don't get hung up on notational nitpicking! A diagram is not meant to be a formal theoretical model but a vehicle for human understanding. You can't show everything on a single diagram and still draw it, so don't try. I can and have made up theoretical models of computation that do show everything, but they are too complex to draw for any realistic program; I don't intend to bore you with these.

A Convoluted Example

I am going to illustrate flow graph notations and the process of using them to design a program. For this purpose I will use an actual program example drawn from the *Smalltalk/V for Macintosh: Programmer's Reference Manual*, Chapter 6 [4]. This chapter describes how to build a user interface using the various facilities of the Smalltalk/V system, including the model-view-controller paradigm (see the article "Modeling Models and Viewing Views," page 297). The class library provides a lot of built-in user interface classes with complicated behavior intended to be used in many different circumstances. I found the example in the reference manual difficult to follow because control jumps all over from object to object (a frequent pattern in object-oriented programs) including reentrant loops in the flow of control into the same object multiple times. I drew a collaboration diagram to "reverse engineer" the program and understand its operation better. The collaboration diagram made the program comprehensible and laid bare the underlying structure in the Smalltalk/V model-view-controller implementation.

I started by modeling the program in full detail and then abstracting the collaboration diagram to focus on essentials by omitting low-level programming details, such as access method "boiler plate." This is a good way to go about reverse engineering or understanding an existing program (including one of your own). However, in this column I will present the example as a design exercise in the forward direction, starting with a high-level view of what we are trying to accomplish and proceeding step-by-step to carry out the design by adding successive detail.

The simple Smalltalk/V application is called "list keeper." Its purpose is to maintain a list of one-line text strings in alphabetical order. The application contains a window with the following parts: a list pane with the sorted list of text strings, a text pane for typing new strings, an "add" button for adding a string from the text pane to the list, and a "delete" button for deleting the selected string in the list. When the user adds an item it becomes the selected string. If the user clicks on a string in the list it becomes selected and it is copied into the text pane.

The purpose of the example in the manual is to teach people how to build user interfaces, including how to construct windows and panes, how to draw into them, and how to manage the flow of control using the model-view-controller paradigm. The latter goal is the one I am interested in for this column.

Figure 1 shows a class diagram for the List Keeper application. Most of the components are taken directly or inherited from existing classes in the library, including **Button, Pane, Window,** and **Application.** The existing classes bring with them a lot of useful behavior, but they also bring interaction rules that must be observed, as the design process will make clear. Reuse is a major goal of object-oriented design, but you must understand how something works before you can reuse it.

Figure 2 shows an object diagram for this application. [In the past we have used the phrase *object diagram* to denote the diagram showing the classes in the system. Other authors have called this a *class diagram* because it describes classes, and from now on I will do the same. I will reserve the phrase *object diagram* to denote a diagram showing object instances; to avoid confusion I may sometimes call this an *object instance diagram*. The phrase *object model* continues to include collections containing both kinds of diagram.] The object diagram shows the individual objects in a List Keeper program together with their links to other objects. I have named the objects to identify them in discourse. The names of the objects are underlined to help distinguish them from classes.

The object diagram shows the model-view-controller structure. The **listKeeper** object is the controller for the application; it coordinates the flow of control in response to external input events from the **addButton** and **deleteButton.** The controller object is connected to three subject (or model) objects that contain semantic data and to two view objects that present the data on the screen for user interaction. The **textPane** (view) is a widget that presents the **textContents** string (model) as an editable line of text on the screen. These are a model-view pair. The **listPane** (view) is a widget that presents the **listContents** string list (model) together with a **listSelection** string (model) as a list of text lines on the screen with the selected string highlighted. The **listContents** and **listSelection** models are jointly mapped into the **listPane** view, a construct that is slightly more complicated than a model-view pairing but not hard to understand. Conceptually model and view objects are directly connected and can communicate, although we will see that the final implementation is somewhat more indirect because of packaging and reuse considerations in the class library. Nevertheless, start a design by building a simple logical model of what you are trying to accomplish, then modify it to accommodate the complexities of an actual class library.

Why start with an object diagram when our goal is to understand flow of control? Because in an object-oriented system, *control flows from object to object along data link*s, so we must understand the objects and their links before we can understand the flow of control.

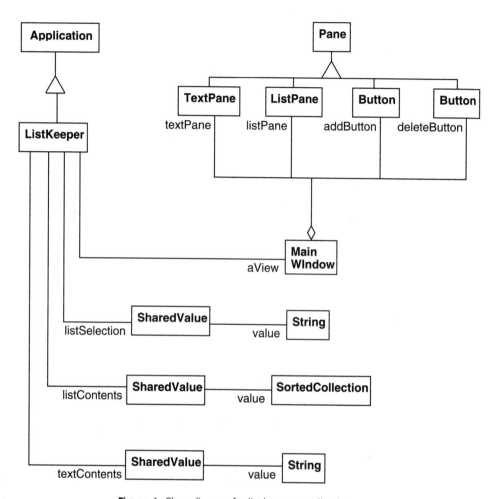

Figure 1. Class diagram for list keeper application

Data Flows

Most program design consists of designing methods (operations, procedures, functions, subroutines, whatever you call them). The main job of most methods is to transform the data state of the system. A *transformation* is a function from data values before the operation

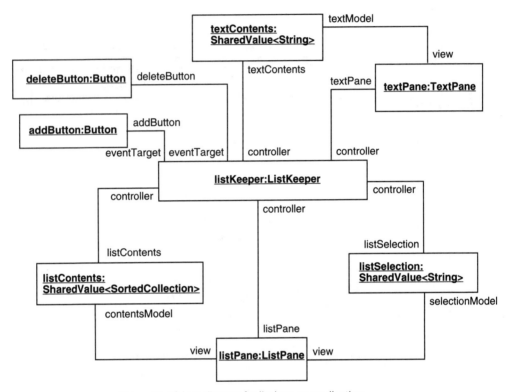

Figure 2. Object diagram for list keeper application

to data values after the operation. A transformation can be shown as a *data flow diagram*. A *pure data flow diagram* shows the functional relationship between *data values*, not between *variables*. A variable is a cell with identity over time; a value is an immutable piece of data of some mathematical type. Variables *contain* a sequence of values over time. A value is the result of a particular computation and is unaffected by time. If we increment the variable x, then there are two values involved, the value of x before the operation (which we might designate simply x) and the value of x after the operation (which we might designate x' using standard mathematical conventions). A data flow diagram for the operation would show the relationship among the values x, x', the number 1, and the *plus* function. Understood in this way, a data flow diagram does not need to show control flow, because the functional dependencies are independent of time.

Figure 3 shows an object-oriented data flow diagram for the operation that occurs when the user clicks the *add* button. This diagram shows functions (ellipses) and values (flows), but I have added a couple of pieces of notation to make it object-oriented. I have drawn object icons enclosing their functions (ellipses) and their internal data values (small boxes). A data value is simply a data flow stored in object, so all data values directly connected by flow arcs have the same value. For example, we see that one result of executing the operation is to copy the text value from the **textPane** object into the **listSelection** and **listPane** objects. The only substantive function is the **add:aString** operation in the **listContents** object, which adds the string from the **textPane** to the old string list value (*list*) to produce a new string list value (*list'*), which is copied into the *contents* value of the **listPane**. I have drawn a dotted line between values *list* and *list'* to indicate that they are successive values of the same variable *list*. In the case of the **listSelection** and **listPane** objects, I have not shown the old values of the variables, because they do not enter into the computation; they are simply replaced by the new values that we see in the diagram.

The data flow diagram tells us what the computation is supposed to do, that is, what the final result is supposed to be, but it does not say how it is to come about. It does *not* imply that the objects communicate directly along the data flow paths. The actual control paths are usually more indirect, so we use collaboration diagrams to see them.

I no longer recommend the use of data flow diagrams for design. The experience of most users has suggested that data flow diagrams are not necessary for detailed design. However, I show them here to demonstrate the strong connection between data flow and control flow. Understanding this connection can help guide the design of control flows in applications, even if the data flow diagrams themselves need not be drawn.

Control Flow

Control can only flow along data links in an object-oriented system. Data links are relationships between pairs of objects. Data links can be semi-permanent (associations) or temporary (arguments to an operation or local variables within an operation), or they can be universal (a global server known to all), but we can represent them all as links between objects in an object diagram. We can optionally show what kind of links they are, that is, the visibility of each reference (universal, association, argument, local). I recommend starting with plain links and then adding visibility information later.

The object diagram in Figure 2 shows the links available within the list keeper application. On the other hand, the data flow diagram in Figure 3 shows the data flows that we want

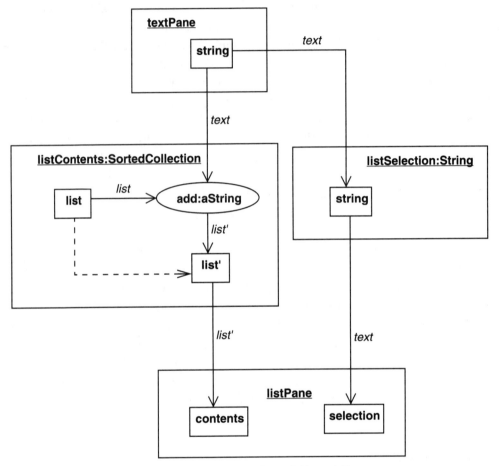

Figure 3. Data flow resulting from clicking add button

to establish. What is the relation between the two diagrams? In an object-oriented system, *all data flows along control paths.* To move a value from one object to another, the object has to pass the value as an argument or a result of a method. Unlike a conventional program, in an object-oriented program you can't separate data flow from control flow; they use the same paths, and *both data flow paths and control flow paths follow data links in the object model.* This is the key to relating data flow, control flow, and object structure and to integrating the three OMT models (object, dynamic, and functional).

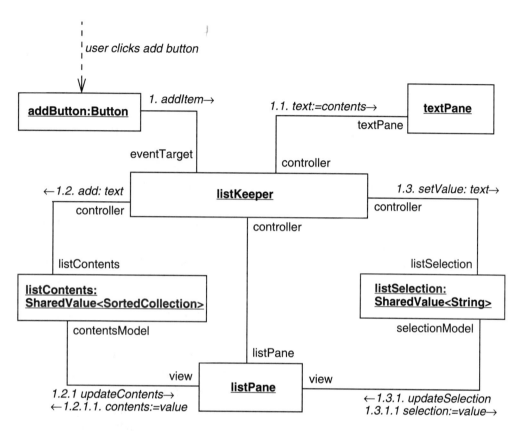

Figure 4. Collaboration diagram for clicking add button

Figure 4 shows a *collaboration diagram*. This is just an object (instance) diagram with control flows indicated by message labels along various interobject links. An arrow shows the direction of control flow. The label includes the message name and arguments. If the method returns a value, it is indicated by an assignment statement (e.g., **selection := value**, which indicates that the result of calling the **value** method on the target object is the value that we call **selection**). The label numbers indicate the sequence of nested operations using a Dewey Decimal kind of notation. Fractional numbers indicate a sequence of suboperations nested within an operation.

The collaboration diagram notation uses Booch's object diagram notation [2] with OMT notation for objects and links. The nested sequence numbering notation is taken from Fusion [3]; most previous authors used a sequential numbering scheme for all the calls within a sequence at any nesting depth, but this made it impossible to distinguish reentrant calls from independent sequential calls.

A collaboration diagram usually describes a single execution scenario, not the general case, but in many cases (such as this one) a single case is prototypical anyway. The general case can be shown using branch conditions on flows. However, in many complicated cases, such as iterated recursion, the general case is too complicated to understand directly and is best understood by examining several typical cases with sample data structures, which are often themselves recursive.

Let me walk through the diagram to explain how it works. The user initiates the operation by clicking the **add button.** The diagram describes the effects of that stimulus. First the **addButton** sends an **addItem** message to the controller, the **listKeeper** object, over the **eventTarget** link. The final implementation does not actually use an association link, but when building a design start with a simple logical model and modify it later as necessary. No matter how it is eventually coded, the button has some kind of reference to the controller, so that's how we represent it for now.

We see that the **addItem** method (number 1) makes three calls on suboperations (numbers 1.1, 1.2, and 1.3). First it sends the **contents** message to the **textPane** object using the **textPane** link; this message returns the local value which we call **text.** Next (number 1.2) it sends the **add:text** message to the **listContents** object with the value of **text** that it just obtained. Clearly message 1.2 must follow message 1.1 because it uses the result of message 1.1. The **add:text** method adds the text string to the sorted list of strings and then calls the **updateContents** method (1.2.1) on the **listPane** object, using the **view** link. The **listContents** and **listPane** are part of a model-view pair (triangle actually, because **listPane** is a view of two model objects).

So far the collaboration diagram has been a direct mapping from the data flow diagram. Messages 1.1 and 1.2 move **text** value from **textPane** to **listContents** by way of the controller **listKeeper.** Where did **listKeeper** come from? It is not in the data flow diagram. The answer is that data can only flow along data links in the object diagram, and in Figure 2 there is no direct link from **textPane** to **listContents,** so we have to propagate the data indirectly through **listKeeper.** Each data flow requires a control flow to actually move the data between objects. In message 1.1 the data flow is in the reverse direction from the control flow, as is typical in access operations that return values. In message 1.2 the data flow is in the same direction as the control flow. In any case, it is fairly simple to convert the data flow of Figure 3 into the control flow of Figure 4, and most people would not have to draw the data flow diagram, but I have shown it to emphasize that it is implicit whether or not you actually draw it.

Back at message 1.2.1, **listContents** sends the **updateContents** message to the **listPane** without arguments. At first this might seem a bit strange. After all, we want to propagate the new list contents value **list'** to the **listPane** so it can update its screen image. Why not just pass it in? In fact, this would be the simplest approach, if this were a stand-alone application, but we want to reuse the existing **ListPane** class within the model-view-controller framework, so we can't just do anything we like. In this framework, subject objects don't pass data directly to view objects. Instead a model object notifies its view object that it has changed, and the view object is responsible for extracting the relevant data from the model object. So **listContents,** the model object, sends a parameterless **updateContents** message (1.2.1) to **listPane,** the view object, which turns around and pulls the data out of the **listContents** by calling it back with the **value** message (1.2.1.1), an access method that returns the list of strings as **contents.** The final effect is to establish all the paths in the data flow diagram, albeit with some indirection in the control flow. A similar flow of control happens in message 1.3 and its suboperations, in which the selection is updated and sent to the **listPane.** Because the contents must be in place in the list pane before the selection can be updated, the selection update sequence (1.3) must follow the contents update sequence (1.2). In the original data flow diagram there was no sequencing relationship between the contents and selection, but the actual **ListPane** class imposes such a dependency, so we must observe it. (Conceivably the **ListPane** could keep track of the selection even before the list is changed. I don't think it does that, but I could be wrong.)

So, to convert a data flow to a control flow, start with the desired data flows, then lay out control paths to propagate the data where it is supposed to go, then add indirection to the control paths to accommodate constraints on the available methods. In the final diagram we have continuous data flow paths and continuous control flow paths that overlap and interlock but that are not identical.

The collaboration diagram is equivalent to another OMT diagram, the sequence diagram (formerly the event trace diagram). A *sequence diagram* is a list of interactions ordered in time, where the objects are shown as vertical bars. Figure 5 shows a sequence diagram for this same scenario. I have shown both calls and returns (using Smalltalk return symbols "∧") as separate control flows. The sequence of calls is much clearer, but the object links are not shown and the one-dimensional layout of objects prevents the use of geographical locality to organize related objects. This illustrates that modeling diagrams have both form and content; different views of the same thing are appropriate for clearly bringing out different aspects of the information. For procedural flow of control, I prefer the collaboration diagram; for real time scheduling, I prefer the sequence diagram because the timing is more apparent.

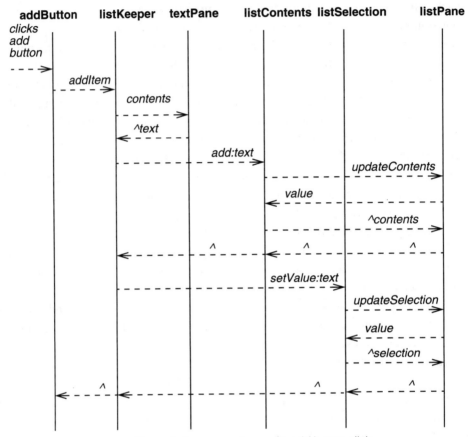

Figure 5. Sequence diagram for add button click

In addition to the sequence diagram, note that several other kinds of diagrams can be derived from a collaboration diagram: A structure chart is a tree of nested procedure calls; just trace out the nested calls and arrange them into a tree. A data flow diagram can be constructed by following the flow of data forward and backward over control paths, then eliding data flows that simply pass through intermediate objects on the way to a final destination.

Full detail

I have outlined the design of the *add text* operation, but the actual implementation is still more complicated and convoluted. Figure 6 shows the full implementation of this operation as supplied by Smalltalk/V. (Actually even here I have left out a few calls, mainly "boiler

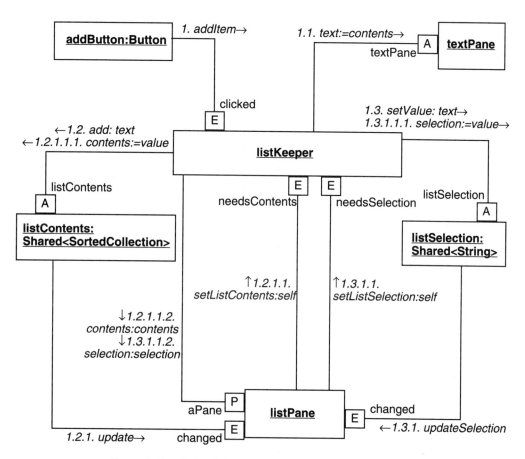

Figure 6. Detailed collaboration diagram for add button click

plate" to package access suboperations.) In this diagram we go beyond logical associations to show how links are actually implemented. I have used the optional visibility notation of Booch. The small box on the end of each links shows its implementation: A indicates an association (a pointer to another object), P indicates a method parameter (an argument), L indicates a local variable (a temporary). The role names show the name of the reference; for an association link this is the name of the instance variable holding the object pointer, for a parameter the name of the argument, for a local variable the name of the variable.

  I have added one more kind of visibility peculiar to Smalltalk/V: an "E" for a Smalltalk/V event, which is a software construct to permit externally binding an action to a trigger issued within a class, that is, a way to bypass encapsulation of classes. A Smalltalk event is a "loose wire" that can be hooked up to other objects at run time. The role name shows the name of the event. For example, object **listPane** triggers event **needsContents** when it is told to update itself; the action that results is specified not in the class code for **ListPane** but by some other object during the program initialization.

In addition to the additional visibility information, Figure 6 shows the actual convoluted control paths used by this application. When a **ListPane** object needs new contents, it does not simply trigger an event that returns the contents (that's how I would have done it, but they didn't ask me). Instead it triggers event **needsContents,** which the programmer must bind to an action that pushes the contents back into the **listPane** object. So in this case the **needsContents** event sends the **setListContents:self** message (1.2.1.1) to the controller **LlistKeeper,** which then gets the list contents across the **listContents** association (1.2.1.1.1) and then sends the contents back to the **listPane** (1.2.1.1.2) across the temporary link established by the **self** argument to message **setListContents** (1.2.1.1). In this more indirect implementation, the **contents** value flows from object **listContents** to object **listPane** indirectly through object **listKeeper,** but the final data flow is the same as before, because **listKeeper** just passes the value along. So if we follow the entire sequence through the left half of Figure 6, we find that control enters each of the objects **listKeeper, listContents,** and **listPane** twice using association, event, and parameter links, all to compute two values—a bit too convoluted for my taste, but it does get the job done.

A similar flow of control occurs on the right side of the diagram within operation 1.3 to move the selection string into the **listSelection** object and the **listPane** object.

This example illustrates the usefulness of collaboration diagrams for following a reentrant flow of control in an actual program. When the subroutine nesting gets deep, the nested sequence numbers get a bit long, but they show clearly the nesting depth and may serve somewhat to discourage excessive nesting of control flow.

Contingent Flow

All of these flow diagrams show a single scenario without contingencies (decisions). It is possible to make up a diagram that shows all possible contingent flows, but you usually don't want to see it, because it is too complicated to be useful. Usually guard conditions, simple branches be shown, and many kinds of iteration can be handled fairly easily. In practice, complicated recursive and reentrant flows are best not seen in the general case but are easier to understand with one or more specific examples; people are good at generalizing from a prototypical example.

Concurrency

This example is totally sequential—it uses subroutine calls (methods), not true interobject asynchronous events—but that's what most programming is anyway. However, there is nothing fundamental about a collaboration diagram that prohibits concurrency. The control flows can be subroutine calls or asynchronous events. Booch indicates an asynchronous event by a half arrowhead, whereas a full arrowhead indicates a synchronous subroutine call. (He also has notations for Ada rendezvous and balking calls that are mainly of use only in Ada.) To indicate concurrent flows, we use letters instead of numbers in the "extended Dewey Decimal" sequence number, with guard conditions to indicate synchronization among concurrent flows.

Other Issues

You can show creation of new objects and links during the scenario using textual annotations or color to show newly -created objects. I've said something about the design process itself; I would also like to say more but that will also have to wait.

Do you have to draw all of these diagrams? Of course not. In complicated cases they are helpful, in simple cases just do it in your head.

References

1. James Rumbaugh, Michael Blaha, William Premerlani, Frederick Eddy, William Lorensen. *Object-Oriented Modeling and Design.* Prentice Hall, Englewood Cliffs, N.J., 1991.

2. Grady Booch, *Object-Oriented Analysis and Design, 2nd ed.* Benjamin/Cummings, Redwood City, CA, 1994.

3. Derek Coleman, Patrick Arnold, Stephanie Bodoff, Chris Dollin, Helena Gilchrist, Fiona Hayes, Paul Jeremaes. *Object-Oriented Development: The Fusion Method.* Prentice Hall, Englewood Cliffs, N.J., 1994.

4. *Smalltalk/V for Macintosh: Programmer's Reference.* Digitalk, Inc., Los Angeles, 1993.

Let There Be Objects
A Short Guide to Reification
November 1992

Making Objects

Most of the object classes in a system are reasonably straightforward. Some of them are real-world objects, such as Airplane, Person, or Theater Ticket. These represent the starting point of an object model, because the purpose of most systems is ultimately to have some effect in the real world. In addition, there are computer representations of real world objects and the means to manipulate them, such as screen icons, simulations, windows, and menus. These are not part of the real world but rather provide handles for the application and its users to represent and manipulate the actual or simulated real world objects. These are the heart of most real applications. Finally there are internal mechanism classes, such as container classes and other kinds of data structures. These objects are not part of the real world at all, but are purely implementation entities that should not appear in an analysis model, as they have no semantic significance. They appear during the later stages of design or during implementation.

In designing a system, there is another kind of object, one that can be created by the designer out of nonobject materials by an act of will. These objects start off life as various kinds of things—functions, control sequences, patterns of relationship—but they are made into objects so that they can be manipulated in some way. They provide a way of uniformly dealing with function and control as well as objects, and they introduce a certain fluidity into the design process.

Promoting a nonobject into an object is called *reification*, from the Latin root *res* meaning *thing*. The word means to take an abstract concept and regard it a a concrete thing. For example, "nature" is a reification of the multitudinous processes that occur in the world. Reification gives reality to something that is not quite real, but it is a concept that humans are quite accustomed to.

Why take something whose natural form is not an object and make it into an object? Usually so that it can be manipulated in some way. The nice thing about data (and objects are primarily data with operations attached to them) is that you can *do* things to it, such as store it and retrieve it, organize it into tables, read it in at run time, operate on it, map it to and from other data, and combine it in various ways.

Reification is basically a design decision—a way of taking a piece of a system and "optimizing" it for the convenience of the designer and programmer. Let's look at some examples.

Functions

In the OMT method, the *functional model* shows the transformations of values. In most programs, functions are called (either explicitly or indirectly as methods) and that's that. They execute but you don't do anything *to* them or *with* them. Most languages permit a function to be passed as an argument to another function, as part of an integration routine, for example. Languages such as Fortran and Ada do not permit functions or references to functions to be stored in variables, however, so in these languages not much can be done to manipulate functions at run time.

Languages such as C and C++ permit function pointers to be stored in variables. A function pointer can be attached to an event in a user interface so that the function is executed whenever the event occurs; the function is called a *callback function*. The callback functions or event types themselves aren't really objects, because they have no identity (you could create several copies of the same function without affecting the behavior of the callback). However, the *mapping* between event names and callback functions—the event table—is an object that reifies the control of the system. It has identity—changes to the mapping affect everything using the mapping. It is manipulable. You can talk about its value and apply operations to it. You can even read it in and modify it at run time.

Functions become objects when you can actually manipulate them, that is, create them and change them. Languages such as Lisp permit functions to be created at run time out of text strings, but most languages are not so flexible. However, you can create *function objects* in most conventional languages such as C++ using function pointers. A function object represents either an actual function or a constructed function. The approach is really the same as what goes on inside of Lisp—direct execution of code is replaced by interpretation of function objects.

The simplest kind of function object (let's call it an Action) contains only a pointer to an actual coded function. You get additional capability by extending the Action class to store the name of the function, count calls to it, and set traps on it (a *trap* is an operation that is implicitly invoked whenever the function itself is executed). More progress is made by adding attributes to the Action object to store the arguments of the hard-coded function. Many functions, such as those from windowing systems, have a lot of optional arguments. Even with function overloading or variable-length argument lists (both of which are problematic from the programming viewpoint), making a function call with a lot of optional arguments can be daunting. The Action object internalizes all the optional parameters—they become attributes of it that can be set one at a time as needed. Furthermore, an Action object can start off with default values for its attributes, and even the default values can be gotten from the environment when a new Action object is created. When everything is ready, an **execute** method on the Action object invokes the actual function with the accumulated parameters.

Figure 1 shows a set of classes for Action objects in a windowing system. The root class **Action** has an association to the event that caused the action and an abstract **execute** method that must be defined by its subclasses. There are two built-in kinds of actions (in reality there would be more): **EventAction**, which causes another event to occur, and **MenuAction,** which causes a menu to pop up. The parameters for these actions are stored with the objects, either as the attributes (**location**) or as the associations (**menu** and **event**). **Function-Action** calls arbitrary hard-coded functions. They can even be changed at run time, but the price paid for flexibility is that they must all have the same argument list, in this case the causing event. Finally, the **SequenceAction** calls a list of subordinate actions. Its code (not shown) simply iterates through the list of actions and executes each one in turn.

You can add other kinds of actions, such as conditionals and loops, and what you get is an interpreter, of course. An interpreter is the reification of function code in a manipulable form. Don't be scared by efficiency concerns; this kind of interpreter is plenty efficient enough for most user interface callbacks, because most of the time is spent executing actual hard-coded functions anyway.

As part of a compiler I wrote a pretty-printer for object values. The **print** routine required several formatting parameters—the maximum nesting depth of embedded objects to print, the amount to indent each level by, and so on. I could have attached all of the parameters to the print method of each object class, but that would have required long calling lists throughout. Instead I reified the print method, by separating a **Printer** object and making all the print parameters attributes of it, such as **maximumNestingDepth, currentNest-**

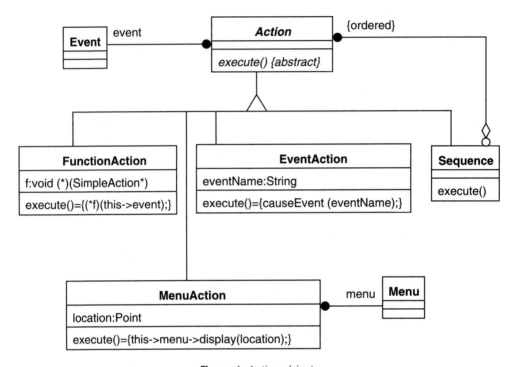

Figure 1. Action objects

ingDepth, indentAmount, and **device** (see Figure 2). The **print** method on each object takes as argument a **Printer** that specifies the formatting parameters as well as the actual output device. You can then do things such as **printer.setIndent (amount)**. To print an object, you do **anObject.print (printer)**. Each class of printable object overrides the **print** method. Objects printing themselves send text strings to the Printer object for formatting and delivery to the actual printer device. Objects can also increase the indent level for a list of nested subobjects and later decrease it again. A **print** method can check the nesting depth and terminate nesting if it is at the maximum. The Printer object keeps track of the indent level and formats the output. This approach permits the setting of formats to be decoupled from the logic of printing each class of object. We have reified the formatting and nesting of the print operation.

Storing parameters and state information in a function object is a widely-used reification technique. An example is a **search** routine that gathers parameters, such as the string to search, the search pattern, where to start looking, whether to search forwards or back-

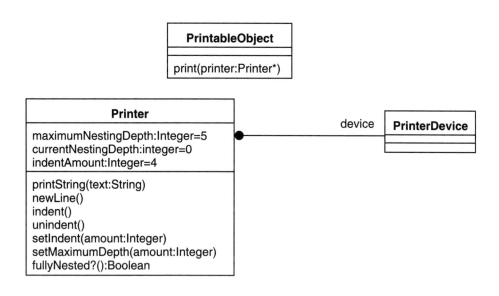

Figure 2. Print object

wards, and whether to consider case (Figure 3). When a **Searcher** object is instantiated, the parameters are set to default values that can be overridden explicitly; the actual invocation of the operation doesn't require any arguments. The application doing the search doesn't have to pass a lot of arguments; they are encapsulated in the reified **Searcher** object. If you make a similar object for sorting, it is possible to have different subclasses of the sort object implementing different algorithms. The application using the sort object need not be concerned with the algorithm, but just with the semantics of requesting a sort. The logic and the optimization of the application can be separated.

The C++ Booch Components® use a similar scheme. In this class library, reified algorithms called "tools" implement filters, searchers, and sorters. Subclasses of each abstract base class implement different algorithms for the same operation with different performance trade-offs.

Control

In the OMT methodology external control is represented by state diagrams. It is a simple matter to reify a state diagram into an object so that the system control can be modified or

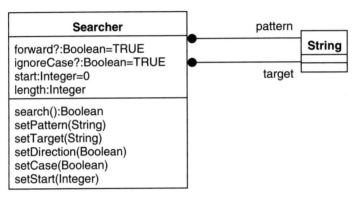

Figure 3. Search object

specified at run time. The only problem is to reify the function calls so they can also be manipulated, but I have already discussed that. Many user interfaces are implemented just so, by a table per state mapping events into actions. Events can be made into objects easily, and there is no reason to restrict yourself to the rather paltry collection of events that comes with a package such as XWindows; you can easily implement a set of user-extensible logical events.

A menu is another kind of event table. It binds text words to actions. A powerful way to implement menus is to break the binding into two steps: the menu object is a user interface object that maps text strings or icons on the screen into logical events (such as "save file" or "draw line"), whereas the state diagram maps logical events into actions (such as actually saving the file). This decoupling permits the user interface layout to be decoupled from the semantics of the application. There is little excuse nowadays for menus that return an integer offset within a list of entries when an item is selected.

A *command* is a semantic operation invoked by the user by manipulating some input widget (such as "save file" or "empty the trash." Representing the execution of a command as an object permits powerful manipulations of commands, one of the most interesting of which is the *undo* operation. *Undo* is an operation applied to previous command executions. You can't very well undo a command unless you keep track of command executions as objects. Most user interfaces only allow the last command to be undone, but there are some user interfaces, such as Emacs, that permit an arbitrary number of previous commands to be undone. The history of the system can be represented as a series of command executions, each of which keeps track of enough information to reverse itself. Executing a command appends a CommandExecution object to the user interface history, containing the parameters of the operation. Each CommandExecution object has an *undo* method that reverses the effect of the command on the system state and removes itself from the execution chain. CommandExecution objects can be arranged into inheritance hierarchies according to their similarities.

Figure 4 shows some CommandExecution objects for a graphic system. Note that each command that operates on a graphic element inherits a reference to its corresponding graphic element. A command such as adding an element doesn't need any parameters except the reference to the element. Changing the parameters of an element, such as color or location, requires that the old colors be saved in the command object. The command hierarchy mirrors the graphic element hierarchy to some extent, as shown by StretchLineCommand and ChangeRadiusCommand, which of course must match the correct kind of element. The DeleteElementCommand could be implemented by storing all the parameters of each deleted object, but this could get large, and the code must be updated whenever the definition of a graphic element changes; a simpler approach is to delete an element by moving it from the drawing window to a "scrap pile" from whence it can be resurrected. Note that the DeleteElementCommand must also keep track of the window that contained the deleted element.

A grammar is a reification of a text transformation with attached operations. Typically parser generators, such as *yacc*, produce code to implement the parser. Code is very inflexible, of course, and *yacc* is notoriously inflexible. A more powerful approach is to represent the parser itself as an object, rather than a piece of source code, which can be fed input sequences, chained to other parsers, placed into known states, and subjected to other operations. Rather than reading input itself, it would be fed input by a callback function attached to a user interface, for example, by binding a **parser.input(Character)** operation to a callback function. We took an approach like that in the implementation of the OSCAR animation system described in our book. The commercial parser generator YACC++™ takes a similar object-oriented approach by producing a parser that is an object that can be linked to a lexer object, bound to callbacks, and used reentrantly. It also introduces the concept of a grammar inheriting from another grammar, so that you can extend a grammar by merely specifying its differences from an original grammar. (YACC++ is a nice product that removes most of the long-standing problems with *yacc*.)

A device driver, such as for a disk controller, modem, or frame buffer, is another example of reification. The state of the device is captured as an object. The events that the device generates are also represented as objects; objects are also used for formatting details, such as bit patterns.

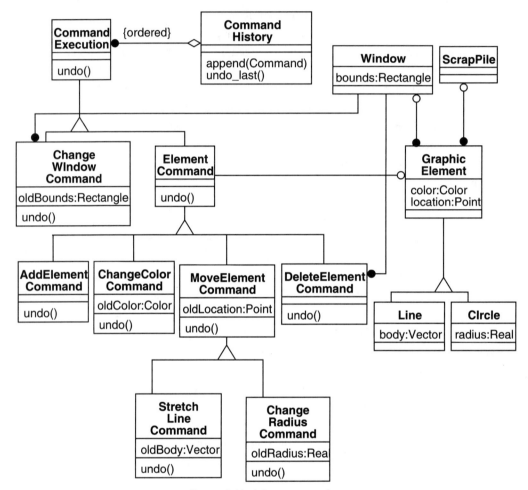

Figure 4. Undoing commands

Profiles

One of the principles of good system design is the separation of concerns: keeping logically distinct things in separate modules so they can be modified independently. One of the issues in designing a complex user interface is specifying a lot of arbitrary parameters, such as font family and size, screen color, window styles, mouse behavior, and so on. Instead of building arbitrary settings into the interface, we can allow users to select their own settings using a *profile file*. At run time, the application (or better yet, the windowing system) reads the settings and uses them. A profile is therefore the reification of a whole pattern of parameter values and setup operations, represented as a piece of data. Many applications can be unaware of its existence because it is processed by the windowing system. The XWindow systems Motif and OpenWindows operate this way.

The whole concept of *context* or *environment* is an example of reification. A context represents the state of a system, represented in such a way that it can be manipulated as an object. For example, in PostScript you can save the graphics state with the **gsave** operation and later restore it with the **grestore** operation. Graphics state has become an object that can be stored, retrieved, and reset. You can think of graphics transformation operations, such as **scale** and **offset**, as operations on the state or context object. A 3-d transformation matrix is actually a similar reification of operations; by making transformation operations into a matrix, they can be manipulated, combined, and simplified mathematically. In this case we have reified a function (the mathematical transformations) that is part of a reified state (the graphics environment).

Rules

Rule-based systems have the most advanced forms of reification. In them, entire patterns of computation and behavior are represented declaratively as rules. At its simplest, a rule-based system is a complicated form of functional model specified as a series of compile-time constraints. At its most complicated, the rules can be defined and modified at run time, so they must definitely be represented as objects. Examples of rule-based systems include:

1. A system of geometrical constraints for layout of VLSI chips.

2. A physics laboratory that allows the user to modify the laws of physics (such as the Alternate Reality Kit).

3. Knowledge-based systems with rules for truth maintenance.

Reification occurs whenever we turn away from hard coding of behavior and instead try to represent the behavior by a piece of data encapsulated in an object. As we saw earlier, simpler forms of reification associate an **execute** method with each behavior object. In a rule-based system, a single rule does not correspond to a single function to be executed; rather, the execution is diffused across the entire set of rule objects in a powerful but complicated way.

```
Object::print (printer:Printer)
{
     printer.newline ();
     printer.output ("Class ", self.class.name);
     printer.indent ();
     for each a:Attribute in self.class.attributes do
         Integer offset = a.offset;
         String name = a.name;
         printer.newline ();
         printer.output (name);
         subobject: Object = self.getAttributeValue (offset);
         subobject.print (printer);
         end do
     printer.unindent ();
}
```

Figure 5. Generic print method

Metadata

Metadata represents the reification of information describing other information. In some languages you can manipulate the attributes of a class at run time: set print formats, attach traps to test constraints or update other objects, and so on. By making a structural entity into an object, the system can share functionality among similar entities. For example, instead of writing a **print** method for each class, most classes can inherit an ancestral **print** method from class **Object** that scans the attributes of the class, prints their names and values according to the format attached to the attribute itself. Figure 5 shows the (somewhat simplified) print method for class **Object** in the DSM language (an object-oriented language that I developed). This generic method works for normal classes that are just collections of independent attributes; it would be overridden when the attribute values are internal implementation mechanisms, such as for a container class like an array or hash table.

Note that the **getAttributeValue** operation extracts the object stored in the attribute slot. An operation like this requires pointer arithmetic, as we are implementing a metaoperation outside the normal semantics of the language.

By using metadata, we have replaced methods on each class by a single generic method and data describing each class. Replacing code with data is almost always an advantage because it makes things more uniform and easier to understand and manipulate.

Models

It is possible to think of an entire model as an object. Building a high-level model and then expanding the level of detail recursively could then be treated as a relationship between models—a high-level abstract model of a system expands into one or more lower level models with additional details. The process of exploring different design alternatives can be thought of as a relationship between multiple versions of a design. The versioning relationship is structured—different versions branch off of other versions at different points in the process. Indeed, the entire design process itself, going from an original high-level abstract model to a fully-developed design, can be seen as a relationship between a series of models.

Optimization can be viewed as a transformation on models, as I discussed in an earlier column. Each transformation is an operation on a model (considered as an object) that produces a new model.

Frameworks (standard patterns of structure and interaction among the objects in a subsystem) could be regarded as metamodels—they describe models. Extending a framework could then be seen as an inheritance relationship between an original framework and its extended version.

How to Use Reification

So when should you use reification? Usually not during analysis; during analysis it is important to understand a system from a fundamental viewpoint that avoids mixing up things that are conceptually different, such as data, control, and function. During analysis in the OMT methodology, think in terms of three distinct semantic models: the object model represents real-world or representational objects, the dynamic model represents sequences of interactions, and the functional model represents transformations of values. For example, map out the sequences of user inputs for a command using state diagrams.

During design consider if and how you want to manipulate things such as functionality and control. If you are just calling functions and following control, then don't bother trying to reify them. If you find that you need to manipulate them a lot, especially at run time, then turn them into objects. You will need to look for common patterns of behavior that allow you to capture a set of state diagrams or a set of functions by a single reified class.

In reifying a function, separate out its optional arguments and store them as attributes of a function object class. Supply default values for each argument so the caller doesn't have to specify them, but provide methods to set them. Look for functions with identical or similar signatures and unify them under a single function object class. You may need more than one reified class, because it is not always possible to make everything uniform. Add composition operators classes, such as sequences, loops, and conditionals, so that you can compose functions without writing little code fragments. Store state information in the function object or the operand object itself. Reduce the number of arguments of the **execute** method (or methods) as much as possible, preferably to zero or to just a single target object.

In reifying control, capture the state of the environment in a single context object. Use this object to get the arguments for functions. Explicitly represent states and events as objects. You may also want to keep track of commands as objects. Consider how the context can be represented textually, so that it can be saved and restored easily. Try to support multiple copies of a context concurrently; then versioning is fairly easy. Try to separate formatting operations from application semantic operations; put the formatting operations into a profile object that can be set up outside of the application itself.

In reifying functions or control, capture all their relevant details in the reified object. Don't use traditional nested subroutines to store information—in a callback function or a device driver, you must always return to the main level, so you can't use the stack or the program counter to hold information. You have to break up an asynchronous request and a response into two separate pieces that communicate through the reified object, not through a subroutine call and return.

Look for the chance to reify an entire algorithm, engine, or package, such as a sorter, a parser, a simulator, or an interpreter. Making these things into objects makes them nonglobal, allowing multiple copies to coexist and to be hooked up or switched on by the main application and used reentrantly.

Reification Is the Object

This column has covered a lot of difficult and subtle points. Just keep in mind the following: Reification is a design technique that converts modeling constructs such as functions and control into objects that can be organized, stored, and explicitly manipulated. Don't use it during analysis. Don't try to use it all the time. Use it when you need to manipulate things at run time. A little bit goes a long way, but when you need it, it can be invaluable.

Forceful Functions
How to Do Computation
October 1993

The Vibrating String

In this column I will show how to approach a problem that is dominated by the need for numerical computation. Such a problem has an important functional model that must be implemented in an object-oriented manner. To illustrate the process I will discuss building a simulator for the vibrating string problem.

The vibrating string is a standard problem in physics texts that serves as an introduction to the physics of continuous systems. It is fairly simple to understand and analyze, and it is also a simple problem to simulate on a computer. It makes a pleasing graphical simulation in which the user can shake one end of the string with a mouse and observe wave motion first hand. In fact, for my undergraduate physics senior project many years ago I implemented a simulation of a vibrating string (in assembly language on the PDP-7—it really was a long time ago). Figure 1 shows a simulator for this problem that I implemented using the design described here.

A discrete vibrating string is a collection of beads connected together by a string under constant tension. If we assume that the deflections of the beads from the axis are small and that they are orthogonal to the axis, then the string exhibits simple wave behavior. If one end of the string is driven externally, deflections in the endpoint propagate from bead to bead down the string as waves at a speed that depends on the mass of each bead and on the tension in the string. By increasing the number of beads we can approximate a continuous string.

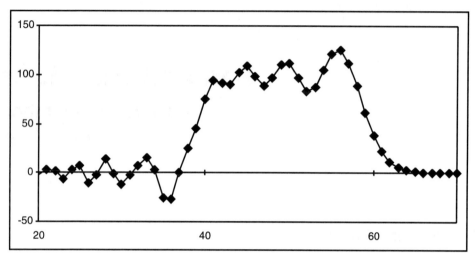

Figure 1. Vibrating string simulation

The functional model is the key to understanding a computational problem. In this problem, the functional model can be expressed as a set of equations showing the forces acting on each bead.

Beads are subject to three kinds of forces: the tension in the string, the drag due to the motion of the beads through a fluid, and an external driving force applied to one or more beads. If the angles are small, we can assume that the forces along the string cancel and that only the transverse components remain. In that case, the transverse forces depend on the slope of the string between two beads $= \Delta y / \Delta x$. The drag force is a complicated function of velocity. The equations on a single bead numbered j are as follows:

$$F_j = T_j + D_j + E_j \text{ forces on a bead}$$

$$T_j = L_j - L_{j+1} \text{ net tension force on bead i = difference between left and right forces}$$

$$L_j = T\frac{y_j - y_{j-1}}{x_j - x_{j-1}} \text{ tension force between beads j-1 and j = force on bead j from the left}$$

$$D_j = D(v_j) \text{ drag force}$$

$$E_j = E_j(t) \text{ external driving force}$$

$$F_j = m_j a_j \quad \text{Newton's law}$$

$$v_j = \frac{dy_j}{dt} \quad \text{velocity}$$

$$a_j = \frac{dv_j}{dt} \quad \text{acceleration}$$

x_j distance of bead along string

y_j displacement of bead from string

m_j mass of bead j

This set of equations defines the forces acting on bead j. At any time, the forces on the bead depend on its velocity v, the position (x,y) of the bead and the two neighboring beads, and a (possibly zero) external driving force $E(t)$.

Some of the functions still have to be defined. The drag force is a function of velocity; its definition depends on the shape of the beads and the medium they move in and is part of the physics of the situation. The external driving force is a function of time; in a typical simulation, it would be applied to one of the end beads in response to a predefined script or the motion of a mouse.

Object Model

We have already determined the functional equations for the simulation. Figure 2 shows a class model for this problem. The main object is a **Wire** (**String** has too much meaning in programming as an array of characters to be used in a different meaning) composed of an array of **Bead**s. Each bead has an integer index within the array, shown as qualifier j. Usually the beads will be equidistant, but there is no reason to build this assumption into the analysis, so each bead contains its location along the wire x as well as its lateral offset y, its lateral velocity vy, and its mass m. The acceleration of a bead is a function of other state variables, so it does not represent an independent state variable; therefore we omit it from the analysis as a bead attribute.

The wire is mostly just an aggregation of beads, but it has an attribute of its own, the tension, which is constant throughout the wire. It is unnecessary to include the number of

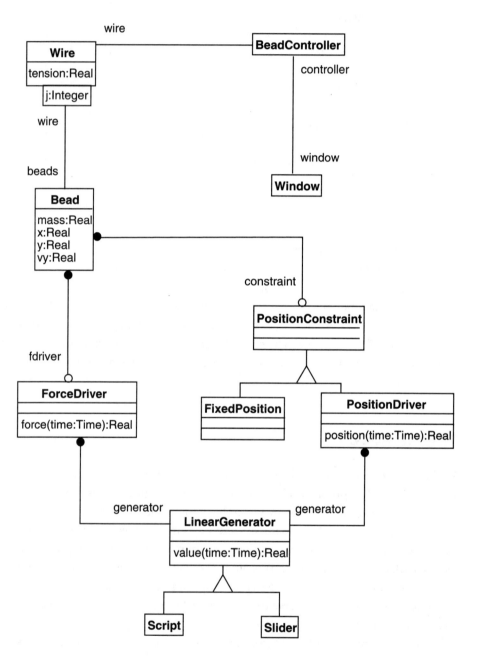

Figure 2. Object model for simulation

beads as an attribute of the wire, because the cardinality of a *many* relationship is an implicit piece of information.

Each bead may also have an association with a **PositionConstraint** object. A **FixedPosition** constraint indicates that the bead's position is fixed and cannot change, regardless of the forces on it. A **PositionDriver** constraint indicates that the bead's position is set by an external position generator, such as a script or a dynamic slider controlled by the user through a mouse. Scripts could be made using various kinds of position generators, such as square waves, sine waves, sawtooth waves, or various combinations, but I will not go into any more detail on them; you can think up various possibilities. We show the generator object as having a *value* function of time; the generator is the reification of a function and not a discrete object with state. (Reification is turning a thing, often a function, into an object so it can be manipulated. Much more on this later. See also the article *Let There Be Objects*, page 183.) Position constraints only make sense at endpoints of the wire, as they prevent any waves from flowing past them.

A bead could instead have a force driver, which supplies an additional driving force to the bead in addition to the tension and drag forces. Both **ForceDriver** and **PositionDriver** objects could be specified in terms of **LinearGenerator** objects, which are generators of real values. Generators can be predefined scripts or window-system sliders controlled by a mouse or other input device. Force drivers can be applied to any bead in the wire.

I have shown a controller object, the **BeadController**, which controls the user interface to the program. The controller knows about the **Window** in which the simulation is drawn. I have not shown any details of the controller or the window, as my purpose in this column is to focus on the computations in the simulation itself. The controller is the only part of the program that needs a dynamic model. The simulation objects always do basically the same thing so they don't need a dynamic model. Their behavior is expressed by the functional model embodied in the equations of motion.

Designing the Operations

The equations of motion show the value dependencies in the simulation. To design an object-oriented program, we must convert the functional equations to operations on objects. Each of the equations becomes an operation on a class. Which class do they go on? In this case it is simple to decide. The entire set of equations describes the forces and parameters of bead j, so the obvious owner of the operations is class Bead (Figure 3).

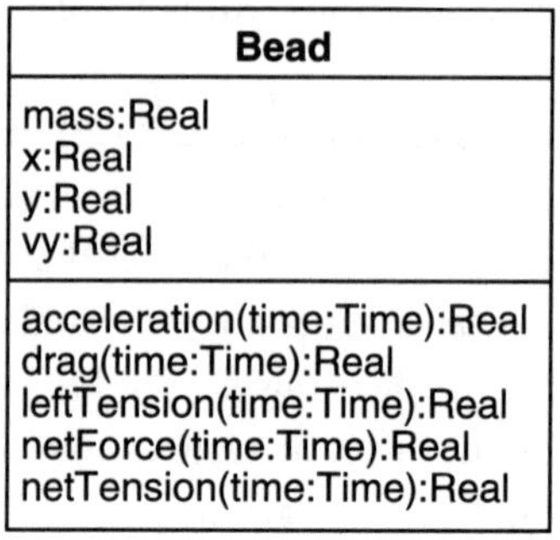

Bead
mass:Real x:Real y:Real vy:Real
acceleration(time:Time):Real drag(time:Time):Real leftTension(time:Time):Real netForce(time:Time):Real netTension(time:Time):Real

Figure 3. Operations added to Bead class

```
acceleration() {
  return netForce()/mass;}

leftTension () {
  if (j < 1) return 0;
  else if (j > wire–>beads–>count) return 0;
  else return wire–>tension * (y – wire–>beads[j–1]–>y) / (x – wire–>beads[j–1]–>x);}

netForce () {
  return netTension() + drag () + fdriver–>force ();}

netTension () {
  return leftTension () – wire–>beads[j+1]–>leftTension ();}
```

Figure 4. Code for operations on class Bead

The driving force is externally imposed, so we make it an operation of the **Driver** object attached to the bead. Making the force driver an object simplifies modifying its form, because we can invent new subclasses of drivers for new kinds of force functions.

It is not always so easy to decide where an operation goes, and sometimes you just have to make an arbitrary decision between two candidate classes. Some C++ code for the operations is shown in Figure 4.

Several of the operations use values from objects other than **Bead**. For example, *leftTension* uses attribute *tension* from class **Wire**. This is not a problem, as **Wire**, **ForceDriver**, and **PositionDriver** j can all be accessed directly from **Bead** j; they correspond to associations with **Bead** in the object model. Don't bother to show access operations explicitly as operations in the object diagram; treat them as implicit from the object model structure. (When you actually program the final code, hide attributes behind access functions.)

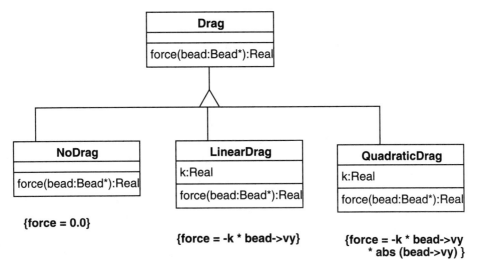

Figure 5. Reified drag function

Reifying the Drag Force

The drag force is more complicated. The formula for fluid friction is quite complicated and depends on the shape of the moving object, the nature of the fluid, and the velocity. In the case of small spheres moving in liquids or thin gases, the drag force is proportional to the velocity or the square of the velocity, respectively. How are we to model the drag force? It is undesirable to wire in a lot of different functions and have a large case statement to choose among them at run time. The solution is to *reify* the function, that is, turn it into an object.

We make up a new class called **Drag** (Figure 5). It represents the particular drag formula appropriate to a given bead. Each bead is associated with one **Drag** object, but one **Drag** object could be associated with many beads (often all beads have the same size and shape and hence the same formula for drag force). A drag object has a public function called **force** that computes the drag force according to its particular formula. The abstract **Drag** class can have many different subclasses, each of which represents a different drag formula (a different shape of bead or a different kind of fluid). For example, there would be subclasses for **LinearDrag**, in which the force is proportional to the velocity of the bead, for **QuadraticDrag**, in which the force is proportional to the square of the velocity, and **NoDrag**, in which there is no drag force. More complicated formulas are of course possible.

Where do the parameters of the formulas go? They are attributes of the drag object, so they can be changed easily, and even varied from bead to bead. For example, the proportionality constant is an attribute of the **LinearDrag** and **QuadraticDrag** objects. The **No-Drag** object needs no attributes, of course. More complicated formulas might have several parameters as attributes.

How does the drag object get access to the velocity of the bead? We could pass the velocity as a parameter to the **force** function, but more complicated formulas might require additional arguments, such as the angle of an irregular bead with respect to its motion. It is more general to make the bead itself an argument of the **force** function, which can then query the bead for its velocity and any other value that is needed in the formula.

Rather than passing the bead as an argument to the force function, each drag object could be associated with a single bead object, but this would preclude the possibility of sharing a single drag object among all the beads. The advantage of sharing a single object is that a global parameter, such as the proportionality constant, could be modified for all of the beads at once as part of the user interface.

Where do the drag objects come from in the first place? They must be created as part of setting up the simulation. The set up is part of the **BeadController** object that represents the user interface (another example of reification). The set up function would test for flags in the user interface and create the appropriate kind of drag object: no drag, linear drag, or quadratic drag. The proportionality constant would also be read from the user interface and stuffed into the drag object.

What about the other formulas that we have already turned into operations on the **Bead** class. Should they also be reified? They could be if we want to be able to select among different formulas. We have already reified the external driving force as a **ForceDriver** object. Newton's laws are safe, so it is probably not worth bothering about the **acceleration** function. The **leftTension** function is definitely a candidate for reification; in more complicated cases it would not be a linear function of the deflection.

Dynamics of Integration

The functions that I have described so far, both the simple operations and the reified ones, represent relationships between values applicable at a point in time. The differential equations for velocity and acceleration, however, represent relationships over time. Any numerical solution must break time into small discrete steps and solve the equations by a process of iterative approximation. Integration is inherently an iterative process, rather than a sim-

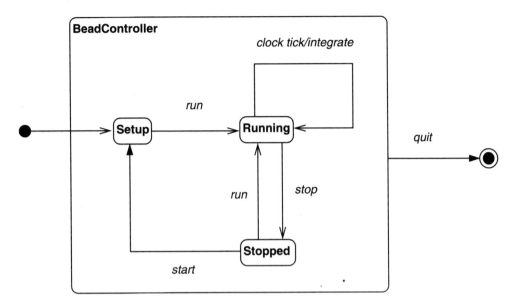

Figure 6. Dynamic model for controller

ple equation. If we are viewing a simulation graphically, for example, we will want to see the beads displayed at uniform time intervals, say every tenth of a second, to give a realistic animation. We will also want to sample the mouse at the same real-time interval to obtain values for any slider drivers. The dynamics of sampling input and displaying output based on real time intervals is properly part of the dynamic model for the **BeadController** object. The dynamic model for this object will also have events to start and stop the simulation and modify simulation and display parameters (Figure 6).

Every time the interval clock ticks, the controller object fires a transition, which reads input, integrates the simulation by the elapsed time, and draws the output. The controller would also have a lot of events to set flags and parameters during setup and running, but I have not shown the individual commands on the dynamic model.

How does integration work? In general, the integration operation must divide the time interval into fine steps so that the errors within the integration are kept within bounds. In more complicated integration algorithms, the step size may vary at run time. The iteration in the integration algorithm is *not* part of the dynamic model. It has nothing to do with external events; it is purely algorithmic. It is part of the functional model. Time steps within the integration algorithm do not have to correspond to real time (provided the integration is completed before the next clock tick).

Bead
mass:Real x:Real y:Array[Time] of Real vy:Array[Time] of Real ay:Array[Time] of Real
acceleration(time:Time):Real drag(time:Time):Real leftTension(time:Time):Real netForce(time:Time):Real netTension(time:Time):Real

Figure 7. Bead object with previous motion parameters

Integration is a complicated study in numerical analysis. The crudest form of integration is just to multiply each derivative by the time interval:

$v[t+dt] = v[t] + a[t] * dt$

$y[t+dt] = y[t] + v[t] * dt$

This is simple enough and allows each set of motion parameters to be computed in terms of the previous ones. However, it is not a very good integration algorithm. Better algorithms use quadratic or cubic curve fitting with one or more refinement steps. The complication is that we have to save two or three previous sets of motion parameters for each bead to be able to do the curve fitting. In theory we could save motion parameters for all previous time steps, but this is not very practical. We need to extend the object model to include these saved values. In general, each motion parameter, such as y (deflection), v (velocity), and a (acceleration) must be an array of values, large enough to hold the previous values needed for curve fitting (Figure 7). As new values are computed, they are inserted onto the top of the array and the oldest values are pushed off the bottom of the array.

The integration operation is another operation that should be reified. Figure 8 shows an abstract integration class with subclasses representing different integration algorithms. The public function on this object is the operation *integrate (beads, time0, time1)*, where *time0* is the initial time (at which the motion parameters are already determined), *time1* is the final time (for which the motion parameters are to be computed), and *beads* is the set of beads whose parameters are to be computed. The name *DE2AIntegrate* stands for second-order differential equation on an array of interdependent values.

The integration operation has to iterate across all the beads in a wire for each internal time step, as well as iterating internal time steps within the larger integration interval. Why

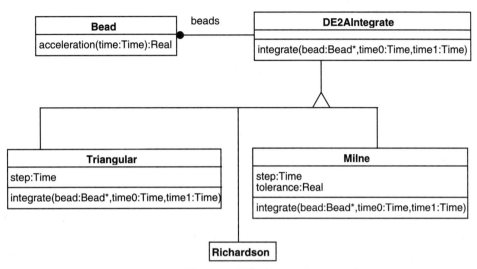

Figure 8. Reified integration operation

not simplify the integration operation to work on a single bead at a time? Unfortunately this will not work, because the force on each bead at each moment depends on the positions of its neighbors, so all the beads must be integrated together. In other words, the iteration across beads must be nested inside the iteration across time, and the two loops cannot be inverted for a simpler object-oriented formulation. This is an example in which we have to think at the system level and not in terms of individual objects.

Higher Dimensions

I have described a physics problem in which all motion is one-dimensional, because the beads cannot move at all in the direction of the wire. How would we extend the model to handle two-dimensional motion?

First the types of the forces should be changed from Real to Vector (Figure 9). The real coordinates x and y should be combined into a vector position z, and velocity and acceleration would also become vectors v and a. The operation to compute *leftTension* should be made exact, without simplifications of small angles. The other operations continue to work fine, provided their Real variables are replaced by Vector variables.

Why not do it this way in the first place? Well, I am not sure I want to pay the cost of this generality. Speed does matter in simulations. However, if we want to be able to change

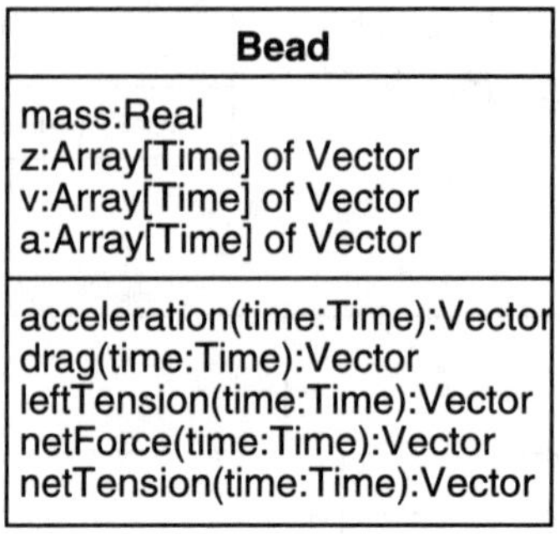

```
┌────────────────────────────────────┐
│                Bead                │
├────────────────────────────────────┤
│ mass:Real                          │
│ z:Array[Time] of Vector            │
│ v:Array[Time] of Vector            │
│ a:Array[Time] of Vector            │
├────────────────────────────────────┤
│ acceleration(time:Time):Vector     │
│ drag(time:Time):Vector             │
│ leftTension(time:Time):Vector      │
│ netForce(time:Time):Vector         │
│ netTension(time:Time):Vector       │
└────────────────────────────────────┘
```

Figure 9. Beads object with two-dimensional forces

the mathematical model at run time by user request, then we need to implement the more general model. The one dimensional model need not be programmed separately. It is sufficient to have two different versions of the reified *leftTension* function, one of which computes the accurate vector tension, whereas the other computes only the simplified y-only component. The selection between the reified functions would be made by the user interface.

How to Handle Computations

For a computational problem it is generally best to build the functional model first. This will usually consist of equations, usually with some explicit or implied iteration. Each equation should then be represented as an operation on some class in the object model. If certain formulas have variant forms then they should be reified: An abstract class should be constructed for each reified operation, with a subclass for each variant algorithm. Each subclass can have attributes for the particular parameters that are needed in its algorithm. The abstract class defines a deferred operation that all the subclasses must implement; this operation performs the computation implicit in the operation. The only arguments to this operation should be general arguments that are needed by all variant algorithms. Instances of reified operations must be created by the user interface, main program, or set-up routine, which are the only places that the algorithm-dependent parameters must be supplied.

The technique of reifying computational operators can be useful for many kinds of engineering calculations with variant models or algorithms, such as structural analysis, aerodynamics, orbital mechanics, and many other kinds of calculations.

Driving to a Solution
Reification and the Art of System Design
July 1995

Get Deliveries Straight

Suppose you are trying to design a system to plan driving routes through the streets of a city or country—maybe for taxi dispatching, or a package delivery service, or retail store home deliveries. One of the components of such a system is an algorithm to decide how long it takes to drive between two locations. Such an algorithm can get quite complicated. On the other hand, it is not a good idea to implement the most complicated algorithm first. Instead it is best to use simple algorithms until the overall system issues are resolved and the major subsystems integrated. How can we build an initial system quickly but still preserve the flexibility to substitute more complicated algorithms later? The solution is to use *reification*, which means to turn the algorithms into objects. I have touched on this topic in other columns, but this is an important topic that bears further examination.

Driving Algorithms

Suppose we have a truck that has to make a number of deliveries in any order. Maybe it is a truck for a furniture store warehouse that must deliver items to several different customers (Figure 1). We want to plan a route for the truck that minimizes the total driving time. This is similar to the well-known "traveling salesman problem" in which the goal is to minimize the total distance traveled. (Actually it is harder, because the driving times may depend on the time of day and therefore be affected by the order of the segments.) A useful by-product

Living room set	1120 Baker Ave.
Lamp	251 Elm St.
Refrigerator	20330 E. 14th St., Apt. 31
Bed and mattress set	14 San Carlos Blvd.

Figure 1. Delivery list

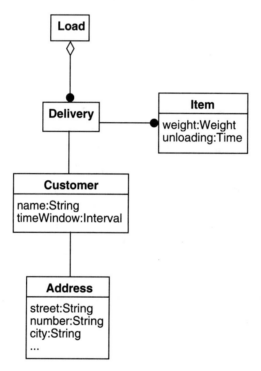

Figure 2. Model of the objects involved in a delivery list

of this algorithm would be an estimate of when the truck will arrive at each customer's house. Figure 2 shows a model of the classes involved in a delivery list.

We can break up the overall planning algorithm in two parts: an outer algorithm (the traveling salesman's algorithm) that tries different orders for the segments to minimize the total time; and an inner algorithm that finds the best route between two locations, possibly exploring different possible routes between the locations. By separating the overall algorithm into two parts, we can modify either the broad strategy or the point-to-point routing independently. The outer algorithm doesn't need to know the route between two points,

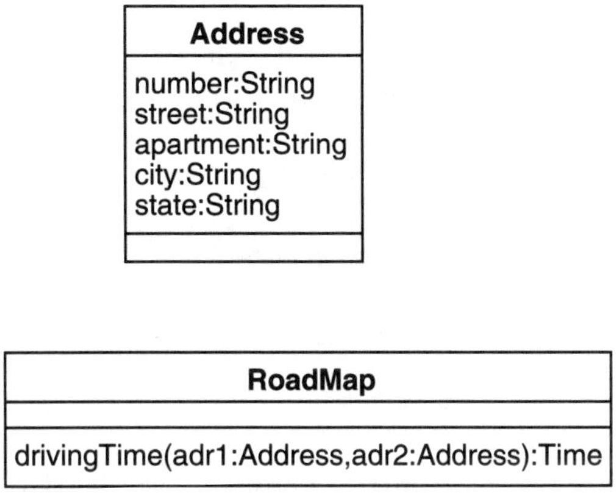

```
            ┌──────────────────────────┐
            │        Address           │
            ├──────────────────────────┤
            │ number:String            │
            │ street:String            │
            │ apartment:String         │
            │ city:String              │
            │ state:String             │
            ├──────────────────────────┤
            │                          │
            └──────────────────────────┘


    ┌────────────────────────────────────────────────────┐
    │                    RoadMap                           │
    ├────────────────────────────────────────────────────┤
    │ drivingTime(adr1:Address,adr2:Address):Time          │
    └────────────────────────────────────────────────────┘
```

Figure 3. Finding the time to travel between two addresses

only the time of the best route, so the interface between the inner and outer algorithm is simple and narrow.

We need to estimate the time required to drive between two addresses without necessarily selecting a route. The outer algorithm will require such estimates to explore good sequences for the deliveries. Now how might we find the best driving time between two points? Clearly we need some way to represent the map of the city or country. The delivery addresses must be located on the map somehow. In Figure 3 the driving time algorithm is implemented by the **Roadmap** class. The arguments to the operation are **Address** objects, which we may assume are basically strings. The road map object must convert the address strings to geographical locations somehow as part of the driving time operation.

We should keep distinct addresses, geometrical coordinates, and locations within a road map. Addresses are basically strings, possibly with some internal structure (such as street, city, state, etc.). Geometric coordinates are pairs of real numbers in some coordinate system (maybe latitude and longitude, but north-south and east-west distances from an origin are probably more useful). Road map locations are more complicated, because they must relate to objects within the road map itself and cannot be treated as stand-alone values; for example, they might be represented by a distance along a particular road segment in the map. Their format will depend on the exact representation of the map, so they may be thought of as auxiliary objects of the road map.

Address objects do not have their own identity, so they are really just pure values. However, we might implement them as real objects with internal state. For example, once an ad-

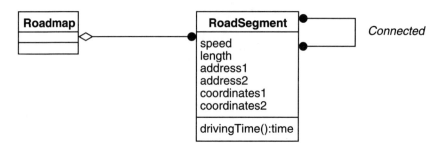

Figure 4. Simple road map

dress has been located on a map, we might choose to save the relationship in the **Address** object itself, rather than recomputing it each time.

We might try different algorithms for computing driving distance. Maybe the simplest algorithm would just divide the straight-line distance between the two points by an average driving speed. The average speed would take into account that roads do not usually connect two points directly. In a city, perhaps we would just sum the east-west and north-south distances, because city streets usually follow a grid pattern. All the road map must do to implement this algorithm is to convert address objects into geographical coordinates. No connectivity is needed within the map.

This algorithm is crude but might suffice in the early stages of the outer algorithm to eliminate very bad orderings, such as zigzagging back and forth across the city to make deliveries.

A more accurate algorithm would find a path over actual road segments in the map and measure its length. Only connected segments are used to make a path (i.e., you can't drive from an overpass to the road below). Presumably any decent map representation will have this kind of information available. The time can still be obtained by dividing the distance by some average speed figure (but this time it is an actual driving speed).

Of course this is not very accurate. Traffic travels at different speeds on different streets, so the algorithm should attach an average speed to each road segment. This would require an extension to the road map representation, but this would not be so difficult, just one additional attribute value (the speed) per road segment. Figure 4 shows a model of this simple road map.

Junctions (including toll booths, highway interchanges, traffic lights, etc.) affect driving time. We really should extend our road map to include road segment junctions. First we need to correct a defect of Figure 4. In our first road map model, we stated that road seg-

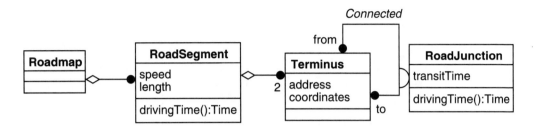

Figure 5. Road map with explicit segment ends

ments were connected to other road segments, but we did not say which ends were connected. Perhaps we could figure this out at run time, but why bother? We introduce another class of object, which I call **Terminus.** This represents a point on a road, in particular the end of a segment. Each segment has two termini (Figure 5). Termini are connected to other termini. An intersection is represented as an n-by-n table of transition times (note that the table is not symmetric, because traveling in the reverse direction may require a different amount of time).

This is certainly a more elaborate version of the road map, with an entirely new class of objects (termini), but the algorithm is not too much different.

Not all roads are open in both directions, and the transit times in opposite directions are often quite different (it may be much harder to get on to a busy highway than to get off of it). A better model is to separate the opposite lanes and treat each road segment as representing traffic in a single direction, as in Figure 6. Now we can distinguish entry and exit termini for a segment; the exit terminus of one segment must connect to entry termini of other segments. This change will actually simplify traversing the graph, because we can always proceed through segments in a positive direction.

We can transform the model a bit more for greater uniformity. Both road segments and junctions are really portions of the road that must be traveled, although their characteristics differ. In Figure 7 we generalize both of them with a new abstract class **TravelSegment.** This class has no attributes, only the deferred operation **drivingTime.** But where has the **Connected** association gone? I have eliminated it by recognizing that road junctions and road segments do the same thing: they connect termini in a directed fashion. Instead of connecting termini owned by particular segments, we allow the same terminus to be the entry and exit for multiple travel segments.

So far I have assumed that the driving speed (and therefore the driving time) for each segment is fixed. As any driver knows, driving times vary at different times of the day. We

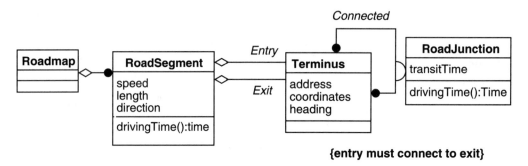

Figure 6. Road map with one-way segment

really should adjust the driving speeds for each road segment according to the time of day. This would require some kind of table for each segment, although we might be able to apply the same table to many different segments. I have shown this table in Figure 8 as **Interval-Table<DayTime,Speed>.** This table maps day-time (a date and a time) into a speed. This makes the road map object considerably larger and it makes the algorithm much more complex.

The interface between the outer and inner algorithms is also more complicated. First of all, the call to the inner algorithm must be modified to include a time-of-day parameter, which affects all the calls in the outer delivery-planning algorithm. The parameter is the time at which the truck leaves the warehouse... or is it the time at which it finishes? A divide-and-conquer algorithm is more difficult, because you can't just divide a path in half and time each part—the time taken by one part affects the starting time of the other part, and therefore affects the parameters under which its elapsed time is computed.

Multiple Algorithms

Even if we can implement a complicated algorithm that takes into account many factors, we don't necessarily want to use it all the time, even in a single program. For example, in solving the traveling salesman's problem for this case, we might want to use a crude but fast estimate of driving time for the first stage of the algorithm. After all, you are not going to drive from point A to the other side of the city and then drive back to a location near point B, and it does not require extremely accurate time estimates to eliminate this route. Only when we start choosing among reasonably direct routes will the detailed calculations matter. So with-

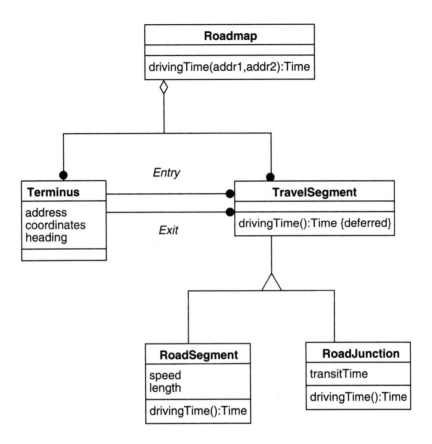

Figure 7. Generalization of travel segments

in a single program there may be a need for multiple implementations of the same algorithm with different degrees of speed and accuracy.

Simple inheritance of an operation bound to a data object is often inadequate for another reason. We may want to separate externally-meaningful data (such as the connectivity
in the road map) from data that parameterizes a particular algorithm. In introducing the
road map with traffic jams at certain times of the day, we had to add a parameter to the driv-
ing-time operation. This certainly will affect all the callers. One possible workaround is to
leave the original calls in the existing code (without the time-of-day argument) and modify
the original operation to call the new operation with a default parameter; after all, this will
be as good as the original algorithm until we get around to changing the calls. This approach

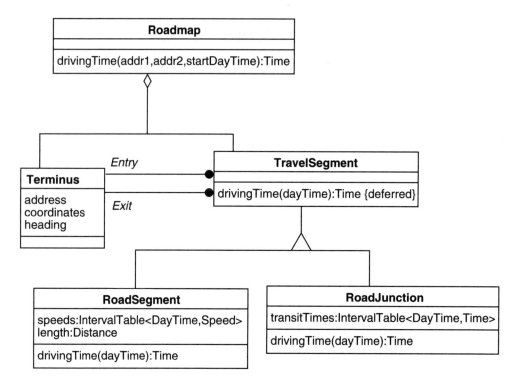

Figure 8. Speeds that vary by time of day

works, but it can lead to a chain of calls to default procedures as the algorithm evolves. Also, the entire program must use the same default values. Even if we adopt the approach of default values, we would like to keep the flexibility to change them without modifying the implementation code of the operation.

We can imagine further variations on the driving algorithm. Different kinds of vehicles might take different routes or drive at different speeds. For example, a parkway might be open to cars but closed to trucks. Or we might have different driving styles for trucks and taxis or for different persons. We do not want to build the driving style into the algorithm as a case statement—this defeats extensibility, even if we pass it as a parameter. We want to be able to supply different implementations of the same operation using the same external data. What changes is not the data but the algorithm itself. Also, as I suggested earlier, we might want different implementations of the same operation within the same program (in this case, a quick and dirty algorithm for preliminary investigation of routes and a slow and accurate algorithm to do the final routing).

Reified Behavior

The solution is to make the algorithm into an object. This is called *reification*, which means "to convert or regard something as a concrete object" (from Latin *res*, thing). We separate the variant behavior (such as the driving style or the algorithm variant) from the variant external data (such as the road map). Each is represented by a different object, but the two objects are associated.

Let's take a look at this algorithm object. It represents finding a route between two points. We make up a class called **Timer** that represents the generic algorithm. Each subclass of **Timer** represents a different variation on the algorithm (Figure 9). Here we have three different concrete algorithms. **QuickTimer** simply measures the straight-line distance between two points; **AverageTimer** measures the time along an actual path on the map using average driving speeds that do not vary during the day; **VariableTimer** allows the speeds to change during the day.

What are the parameters of the algorithm? At the very least, the algorithm requires the starting and ending locations. These must always be supplied; there is no point to having default values for them. So we can define a deferred operation **findTime(start: Location, finish:Location)** that returns the best time.

What about the time-of-day argument? We could include it in the argument list for the operation. Another approach is to make it an attribute of the algorithm object **Variable-Timer** itself. The attribute value can be set once in an outer loop and need not be passed into an inner loop scanning possible road segments; the inner loop need not be aware of it.

As a bonus, we can store multiple results as attributes of the **Timer** objects. For example, the **AverageTimer** and **VariableTimer** algorithms actually find a path as part of the work of estimating the travel time. We can store this value as an attribute of the algorithm object. If the caller doesn't want it or can't handle it, then the caller doesn't have to take it. Algorithm objects are excellent for handling multiple return values, especially in cases when some of them may be optional or may be meaningless to some of the callers.

We can even go further and separate the reified algorithm into parts to permit greater flexibility of change. We can separate the time-estimating algorithm itself from the various rules that affect computation of the time, such as driver's driving styles and the vehicle used (Figure 10). In this model the **Timer** object/algorithm uses a **DrivingStyle** object with two parts, **DriverStyle** and **VehicleStyle**. The **Timer** algorithm calls its **DrivingStyle** object to obtain the time for each road segment, because the time is affected by the driving style. The **Timer** object is still responsible for exploring and evaluating the overall sequencing of seg-

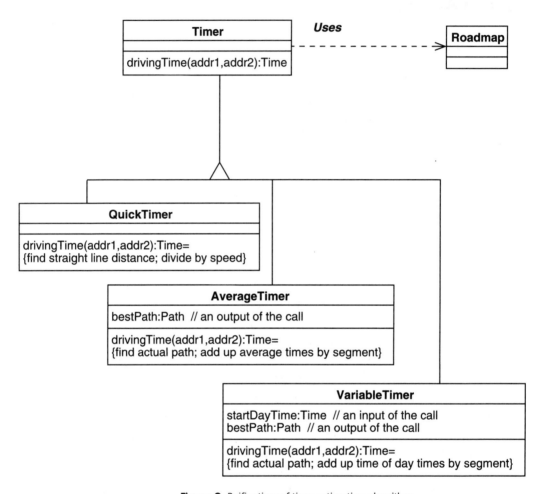

Figure 9. Reification of time estimation algorithm

ments. The association between **Timer** object and **DrivingStyle** object is established by the main program, making changes to policy easy to implement.

Creating algorithm objects

Where does an algorithm object come from? It must be created by the program itself at some level, possibly the setup portion of the program. You can't completely eliminate the

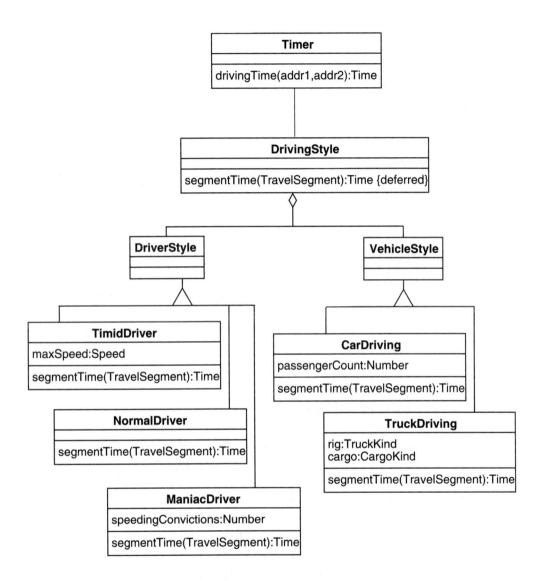

Figure 10. Reification of driving style

algorithmic dependencies from a program, but you can isolate them to a limited number of explicit places.

Some algorithms may depend on nongeneric parameters of the algorithm itself. For example, the path-finding algorithm may search a certain number of paths before selecting the best one that it has found. Algorithm-dependent parameters must be set in the outer program, not in the inner program in which the nongeneric parameters are hidden. They can be set in two ways: they could be set by default by the constructor method or they can be set explicitly by the outer-level caller. In either case, they can be overridden individually, which is a nice advantage of algorithm objects, especially when there are a lot of optional arguments. The algorithm object is then passed to the inner program, which need not know anything about the algorithm-specific parameters. This is far superior to the traditional approach of passing all the parameters through as calling arguments over several levels of calls. The object approach allows an outer-level caller to communicate with an inner-level procedure without creating dependencies at the intermediate levels.

The intermediate-level callers can also rebind some of the parameters. You can think of an algorithm object as a *closure*. A closure is a partially bound function.

Algorithm objects have other advantages. You can represent exceptions as attribute values of the algorithm object. Again, this allows communication to skip several levels of calls without disrupting the intermediate levels, who can simply ignore things they don't know about.

Algorithm objects are discussed in the *Design Patterns* book [1] under the title *Strategy Pattern.*

Minimizing Dependencies

Maybe we don't really need all this complexity in a simple planning program. My point is that you should design systems in such a way that extensions are straightforward to add. The main design rule (for *any* field of design) is *to minimize unnecessary dependencies* and to carefully define and structure necessary dependencies.

In this article I have examined how to minimize and structure the dependencies on an algorithm that is used as part of a larger system. What kind of dependencies are there?

First there is the dependency between a call and the procedure that implements it. By separating the specification of an operation and its implementation as a procedure body we can minimize the effects of changing the implementation. The procedure body can change without changing the many calls that use it. This is an old idea in computing that far predates object-oriented thinking.

Extending an algorithm often requires extension of the data that it uses. The driving algorithm and the road map are closely linked together. They depend on each other. To minimize dependencies between the algorithm and road map data we combine the algorithm with its supporting data. The result is an object. This is of course the essence of the object-oriented approach. The object's class contains the implementation of the algorithm as well as the data format. Data formats and algorithm implementations can be freely changed, as long as the operation presents the same interface to its callers. Each client is written in terms of an abstract class that defines the interface of the driving algorithm and nothing more. The algorithm and data format depend on each other, but the dependency is encapsulated within the class boundary and hidden from the outside world.

There may also be variations in the algorithms themselves, even on the same data. In this case we represent the algorithm itself as an object that knows the representation of its dependent data. Encapsulation is no good here; the algorithm object must be able to manipulate and traverse the data, so they are dependent on each other, but the entire package forms an encapsulation boundary to the outside world. I call this design mechanism *reification of behavior.*

Things are not totally free, of course. *Someone* has to create the reified object and populate it with data. That someone is the main program. You can minimize dependencies but you can't eliminate them entirely. However, the main body of the program is independent of the driving algorithm and data format.

References

1. Erich Gamma, Richard Helm, Ralph Johnson, John Vlissides. *Design Patterns: Elements of Reusable Object-Oriented Software.* Addison-Wesley, Reading, Mass., 1995.

Case Studies

I HAVE written many columns about one aspect of modeling or another, but occasionally I have found it useful to demonstrate the overall modeling process by citing a case study. It is difficult to find good examples that are both short and reasonably complete as well as understandable to the general reader without particular domain knowledge. Furthermore, short examples tend to be overly simplistic, often little more than toy problems, but this cannot be helped, because there is no space to explain a real problem of any size even in most books. I have found it better to show a toy problem in full detail than a real problem in superficial detail.

The Evolution of Bugs and Systems was the first column I wrote. It is based on a small evolution simulation I had made after reading a "Mathematical Recreations" column in *Scientific American*. Simulations are excellent object-oriented examples because the programming-language objects are a direct mapping of the simulated objects. You simply have to understand the problem and the object-oriented model is practically done. This particular problem is small, almost trivial, but I have used it many times as a class exercise in teaching object-oriented analysis and design courses. At first I had tried to use more realistic examples, but after awhile I realized that beginners need simple examples to focus on the basic concepts, and that even simple examples are not so simple the first time. (I have combined the original two-part article into a single article here.)

Objects in the Constitution shows the use of object-oriented modeling to represent a real-world institution, doing *enterprise modeling*. Object-oriented models are excellent for representing real-world organizations, better in my opinion than BPR (business process re-engineering) and other methods that put a big stress on functions and processes, because organizations are fundamentally about objects that maintain themselves in spite of outside forces. It is an oft-observed fact that organizations are more stable than the processes they support, so representing the objects is as important or more important than representing the processes.

The Evolution of Bugs and Systems

November 1991, January 1992

OBJECT-oriented development provides a seamless path from analysis through design and implementation. You don't have to change notation at each stage of development, but this doesn't mean that all stages of development are the same or differ just in the amount of detail. The different stages focus on different aspects of a problem and emphasize different object-oriented concerns. In this article I will illustrate object-oriented analysis and design using a simple example.

Creeping Bugs

We will consider an evolution simulation based on a *Scientific American* "Mathematical Recreations" column (May 1989). The goal is to simulate the evolution of "bugs" in a simple two-dimensional world. The world contains bugs and bacteria, which the bugs eat. The bacteria are "manna from heaven." They appear at random and persist at fixed locations until they are eaten. Bacteria do not spread, age, or reproduce. Bugs move around the world randomly under control of motion genes. Each bug has a variable position and orientation within the world. For simplicity, time is divided into uniform time steps. During each step, each bug rotates randomly to a new orientation, then moves one unit forward in its new direction. Rotation is controlled by the motion gene, which codes for a probability distribution of rotating by an arbitrary angle from the previous orientation. Initially the probability distribution is uniform, so a bug performs a random walk. For simplicity, we divide the world into uniform cells with a finite number of angles, such as a hexagonal grid with six possible angles. A bug eats any bacteria it finds within its cell, gaining a fixed amount of weight for each meal. Each time step the bug loses a fixed amount of weight to maintain its metabolism. If its weight becomes zero, the bug starves. If its weight exceeds a certain "strong" value, then the bug reproduces by splitting itself into two identical bugs, each with half the original weight. Each new bug suffers a single mutation in its motion gene, modifying the probability distribution.

If you program this simulation and choose appropriate values for the various parameters so that all the bugs do not die out quickly, over time you observe a kind of evolution. At first the bugs jitter about randomly, but over time they evolve so that they move more or less in straight lines, with an occasional turn to the left or right (but not both for any one bug). The explanation is that bugs that move randomly tend to eat up the food supply in one place and starve, whereas bugs that move in lines have a better chance to find new food, but they must turn occasionally to avoid getting stuck against the edges of the world.

This problem is well-suited to an object-oriented approach and is fairly simple to program. There is some ambiguity in the specification, and many possible extensions can be considered, such as carnivorous bugs. I will illustrate my solution to it using the OMT notation described in the book *Object-Oriented Modeling and Design*. I cannot show all the details that would accompany a full solution of the problem, but I hope to touch on the major points, at least.

Stages of Development

To solve a problem, you must identify a problem, describe what you need to do about it, decide how to do it, and then go and do it. These steps are the development stages of *conceptualization, analysis, design,* and *implementation*. Other things you might do include verifying that you actually solved the problem and carefully describing your solution so that someone else could repeat it. These steps correspond to *testing* and *documentation*.

Of necessity, methodology books (including ours) lay out the development process as a sequence of steps. This pedagogical need has been misinterpreted as the infamous "waterfall diagram," showing development as a one-way flow of information through well-defined rigid stages. In practice, the distinction among the stages is not always clear cut, because software development is a creative act that requires some judgment from the practitioner. More important, the development of any real system involves a lot of iteration within and among stages, more of a "whirlpool" than a "waterfall."

Analysis, design, and implementation could be called "synthetic" stages of development. During these stages the designer must synthesize a system out of a jumble of potential requirements and parts, striving for a result that is both understandable and efficient while solving the problem. During synthesis it is useful to have a well-defined notation to specify exactly what has been created at any step in the process. The development notation should flow easily from stage to stage so that work will not be lost, ignored, or repeated as the design process proceeds. We claim that an object-oriented modeling notation can be used throughout the development process without a change in notation or reenty of information.

First I will focus on analysis. The analysis model forms the framework on which the entire design is built and fleshed out.

Analysis

During analysis we identify *what* must be done without saying *how* it will be done. During analysis, we identify the object classes in the problem domain, their significant attributes, and the relationships among objects. We capture this information in a *class diagram*. The class diagram describes a snapshot of information at a point in time.

The first step is to identify object classes and describe them briefly. Table 1 shows a model dictionary in which we have identified five object classes from the problem description: Bug, Gene, Bacterium, Cell, and Grid. You should always prepare a model dictionary containing a brief description of every class, attribute, operation, relationship, or other element of a model. A simple name by itself has too many interpretations.

Table 1: Model Dictionary

Bug

> An organism that inhabits a cell, moves under control of a motion gene, eats bacteria it finds, and reproduces by fission under suitable conditions. The bug dies if it doesn't eat enough

Gene

> A set of discrete values that codes for the probabilistic motion of a bug. Genes are copied and mutated during bug reproduction.

Cell

> A discrete location within the grid world that contains (possibly multiple) bugs and bacteria. The cells are uniformly spaced within the grid.

Bacterium
> Food for bugs. Each bacterium is worth a specified amount of weight when eaten. Bacteria are created randomly on the grid and persist on the same cell until they are eaten.

Grid
> A tessellated world inhabited by bugs and bacteria. Bugs can move to neighboring cells. The edges of the grid block motion.

Object Model

Figure 1 shows a *class diagram* for the "Bugs" simulation. A class diagram is a graphic representation of the classes in a problem together with their relationships, attributes, and operations. Each class is shown as a box with the name of the class in the top part, an optional list of attributes in the second part, and an optional list of operations in the third part. We have omitted operations from the first diagram.

Each bug has a weight and an age, a direction of movement, and a weight at which it is "strong" enough to reproduce. These attributes have been pulled directly from the problem statement. Similarly, each bacterium has a food value. A gene contains an array of rotation factors, each an integer. We want rotation factors to be discrete values subject to quantum

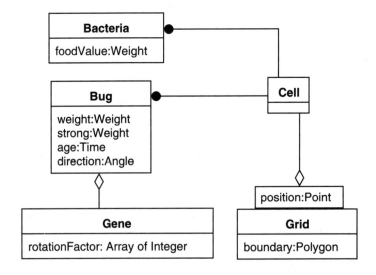

Figure 1. "Bugs" object diagram

mutations, therefore we have represented them as integers, but we have not yet said how a rotation factor value maps into a probability; we must specify this mapping during design. Finally, we have called the world Grid to capture its discrete nature within our simulation. The boundary of the grid is a polygon, although in the first version of this program it will likely be a simple rectangle.

More important even than the attributes of an object are its relationships to other objects. Relationships indicate how objects interact, how information flows among them, and how objects can be assembled into a complete system. Relationships affect the organization of the entire system, whereas attributes (and operations) are often used by only a single class. Relationships include association, aggregation, and generalization.

Association is any relationship among the instances of two classes. In most cases, binary associations are sufficient. A binary association is indicated by a line between two classes (or a loop on a single class), with a *multiplicity* symbol at each end to indicate how many of each class may be related to an object of the other class. For example, each cell may contain zero or more bugs and zero or more bacteria. The line between Cell and Bug indicates an association; the black dot next to Bug shows that "many" (zero or more) bugs may be associated with a given cell; the lack of a symbol next to Cell indicates that exactly one cell is associated with a given bug. An association and its two ends may have names, but they may be omitted if there is no ambiguity.

Aggregation is a special kind of association, indicating a part-to-whole relationship. For example, a gene is part of a bug. The diamond next to Bug on the line from Gene indicates that Bug is the aggregate and Gene is the part. The lack of a multiplicity symbol on either end indicates that each bug contains exactly one gene and each gene is part of exactly one bug. In the case of a one-to-one relationship such as *Gene is part of Bug*, the two classes could be merged into a single class containing all the attributes, but we choose to distinguish Gene and Bug because they have distinct names in the application domain and a clear separation of properties.

A grid is composed of many cells, as shown by the aggregation line between Cell and Grid. Each cell has a unique position within the grid that distinguishes it from all other cells. The position is not really an attribute of Cell; rather it is an attribute of the Cell-Grid association, because it defines the position of the cell uniquely with respect to the grid. The association line between Cell and Grid with the box next to Grid is a *qualified association*. The *qualifier* in the little box indicates an index value unique within the qualified class. A grid and a position determine a unique cell; a cell corresponds to a grid and a position. There is a one-to-many relationship between Grid and Cell; there is a one-to-one relationship between the pair (Grid, Point) and Cell.

Why bother to even have a Grid class? After all, the grid is unique within the problem, and it seems wasteful to represent associations to fixed global objects. Don't fall for this reasoning. If you build unique global objects into your problem, you will often find that you eventually want to extend the problem to accommodate multiple instances of the "unique" object. Therefore define a class for each object in the system, even those that you think are unique, and define associations between those classes and other classes that depend on them.

This completes the basic class diagram. It defines a snapshot of a system at a moment in time, in terms of classes, their attributes, and their relationships. The goal is to include enough information, and just enough information, to fully define the state of the system and the objects in it without redundancy. Don't show redundant attributes during analysis. For example, we could replace *age* by *birthDate*, but we would not show both at once, because to do so would indicate more freedom than is actually present in the system. Don't show attributes or associations that are derivable from other attributes or associations. For example, don't indicate *position* as an attribute of Bug; a unique position value can be derived by navigation from Bug to Cell to Grid. Don't show associations between classes as attribute values. For example, we could have an attribute *gene* within Bug and an attribute *bug* within Gene, but this again would indicate that the two values could be set independently, which they cannot. Associations should always be used for showing relationships between objects because they are inherently bidirectional; pointers (attribute values referencing other objects) are inherently an implementation concept and do not belong in analysis.

What is not present in this analysis object diagram? First of all, this diagram contains no inheritance (or *generalization*, as the relationship between the classes is called). Some readers will be shocked that I dare to describe an object-oriented problem without using inheritance. It is true that an object-oriented language or notation needs the concept of inheritance to be fully object-oriented. But that doesn't mean that you have to *use* inheritance on every problem. The real essence of an object-oriented analysis is not inheritance, but thinking in terms of objects. An object-oriented model is object-oriented because the potential to add inheritance to the model is always present. For example, we could specialize Bug into Herbivore and Carnivore subclasses in the future. Inheritance may or may not be necessary in the analysis of a particular problem; don't think you have to use it all the time.

What else is missing from the analysis model? You might note the absence of methods. Although some authors would disagree, we feel that identification of application-domain objects should come first. The class diagram defines the universe of discourse on which behavior operates. It is important to define what something *is* before describing what it *does*.

Once the classes and their structural relationships are identified, you can describe what they do. Operations can then be added to the model.

The analysis model does not attempt to encapsulate information. The analyst should take a "God's eye" view of the problem and capture all the information available. Accessing attributes and traversing associations are legitimate sources of information that do not require any special dispensation. How can you make a good design if you conceal information from yourself? Encapsulation is a design construct, intended to limit the effect of changes within an implementation; it is not an analysis construct.

Dynamic Model

The *object model* specifies the structure of the objects in the "Bugs" simulation. During analysis, you must of course define the behavior that you want your system to have. Behavior can be specified by the interactions that occur between objects and by the transformations that objects undergo. In the OMT methodology, interactions are specified by the *dynamic model* and transformations by the *functional model*.

The dynamic model specifies the external interactions of the system with outside agents. The dynamic model is represented graphically by state diagrams, one for each class with dynamic behavior. Figure 2 shows a *state diagram* for class Bug and class Grid. The state diagram shows the life history of a bug. Each rounded box is a different state. The behavior of a bug is very simple. It only has one state, Alive, during much of its life. The other states are initialization or termination states. An arrow between states shows a state transition in response to an *event,* which is an interaction between objects. The open circle labeled "birth" points to the initial state of the object, the state Alive.

The grid has an even simpler life history. When it is born, it populates itself with bacteria and bugs. On each clock tick, it generates some bacteria at random locations in the grid.

The only event a bug responds to is *clock tick*, that is, the passage of a unit of time. The passage of time may be regarded as an event from the universe to an object. When an event occurs, the object takes a transition from the current state labeled by the event. When a transition occurs, an object may perform an operation and transition to a new state. When *clock tick* occurs, the bug performs operation "step" and returns to the Alive state. The bug also responds to two possible conditions, shown as transition labels in brackets. A transition occurs whenever one of the conditions becomes true. If the bug starves (weight = 0), then

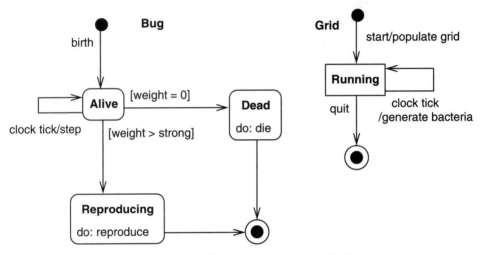

Figure 2. State diagram for class Bug and Grid

it transitions to state Dead, where it performs operation "die" and then ceases to exist (shown by the bull's eye). If the bug gets fat enough (weight > strong), then it transitions to state Reproducing, where it performs operation "reproduce" which creates two new bugs to take its place. The original bug then ceases to exist. (We could have drawn the state diagram so a reproducing bug made a single copy of itself and continued to exist, but the way I have drawn the diagram is more symmetric.)

The event *clock tick* affects every bug. In what order do the various bugs perform their operations? For this simulation, it doesn't much matter, so we don't specify it. *Objects are inherently concurrent.* Because all the major object-oriented languages are sequential, during design we must serialize the execution of Bug operations, but during analysis a concurrent viewpoint is just fine.

This state diagram completely defines the behavior of the system. All operations are ultimately initiated by clock ticks. But where do we specify the effect of an operation? That is done in the functional model.

Functional Model

The functional model specifies the effect of operations on data values. It is expressed by *operation descriptions*, one per nontrivial operation. The only top-level operation on Bug is the *step* operation on Bug, but we can define suboperations to simplify the specification and make it readable. In the pseudocode shown in Table 2, a semicolon between statements denotes sequential ordering and a double line denotes concurrent ordering (statements that can be executed simultaneously or in any relative order).

Table 2: Suboperations for Bugs application

Bug::step () is
    growOlder ||
    move to a new direction and location ||
    metabolize then *eat* the bacteria found in the cell at the bug's location.

Bug::growOlder () is
    add the simulated time step to the age.

Bug::move () is
    rotationAngle := generate a random angle using the rotationFactor in the gene;
    rotate the direction by the rotationAngle;
    offset the location by one unit of length in the new direction.

Bug::metabolize () is
    subtract the "cost of living" from the weight.
    [Initially let this be constant. Later we might want it to be a function of the
    weight, i.e., big bugs expend more energy to stay alive.]

Bug::reproduce () is
    create a new Bug by copying the original Bug;
    divide the original weight among the two bugs [initially divide it evenly] ||
    set the age of each bug to 0 ||
    separately *mutate* the gene in each Bug.

Bug::mutate () is
    randomly modify one element of the gene's rotationFactor.
    [The details of this operation can be tailored to the physical representation of the
    gene, since we simply need some kind of mutation. Essential to the concept of
    mutation is an *integer* encoding of the gene, because genes are fundamentally
    discrete codes.]

Grid::populate (nbugs, nbacteria) is
    generate *nbugs* bugs at random locations in the grid ||
    generate *nbacteria* bacteria at random locations in the grid ||
    initialize other grid parameters (to be determined).

Three Models

The analysis is now complete and described by three separate but related models. The object model describes the information structures of the system. The dynamic model describes the external stimuli that initiate activity on objects and the operations that are invoked. The functional model describes the computations on values performed by each operation. Together all three models describe what a system does with minimal constraints on how it must be implemented.

As a final step of analysis, you may summarize operations from the dynamic and functional models onto the object model. Figure 3 shows the "Bugs" object diagram with operations allocated to classes. Operations that update attributes have been allocated to the class owning the attributes. For example, *growOlder* and *metabolize* have been assigned to Bug.

We can use the analysis model to answer all kinds of questions about the system we are building. We can ask and answer queries about the state of the system, about the response of the system to stimuli, about how values are computed. We can execute the simulation to a certain level of detail. We cannot completely execute the model, because we left some details open, such as the mapping of the gene rotation factors into probability vectors. We omitted these details because we did not care exactly how they are implemented during these analysis phase.

Designing Bugs

During design, we must resolve any open issues and expand out the details of any loosely specified operations. We must also transform and optimize the analysis model so that it is efficient enough for implementation. During implementation we must map the design into a specific programming language and satisfy all of the rules and conventions of the chosen language.

I make a somewhat arbitrary but useful distinction between *design* and *implementation*. During design, we build a solution to the problem, but in an idealized medium, without worrying about the peculiarities of the programming language or database. We do worry about computational complexity and are concerned about providing algorithmic data structures and optimizations for efficient computation.

In a larger and more complex problem, the first step of design would be to choose a system architecture and to make high-level policy decisions about the strategy of solving the problem. The few architectural issues in this small problem will be treated as part of a single

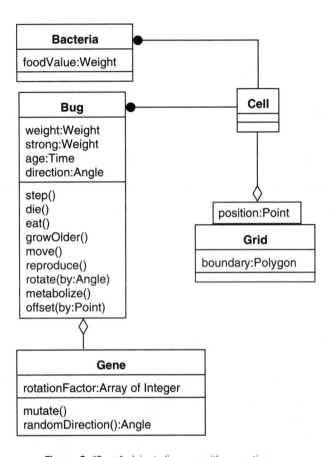

Figure 3. "Bugs" object diagram with operations

design phase. If we expanded the problem to include graphic displays, control panels, statistics, and archiving of simulations, we would probably want to separate the system design and object design phases.

Design

During the design phase we start with the analysis model and expand it into a design model. During design, the object model becomes the focus for integrating the information from all three analysis models (object, dynamic, functional). There is no sharp break with the analysis model; instead information is gradually added and transformed to build the design model from the analysis model.

During design the main focus becomes the expansion and realization of operations as methods on object classes, together with clarifications and modifications to the object diagram needed to facilitate implementing methods. There is a shift away from "what we need to do" and toward "how we do it." The design process for the "bugs" simulation has the following steps:

◆ Design a control architecture to implement the dynamic model

◆ Realize the operations in the functional model as methods on objects

◆ Transform the object model for more efficient use

Dynamic Model

At the end of the analysis we summarized operations on classes in the object model. Association and attribute access operations should be omitted from the object model during the design phase. These are "junk methods" that may easily be handled as implementation details; worry about the substantive operations during design.

The first step is to remove some of the idealistic assumptions about the execution environment. During analysis, we treated the clock tick event as acting concurrently on all the bugs as well as the grid. Because most major programming languages are sequential, it is more convenient to process all the effects of each event sequentially, and there is no real need in this simulation to process all the actions concurrently (as there would be in a cellular automaton, such as the Game of Life). Therefore we make the architectural decision to apply the clock tick event to the bugs in the grid sequentially. Because **Grid** already responds to the clock tick event, we can make it responsible for invoking the step operation on each bug in turn. Sequential implementation of control is the simplest and most common way to handle small applications.

We assume that the operating system can generate periodic time events that trigger a user-specified procedure, which we designate to be the method **Grid::clockTick**. Pseudocode for this method is as follows (by default, operations and attributes apply to the current object):

```
Grid::clockTick ()
    do fertility times:
        generateBacterium;
    for each bug in the grid:
        bug.clockTick;
```

The Bug state diagram can then be represented by the following method:

```
Bug::clockTick ()
    step;
    If weight = 0 then die;
    if weight >= strong then:
        reproduce;
        die;
```

In the state machine for this example each clock tick event always invokes the same response, so we implement it as an operation on the grid and bug. In highly interactive systems, such as user interfaces, it is often desirable to implement a control mechanism with an explicit state machine. In an object-oriented model true concurrency is represented in a straightforward way, because objects are inherently concurrent, but the major OO programming languages are sequential, so implementation can be a problem. Control and concurrency are topics for one or more whole columns, so I will not treat them fully now.

This completes the expansion of the dynamic model. The rest of the design process is the expansion of the operations in the functional model.

Functional Model

The operation **Bug::step** was described by a high-level pseudocode description. Now we fill in the details and pick a sequential ordering of the concurrent suboperations:

```
Bug::step()
    growOlder();
    move();
    metabolize();
    count := grid[position].nBacteria
    if count > 0 then
        eat (count * Bacterium.foodValue);
        grid[position].nBacteria := 0;
```

Operations **growOlder, move, metabolize,** and **eat** are simple functions that update the attributes of **Bug**. I show **move** as a typical example:

```
Bug::move()
    rotate (gene.randomDirection());
    offset (direction);

Bug::rotate (delta)
    angle := (angle + delta) mod 360;
```

Here is the pseudocode for bug reproduction:

```
Bug::reproduce()
    create a new bug;
    copy direction and location to new bug;
    attach new bug to the grid;
    copy weight/2 into the new bug and subtract it from the existing bug;
    set the age of each bug to 0;
    create a new gene in the new bug;
    copy the rotation codes into new gene;
    mutate each gene independently;
```

The remaining operations are mapped into methods in a similar way.

To summarize, events on the dynamic model trigger top-level operations, which may be expanded in terms of other operations in the functional model. Because the original operations are so simple, there is little expansion to do. In a more complicated example we would have to introduce one or more levels of intermediate operations.

Object Model

We now optimize the object model by applying to it a series of transformations that change its form but leave its fundamental meaning unchanged. The purpose is to make the model amenable to efficient implementation. Figure 3 shows the object model that we devised during analysis. We now describe several kinds of transformations that we apply to produce the final design model. The purpose of the transformations is to expand detail, integrate information from other models, and to optimize the access paths.

The first kind of transformation is the modification or clarification of attributes. Figure 4 shows one of these transformations. During analysis we simply said that **Gene::rotation-**

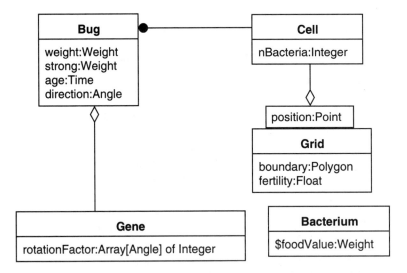

Figure 4. Object diagram after some transformations

Factor was an array of integers on some unspecified domain, but now we further specify that it comprises one integer value for each possible rotation angle. The probability of rotating by a given angle is proportional to the negative exponent of the integer value. (This last piece of information is not visible on the diagram, but would be described in the model dictionary.) We will eventually want to optimize this computation further so we do not have to take exponents all the time, but that is a low-level local optimization that can wait until implementation. During design, it is important to specify high-level algorithms and optimizations of a broad importance.

A second kind of transformation is the elimination or collapsing of unnecessary information. In this simulation, bacteria do not have identity. It does not matter which bacterium a bug eats, because the bacteria are indistinguishable. All that matters is the number of bacteria associated with a given cell. Therefore we replaced the **Cell–Bacterium** association with the number of bacteria in a given cell, making it the attribute **nBacteria**. The class **Bacterium** no longer has any instances. It survives only as a repository for the food value of a bacterium, which is constant across all bacteria. The dollar sign indicates that **foodValue** is a class attribute shared by all instances of the class. Of course, this design decision precludes the possibility of bacteria of different weights, but any design decision removes some freedom from a design. If we want variable-size bacteria in the future, then we can revisit this design decision.

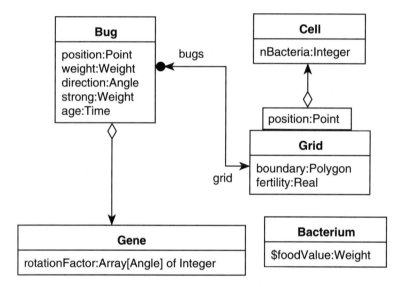

Figure 5. Object diagram after all transformations

Of course, we must check with the customer to make sure that all bacteria really do have the same value. Often you discover some optimization that you would like to make that you suspect doesn't matter to the customer, but you should verify the clarification with the customer. Always try to clearly separate design decisions from requirements statements.

Why not just use a fully general design? Well, you wouldn't be wrong if you did, but I felt that the added complexity was not needed yet, and I wanted to get the job done quickly. Learning how to trade off generality against simplicity is a matter of judgment that takes experience.

The third kind of transformation is the modification of associations to optimize access within the application. Figure 5 shows such optimizations between **Bug**, **Cell**, and **Grid**. We know that we need to find the bugs in the grid. Having to scan all the cells in the grid to find the bugs is very inefficient. Therefore we introduce a one-to-many association between **Grid** and **Bug** to represent the path **Grid–Cell–Bug** directly, without including **Cell**. This is a *derived* association; it does not represent new information, rather it is derivable from the original base information. We don't need the position as part of this "shortcut" association, so we leave it out.

In a simulation of a large grid, we might have millions of cells, the majority of which have no bacteria at any moment. We would probably want the implementation size of each cell to be small. The most spatially-efficient implementation would be to store only cells with non-zero bacteria counts in a hash table, but dynamic allocation and hashing cost execution time. If we can afford the space, the fastest approach is to represent the grid as an array of cells, each cell containing only its bacteria count. In any case, we do not want to store the position or any pointers in a cell. We would also prefer to avoid two-way associations, which are more costly to update.

For the reasons mentioned above, we want to eliminate the direct association between **Bug** and **Cell**. Also we would prefer to deal with bug motion in terms of positions and not cells. Therefore we have replaced the association from **Bug** to **Cell** with a *surrogate*, that is, a value that stands for an object. The surrogate consists of the position of the cell and the pointer to the grid. The pair of values uniquely correspond to a single **Cell**. To implement the surrogate, we add the attribute **position** to the bug; the grid pointer is already present as part of the **Bug-Grid** derived association.

An arrowhead indicates an association that can be traversed in one direction only. Notice that all the associations to **Cell** are now incoming. There is no way to get from a **Cell** to a **Grid** or a **Bug**. This is an acceptable constraint in the current problem, because we can easily keep track of the context any time we access a cell.

Although the model has been transformed, it still represents the same information, but some of the access paths are a bit different (and more efficient to traverse).

We could have gone further and removed the pointer from **Bug** to **Grid**, as we removed the pointer from **Cell** to **Grid**, because the **Grid::clockTick** operation ultimately calls all the other operations, and we could simply pass the grid along as an argument. However, this transformation would add an argument to most of the methods of **Bug**. In this simulation we will have only a hundred or so bugs at a given time, so the cost of an additional pointer is small and not worth complicating the methods. We might have a million cells, so reducing the size of a cell was worth the additional complication.

We note that after our transformations the time cost of a step of the simulation is proportional to the number of bugs and newly-created bacteria and is not affected by the number of cells or existing bacteria. The time cost of simulating one bug step is constant. Storing nonempty cells in a hash table would not change the complexity, because hashing is constant time, but hashing would increase the proportionality constant. Always understand the computational complexity of your algorithms before you attempt to optimize them. It is harmful to complicate your design by optimizing unimportant cases.

I explained design in a clear sequence: determine top-level operations from the dynamic model, derive lower level operations from the functional model, and then optimize the object model accordingly. In practice design proceeds with some guessing ahead and jump-

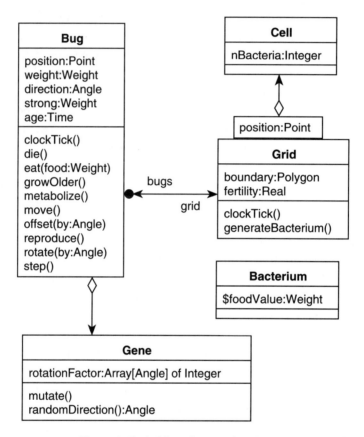

Figure 6. Final object diagram after design

ing around, so don't feel you have to follow the steps of a methodology in a rigid order. Development is always iterative.

Figure 6 shows the object diagram with operations. In the design model, we show operations that perform semantic computations. We omit operations that merely access attributes and create and destroy objects. We are concerned with establishing the logic of the algorithms, not with language issues such as encapsulation of attributes. During design, we may assume that attributes are accessible to operations and that the object network can be freely navigated. These things we omit from design are important, but they vary widely from language to language and are best deferred until the implementation phase.

Implementation

I use *implementation* to indicate the mapping of a design into a particular language. During implementation, you must fully map your design into a specific programming language, dealing with the quirks of the particular language (and they all have many quirks!). You must adapt your model to accommodate the syntax and semantics of the language, which may require extensions to notation, conventions on usage, or annotations. You must account for boundary conditions, such as initialization, termination, object creation, object destruction, and object copying. You must use the naming conventions of the language and your work environment. You must define encapsulation and introduce dummy operations to enhance encapsulation; access methods must be defined.

Figure 7 shows an implementation model of the "Bugs" simulation in C++ (a language with a great many quirks). You can recognize the design model within the diagram, but there are some extra classes and a lot of extra methods, as well as C++ syntax for attribute and argument types. Most of the new methods have been added to encapsulate access to attributes or to other objects. They do not affect the logic of the program, but they are necessary to good object-oriented programming style.

During implementation you should specify the visibility of operations. We have indicated public visibility by a plus sign and private visibility by a minus sign (in C++ we might also distinguish protected visibility). Public operations are freely accessible; private ones are not accessible outside the class. In general, attributes should be private and accessed outside the class using only access methods.

We indicate an embedded *pure value* by a solid diamond on the aggregate end of the association. Although pure values may be implemented as C++ classes and have methods, they have no individual identity and can be embedded within other objects without loss of generality. For example, we have made **Direction** into a class so we can define methods on it, but it can be embedded in Bug as a data value because its only purpose is to encapsulate angle values. Similarly **CellLocation** and **Point** are pure data structure types. We have embedded **Gene** within Bug because **Gene** and **Bug** are in one-to-one correspondence anyway.

During implementation you must specify the implementation of associations. In C++ associations can be implemented as pointers. An arrow from one class to another indicates that the association is implemented as an attribute in the class at the tail of the arrow. The name of the attribute is shown on the arrowhead. For example, **CellLocation** contains an attribute **ptrGrid** that is a pointer to a **Grid** object. An arrow with a black dot ("many") is implemented as a set unless specified otherwise. **Grid** contains a pointer to a set of bugs, whereas **Grid** contains a pointer to an array of cells; the array indices are points. If an asso-

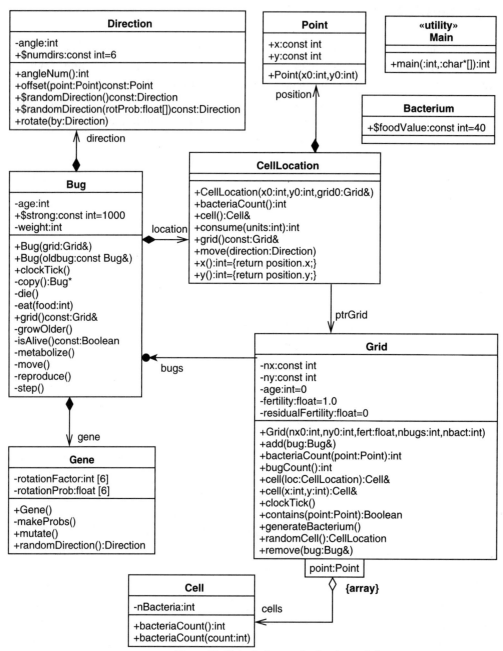

Figure 7. Object diagram for implementation

ciation is implemented in both directions (such as **Grid-Bug**) any update must change both ends (**Bug.location.ptrGrid** and **Grid.bugs**).

We added a new attribute, **rotationProb,** and a new method, **makeProbs,** to class **Gene.** When a gene is created and its **rotationFactor** values are mutated, the method **makeProbs** takes the exponential of each factor, normalizes it, and stores the probability in the vector **rotationProb,** so that the computation of random values is more efficient. This kind of low-level optimization belongs to implementation, not object design, because it depends on the details of the language and does not affect the large-scale algorithm.

Several methods just encapsulate data access. We need to obtain the number of bacteria at a given location. This could be obtained by traversing the association network, but it is best not to traverse more than one association link within a given method, otherwise the code depends too heavily on the low-level data structure. A bug can ask for **bacteriaCount()** on its location, which calls **bacteriaCount(point)** on its grid, which in turn indexes its **cells** array by the point and calls **bacteriaCount** on the resulting cell. There is no information or new semantics here, so there is no need to list these methods during design. These encapsulation methods can be written almost mechanically during implementation, but they *should* be written or you will regret it later when your implementation changes.

In this implementation, I simplified the grid boundary to be a rectangle and replaced the **boundary** attribute with the dimensions **nx** and **ny** of the rectangle, but a more general implementation would not be difficult, provided other classes use the method **Grid::contains(Point)** to test whether a point is actually in the grid.

The implementation diagram in Figure 7 is an actual diagram from the Object Modeling Tool, an object model editor that I wrote that generates C++ code (among other things). The tool also contains popup text forms to specify additional information about classes, attributes, and methods beyond that shown on the diagram, such as text descriptions of each entity and other C++ semantics. During implementation a textual information peculiar to a particular language is needed. This information can be specified nongraphically. Although I have discussed generating C++ code, similar low-level decisions must be made for other object-oriented languages.

Summary

This completes the walk through of the "bugs" example. It was intended to illustrate what goes on during analysis, design, and implementation. I have tried to show a seamless approach to software development in which we first build an analysis model based on the problem statement, then augment and transform it to produce a design model, which is then mapped into a particular programming language. I have also shown the use of three modeling views—object, dynamic, and functional—during analysis. During design we integrate the three models onto the object model in a kind of "symmetry breaking" process that generates the operations on the object classes. During design we must partition the system into coherent pieces and address computational complexity issues, but low-level optimization and encapsulation of attributes and access paths belongs to the implementation phase.

This walk through has been fast and I have had to gloss over many important points. In future columns I will go into more detail on some of them.

Objects in the Constitution
Enterprise Modeling
January 1993

The Constitution as Architecture

As I write this article, the United States has just completed its 103rd biennial election under the Constitution inaugurated in 1789. The U.S. Constitution is a masterpiece of brevity: the original document is only four printed pages long, whereas some state constitutions (such as New York's) run into hundreds of pages of arcane detail. The Constitution is an example of "political architecture"; it lays out the framework of government without specifying all the details, just as a software architecture describes overall structure and not the details of individual procedures.

One of the major uses of object-oriented modeling is *enterprise modeling*, which is the process of understanding a complex social organization by constructing models. Many organizations are poorly understood even by those people who are part of them, and building an object model can force people to ask questions that clarify how the organization actually works. The precision required to construct an object model often exposes ambiguities that are not apparent from a natural-language statement.

In this column I show some models of the U.S. government based on the U.S. Constitution. The Constitution is one of the few definitive specifications of a complex human organization, so constructing a model is easier than it would be for a typical company, but we will see that the modeling process exposes some ambiguities even here.

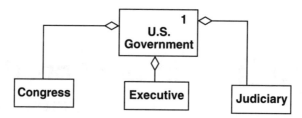

Figure 1. United States government

The Object Model

Figure 1 shows a high-level object model of the U.S. government showing the three branches of government, each of which is expanded in turn in Figures 2-4. Figure 2 shows the executive branch. I have made a distinction between an *office* (such as Presidency or Senate Seat) and an *officer,* a person who holds an office. An office is part of the government branch, shown as an aggregation relationship. An office may or may not have an officeholder at a given moment. Note that there is no class **Officer**; an officer is a role of the Office-officer-Person association, not a distinct class. This association is optional in both directions: an office may be vacant, and a person may or may not hold an office. (I have assumed that a person may only hold one office. If this is incorrect, then the multiplicity should be *many* and not *optional.*) Do not fall into the trap of confusing a role with a class!

There is something a bit funny about this model. Because it is a model of the U.S. government, there is only a single instance of the model (there are other governments with similar structure, but we would be stretching things to claim that this model is general purpose). I have borrowed an idea from Embley, Kurtz, and Woodfield [1] and called **U.S.Government** a *singleton class,* that is, a class that has only a single instance (indicated by the "1" in the upper right corner of the class box). I have not marked Congress, Senate, Executive, Presidency, etc., as singleton classes because their cardinality can be derived from the uniqueness of the **U.S.Government** class and the one-to-one associations to the other classes.

Note a constraint in the model. The Constitution stipulates that no member of Congress can simultaneously hold a civil office. This is indicated by saying that the set of officers (**office.officer**) and the set of Congressional seat holders (**seat.incumbent**) are disjoint.

Figure 3 shows the judicial branch. The Constitution explicitly mandates a single Supreme Court (which is unique since Judiciary is unique) but some indeterminate number

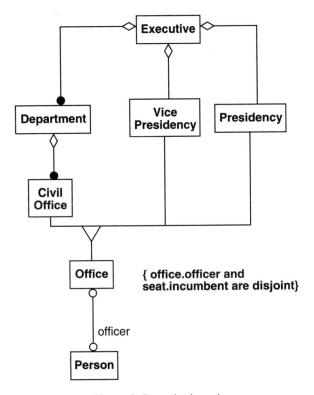

Figure 2. Executive branch

of inferior courts. On the other hand, the rights and privileges of judges are similar for all Federal courts, so we use generalization to **Court** and association to **Person** to identify judges.

Figure 5 shows the composition of Congress. There is a slight difference between House and Senate seats. Each state has exactly two senators but the number of House seats is proportional to state population as of the previous census. (The model dictionary must clearly define the meaning of the attribute *population* as applying to the previous census, not the current moment. Isolated words are frequently ambiguous). House seats come up for election every two years, whereas Senate seats are divided into three classes (that's the word the Constitution uses, although I doubt they were being object-oriented), one of which comes up for election every two years, so senators serve for six years per term. The Constitution specifies that the partition be as even as possible, which I have indicated by a constraint. In-

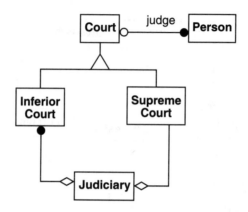

Figure 3. Judiciary branch

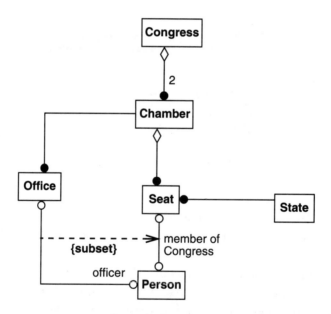

Figure 4. Congress (generalized)

terestingly, it does not specify that the two Senate seats from a single state should be from different election classes, although the members of the initial Congress sensibly added that constraint in partitioning the seats.

The number of House seats per state is proportional to the population of the state. Unfortunately, we have a little problem with integer arithmetic here, as the Congress is com-

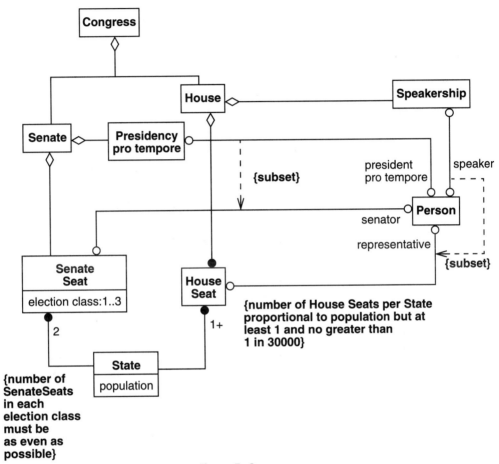

Figure 5. Congress

posed of real persons each of whom has one vote. It turns out that the method of allocating the fractions has been a major issue for the past 200 years, because there are several different mathematical ways of doing it that yield different results. In fact, this year Massachusetts won and later lost an attempt to capture a seat from Washington based on a dispute as to the proper formula. The algorithm for allocating seats belongs in the functional model. (I won't show it because I don't know exactly what it is right now.)

Figure 4 shows the same model of Congress using generalization to reduce duplication. The Constitution uses the word "house" to mean either House of Representatives or Senate, but this usage is easily confused with House of Representatives, so I have used the word "chamber" instead. Such potential ambiguities occur frequently in natural language. I feel that it is best to avoid possible confusion by choosing unique names, even at the expense of modifying the names used in the actual specification documents, but that is a matter of judgment.

We can clearly see the similar structure of both legislative chambers, but we have lost a little precision, because House and Senate are now treated as instances of Chamber and we cannot see the variations between them. We could of course combine the two models, but then the diagram would be rather cluttered. Modeling often poses such choices between understandability and precision. Keep in mind that the purpose of a model is to help you accomplish a task and not to prove mathematical theorems, so usually you should choose a simpler representation rather than a contorted model that ekes the last iota of precision out of a situation using notation. No diagram is complete by itself anyway; they all require text commentary and human understanding, so don't be afraid to use textual commentary to clarify a model.

On Figure 4, I have indicated that a person can hold at most one seat in Congress. The Constitution does not actually *say* that a person cannot serve in both bodies simultaneously, although I'm sure that the framers did not intend to allow it. This is an example of the kind of unstated assumption that an object model can make explicit.

The House has a speaker and the Senate has a president pro tempore, as well as other unspecified officers. Note that the speaker is an association between the House and Person, not Seat; the person is elected directly to the office.

Modeling Elections

The Constitution devotes a good amount of space to describing how Congress and the President will be elected. Because elections inherently involve changes over time, we need to confront the trickiest aspect of modeling: the treatment of time and the behavior of objects over time. All three modeling views (object, dynamic, functional) will be involved, but first we will look at the object model. There is a fundamental tension in an object model between an object *at a point in time* and an object *over time*. In the first case, we capture a snapshot of a situation at some moment in time, for example, at the time of an election. In the second case, we capture the history of an object over a series of changes over time, for example, the history of elections for a particular congressional seat. The two are closely related, of course. For a snapshot, we must clearly indicate the time for which it is valid; events and operations

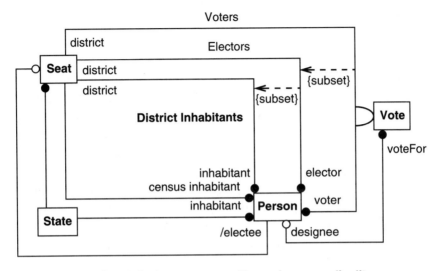

{seat.electee = person with maximum cardinality
of voteFor who meets qualifications}

Figure 6. An election at a moment in time

change the state of the entire system. On the other hand, we do not try to *change* a history, just add to it as time goes on. Both views can appear in a single model, but they must be clearly distinguished.

Figure 6 shows a single election for a congressional seat. There are several things shown on this diagram. First we indicate the *electors* for a seat, as shown by the Seat-Person association. Electors are the persons constitutionally entitled to vote for an office; in other words, they are the voters. The Constitution gives a functional constraint for this association: "qualifications requisite for electors of the most numerous branch of the state legislature." There is another implicit requirement for House (but not Senate) elections: the voter must live in the election district assigned to the seat (association Seat-inhabitant). This requirement is not actually stated in the Constitution, and I believe that an at-large election of representatives for a given state would be legal, if not politically likely, but I have modeled the constraint as it exists in practice.

The number of inhabitants per seat within a state must be approximately equal (the definition of "approximate" is a matter of intense legal and mathematical argument). The number of inhabitants is the count as of the last census, not the count at the moment of the election; we need separate association for "census inhabitants", a historical association that changes every ten years, and "current inhabitants," an association valid at the time of the election. One of the necessary skills in modeling is to separate distinct things with similar names.

Not every eligible elector votes, of course. The seat-voter association is a subset of the seat-elector association. We call an instance of the seat-voter association a **Vote** and promote it to an association class, that is, a link that has properties and is treated as an object. The one property of each vote is that it is a vote *for* some person, which we call the *designee,* indicated by an association between **Seat** and **designee Person**. Don't be fooled just because **Person** appears twice in conjunction with **Vote**; they are not the same object. One role is the voter and the other the person voted for, but both are objects of class **Person.**

The winner of an election is the *electee,* a derived association determined by the person who receives the most votes as designee. In fact, the Constitution does not say that elections are decided by plurality, rather than by majority vote with a run-off, for example. Building models helps to identify ambiguities such as this one. Probably the framers assumed that their intent was obvious, based on previous custom, for example.

In fact, the derivation constraint is a bit more complicated, because the electee must also be qualified for the position. The Constitution specifies that a Representative or Senator must "be an inhabitant of that state in which he shall be chosen." This constraint is shown by the state-inhabitant association. Note that a representative need *not* reside in the voters' district, although in practice it would be political suicide not to do so. The qualification applies only at the moment of election; a representative could presumably move to another state after election. However, we must take some care with the representation of these historical constraints within a snapshot model. For example, at the moment of election, the winner becomes the electee but not immediately the incumbent.

Suppose we want to represent the history of elections and officeholders over time. Figure 7 shows such a model. In this model, we have omitted the more transient relationships, such as inhabitants and electors, because these are more appropriate to the snapshot model rather than being information we would like to preserve. If we are going to combine the results of several elections within a single model, we need a way to distinguish a particular election for a particular seat; we call this a **Contest**. Each contest is identified by the date that it occurs. The number of votes for each person is a link attribute of the association between **Contest** and **designee.**

Similarly, we distinguish a period of time for which a person holds a seat as a **Term,** identified by its start and finish dates. The same person may serve several terms, so we do not make **Term** a link class, which would represent a single unique link between a seat and an incumbent.

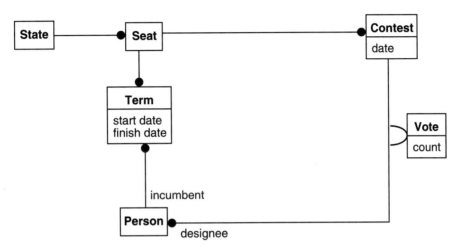

Figure 7. An election history over time

A historical model such as this is more suitable for storing records about what happened in the past; a snapshot model is more suitable for actually simulating changes as they occur and performing operations.

Dynamic Model

Figures 8 and 9 show a dynamic model for a congressional seat. I have broken the model into two concurrent parts: the occupancy of the office (Figure 8) and the election process. In the American system, the winning candidate does not assume office immediately after the election; there is a two-month opportunity for "lame ducks" to do mischief even after they have been defeated (originally it was an entire congressional session, so I suppose we should be grateful for progress). An office itself may be occupied or vacant. It becomes vacant if the incumbent dies, resigns or is expelled. The office also becomes vacant if the term expires and no successor has been elected (perhaps the electee has died, for example).

The election process is related to the occupancy of the office but not totally coincident. Scheduled elections happen every two years (for House seats). Once the election is complete, there is an electee (ignoring the possibility of ties or other electoral difficulties). The electee may or may not be the same as the incumbent, if any, but in any case the electee only takes office when the scheduled term begins and the electee is sworn in. I show this on the

Office

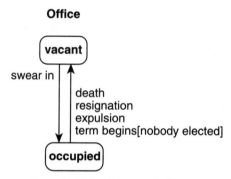

Figure 8. State diagram of office

Election

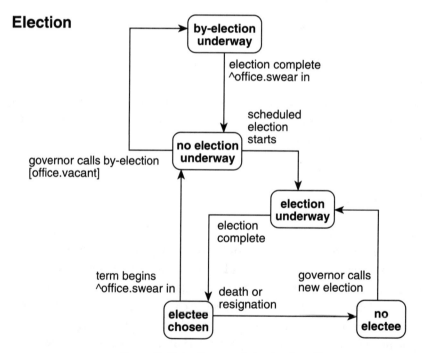

Figure 9. State diagram of election for office

election complete transition by the notation "^office.swear in", which indicates a "swear in" event transmitted from the **Election** substate to the concurrent **Office** substate.

If the incumbent dies, then the governor calls a special by-election to elect a replacement for the remainder of the term, unless a regular election is about to occur anyway. The

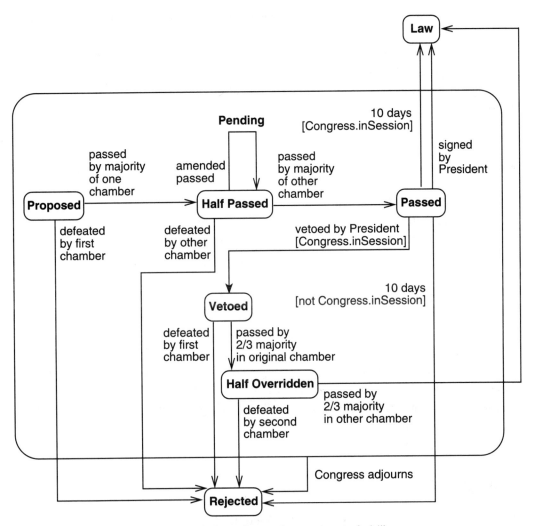

Figure 10. State diagram for enactment of a bill

winner of a by-election is sworn in immediately; there is no interval during which there is both an incumbent and an electee.

Treating the situation as two interrelated but concurrent substates simplifies understanding of the situation, as many combinations can occur.

Figure 10 shows the state diagram for a bill in Congress. This diagram is fairly straightforward. Note the use of elapsed-time events with conditions on other objects. For example, a passed bill becomes law if 10 days elapse (an event) and Congress (another object) is in session (a state of the other object).

If Congress adjourns, all pending bills die, as shown by the transition from the super-state **Pending** to the **Rejected** state. The use of superstates to group several states is similar to the use of superclasses to group classes; the transitions on superstate are inherited by all the substates.

Reflection

The Constitution is *reflective,* that is, it describes itself, in that it provides a process for its own amendment. It also provided for its own initialization, including handling "heritage code" (debts contracted under the Articles of Confederation).

Conclusion

My point in this article was to show how an organization can be modeled to understand and explain its structure and behavior. The Constitution is fundamentally a textual document, with hundreds of pages of legal decisions hanging off of every sentence, so no model can make it more definitive. Many organizations, however, do not have a binding written spec-ification, and object-oriented enterprise models can help greatly in providing concise, pre-cise explanations of how they work.

References

1. David W. Embley, Barry D. Kurtz, Scott N. Woodfield. *Object-Oriented Systems Analysis: A Model-Driven Approach.* Yourdon Press, Englewood Cliffs, N.J., 1992.

Design Process

A METHOD can be divided into two major parts: the modeling language (*what*) and the process (*how*). The modeling language includes the modeling concepts and the notation to represent them. The model captures the final result of the development process, much like a theorem captures the final result of a mathematical proof. Before telling how to develop a model, it is necessary to describe the elements of modeling. In the course of describing the modeling elements, I have suggested some guidelines on how to discover and choose good models. Nevertheless it is necessary to describe the development process more directly and completely. In this part I have included a number of articles about the development process at various stages of development.

Getting Started: Using Use Cases to Capture Requirements describes use cases as a good way to obtain a user-centered view of the system requirements. Ivar Jacobson has popularized the term and the concept, which has a long history in computer development under such names as *operations concept document*. Almost all methods have adopted use cases for gathering requirements.

The Life of an Object Model: How the Object Model Changes During Development describes the different way in which models are constructed at different stages of the life cycle. The model provides a language, but just like a natural language the modeling language can be used for different purposes. What you do during analysis is not the same as what you do during detailed design.

One of the biggest problems I had with the original OMT book was the separation of classes into real-world domain classes and internal design classes. This missed the point that some user-visible classes are meaningful during the analysis although they do not represent real-world concepts. *Objects in the Twilight Zone: How to Find and Use Application Objects* describes these "twilight zone" classes that represent aspects of the computer system visible to the users. Because they are part of the computer application itself, they are not arbitrary parts of the design solution but instead are parts of the requirements. I called them *application classes* because they carry the weight of the application itself. Once I discovered them, many of the problems in my development process fell into place.

Virtual Worlds: Modeling at Different Levels of Abstraction illustrates another aspect of modeling that often confuses beginners (as well as many experienced modelers, including some methodologists). The real world does not have objects in it. The objects are in our minds, an abstraction of the seamless web of reality. Our minds and languages are attuned to creating objects, so we don't think about this much, but all thought, language, and modeling is a process of abstraction. Critical to abstraction is choosing the right level of detail, but there is no one "right" level. Most problems can be approached from multiple levels of detail simultaneously, layered virtual worlds built on top of each other. This is not a mathematical construct; it is the way we think, and it is built so deeply into us that it happens automatically. In building explicit models, however, it is sometimes necessary to think of it explicitly.

Modeling Models and Viewing Views is less general: it describes the model-view-controller framework that was popularized in Smalltalk but used far more widely in many applications. This kind of framework is an *architectural pattern*. A number of people are cataloging such large-scale patterns so that others can emulate them.

The end result of most application models is code. Converting class models to class declarations is reasonably straightforward, because OO languages support most of the concepts directly, but state models are harder for many people to program. *Controlling Code: How to Implement Dynamic Models* describes the kind of code necessary to implement state models.

Getting Started
Using Use Cases to Capture Requirements
September 1994

User-Centered Analysis

What is the most important aspect of modeling and design methodology? Formal consistency, reusability, efficiency, faithfulness to object-oriented principles? No. None of this matters a bit *if you don't solve the right problem.* There is no internal check that a model or a program is correct. Developers must ask users or domain experts what to do, capture their needs in some form, and then verify that the captured requirements are correct. The requirements must be expressed in some structured way, but they must still be understandable to the users who must verify them.

User-centered analysis is the process of capturing requirements from the user's point of view. The designer must then map the requirements into the computer domain for solution. Don't assume that stating requirements in users' terms will eliminate all problems. In a large system with many interactions, nobody may understand the consequences of each requirement. The purpose of analysis is to explore the consequences of an initial problem statement and come up with a complete, correct model of a problem. You can't just write down all the requirements; you have to start with an initial approximation of them and then refine them while exploring their interactions, implications, and mutual inconsistencies.

Most methodologists now agree that user-centered analysis is the best way to solve the right problem. Capturing the user's needs is a major focus of several methodologies, including Rubin and Goldberg's OBA [1] and Jacobson's OOSE [2]. Jacobson's *use cases* in particular have been well received by just about every methodologist including us. We feel that use cases fit naturally on the front end of the published OMT process [3] and supplement the existing user-centered features of the method.

Use Cases

An *actor* is an outside entity that interacts directly with a system. Actors include both humans and other quasi-autonomous things, such as machines, computer tasks, and other systems. More precisely, an actor is a role played by such an entity. One person can play several roles and thereby represent several actors, such as a computer system operator, a database administrator, and an end user. Objects that are indirectly connected to the system are not actors, because their needs must be communicated to the system through an actor.

Each actor uses the system in different ways, otherwise the actor would not be different. A single actor can also use the system in fundamentally different ways. Each way of using the system is called a use case.

A *use case* describes the possible sequences of interactions among the system and one or more actors in response to some initial stimulus by one of the actors. It is not a single *scenario* (a specific history of specific messages exchanged among system and actors) but rather a description of a set of potential scenarios, each starting with some initial message from an actor to the system and following the ensuing transaction to its logical conclusion. Normally each use case focuses on some purpose for the actor. For example, the database administrator (DBA) might have a use case for "installing a database" which begins when the DBA starts the installation program and concludes when the installed database is complete. Another use case would be "adding a user to the database" which begins when the DBA runs the "install user" command and concludes when the user is authorized on the database. An end-user use case might be "printing a report" which begins when the user selects a database table and concludes when the report is printed.

A use case involves a sequence of interactions between the initiator and the system, possibly involving other actors. It follows a thread of control in and out of the system, but in the final system it might be interleaved with other threads. The system is considered as a "black box"; we are interested in externally-visible behavior. A use case can include choices, iterations, and parameters. It is a description for a set of scenarios, in the same sense that a class is a description for a set of objects. There should be a finite number of use cases for a system, just as there are a finite number of classes, whereas there are usually an infinite number of possible scenarios and objects. You must enumerate all the use cases of a system, otherwise you don't really understand what it does.

Use Case: Assign Seat

Summary: A passenger with a reservation on a flight requests a seat assignment. The system obtains information from the passenger and then attempts to make an assignment. The assignment is given to the passenger or the passenger is told that no assignment is presently available.

Actors: Passenger

Preconditions: The passenger has a reservation on a flight by the given airline

Description: A passenger requests a seat assignment on a flight. (This may be implicit as part of checking in or may be an explicit request by the passenger.) The system (in the form of the agent) asks for the date of the flight, the flight number, departure airport, and passenger name. The passenger supplies the information. Instead of name, the passenger can supply frequent flyer number with the airline. [Exception: Too early to make assignment.] The system finds the reservation. [Exception: No reservation found.] If the reservation already has a seat assignment, it is given to the passenger who is offered the opportunity of changing the assignment. If there is no assignment or the passenger wants to change, the system requests seat preference. The system uses the information, including frequent flyer level, to try to find a suitable seat assignment subject to previous assignments and the policies of the airline. If necessary, the system asks additional questions: would the passenger accept a bulkhead seat, would the passenger accept a seat in an emergency exit row? The system proposes a seat assignment. If all the passenger's preferences cannot be satisfied, then the system proposes the best match it can find. [Exception: No assignment possible.] The passenger can accept the assignment or ask for changes, in which case another assignment is attempted. The use case concludes when an assignment is made and accepted.

Exceptions:

Too early: Raised if the current date is too early, based on an airline algorithm that includes fare category and frequent flyer level. The passenger is advised when seat assignments will be possible and the use case terminates.

No reservation found: Raised if no reservation can be found. The information is rechecked and searched if necessary for a partial match. If still no reservation can be found, then the passenger is advised to obtain one and the use case terminates.

No assignment possible: Raised if no assignment is possible based on an airline-dependent formula that includes number of unassigned seats, days until departure, fare category, and frequent flyer level. The passenger is advised to obtain an assignment on check in. If this is part of check in, then the passenger is placed on standby in the order of arrival. The use case terminates.

Postconditions: If this is part of check in, then the passenger either has a seat assignment or is on the standby queue in order of arrival. Otherwise none (may fail).

Figure 1. Use case specification

In defining a use case, group together all transactions that are "similar" in nature, which a user would think of as being variations on a theme. A typical use case might include a main case with alternates taken in various combinations and including all possible exceptions that can arise in handling them. For example, a use case for a bank might be "performing a transaction at the counter." Subcases would include making deposits, making withdrawals, and making transfers, in various combinations, together with exceptions such as "overdrawn" or "account closed." These subcases are all similar, in that they require much the same set up and interaction sequences. On the other hand, the use case "applying for a loan" is quite different; the customer will probably deal with different bank personnel, have to fill out a lot of forms, and wait a few days to finish this use case.

Use cases are written as natural language text descriptions expressed informally. The descriptions express *what* happens from the user's point of view. The details of *how* the system works internally are irrelevant to a use case. The description includes the events exchanged between objects and the system operations performed by the system, but only those operations visible to the actors.

Figure 1 shows a sample use case for "assigning seats" for airline flights. This use case could be used alone (if a passenger calls up for a seat assignment) or as part of a larger use case "check in for flight." In this use case the system includes the airline computer and the clerk at the counter or on the telephone.

Combining Use Cases

Jacobson describes two ways of combining use cases, *extends* and *uses* (Figure 2). *Extends* embeds optional new behavior into a complete base case. For example, we might have use case "check in for flight" in which a traveler hands tickets to a clerk, answers some questions, and ends by receiving a boarding pass. Use case "check baggage" extends the base case "check in for flight" by having the clerk ask about baggage, collect and tag the baggage, and finally staple a claim check to the customer's ticket. The actual behavior includes both use cases. The base case "check in for flight" is meaningful and complete in itself so it is possible to separate the additional functionality "check baggage" as an extension.

Uses embeds a fragmentary subsequence as a necessary part of a larger case. The embedded use case is a kind of behavior subroutine. For example, the use cases "process automated teller machine transaction" and "process automated telephone bank account inquiry" might both *use* the subordinate case "validate password" which requests a password and

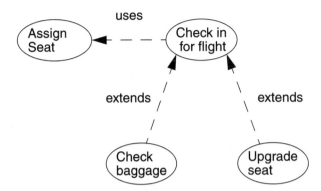

Figure 2. Combining use cases

verifies it. The *uses* relationship permits the same behavior to be embedded in many otherwise unrelated use cases.

What is the purpose of use cases, given that they are often informal and do not carry complete semantics? They force the analyst to confront the purpose of a system, namely to implement functionality. Use cases are a way of specifying functionality in a manageable way, organized into categories of functionality from a user's point of view. By trying to enumerate first the actors, then the use cases, there is less chance of forgetting important parts of the system.

Use Cases and OMT

When should you make up use cases? In our book [3] we recommended making scenarios as part of building a dynamic model, but use cases serve a broader purpose than just control. They provide a first cut at the functionality in an application, so they can be captured right at the beginning of the analysis. I would advise the following approach:

1. Identify the boundary of the proposed application. For example, is a clerk part of a system or is the clerk actually the actor whom the system serves? Identify the objects just outside the boundary that interact directly with the system (objects that send and receive messages, including messages such as commands, signals, output messages and output displays).

2. Classify the outside objects by the roles that they play in the application. Each role defines an actor. Make a list of actors. State the purposes of each actor in using the system.

3. For each actor, think of the fundamentally different ways in which the actor uses the system. Each way of using the system is a use case. Group different scenarios into the same use case if they appear to be variations on a single theme.

4. Make up some specific scenarios for each use case. Plug in actual parameters; don't try to be general. The purpose is to ground your thinking in concrete examples. You can then generalize to the full use case with less danger of forgetting something or violating common sense.

5. Determine the interaction sequences. For each use case, identify the message from the actor that initiates the use case. Determine if there are preconditions that must be true before the use case can begin. Determine the logical conclusion of the transaction: when is the thread of activity complete? There is some judgment about how broadly to define a use case. For example, is "applying for a loan" complete when the application is turned in, when the loan is granted, or when the loan is finally paid off?

6. Write a prose description of the use case. Identify the sequence of interactions that occur in a normal transaction together with the system operations that are invoked. Specify rules for choosing among variations and iteration.

7. Consider all the exceptions that can occur in handling a transaction and specify how they affect the use case.

8. Look for common fragments among different use cases and factor them out into base cases and additions. Determine if the additions are optional or mandatory and specify where they go in the main sequence.

Domain Models

Most applications are built on some problem domain that supplies the underlying semantics of the application. A problem domain is an area of real-world expertise, such as mechanical engineering, stock trading, or travel.

Domain classes are classes from a problem domain that are meaningful outside of any application. They carry the semantics of a problem domain in terms meaningful to domain experts. For mechanical engineers, classes such as *force, stress, strain,* and *beam* are meaningful; for stockbrokers classes such as *stock, bond, trade,* and *commission schedule*; for travel agents, classes such as *flight, reservation,* and *airport.* Every field has its own particular terminology, and jargon words usually identify important concepts that are often domain classes. Because domain classes are meaningful by themselves, they can be found and modeled as part of a domain analysis without considering a particular application. *They do not need to be driven by use cases.*

Application Models

An *application model* is a model of a particular application. It goes beyond the real-world domain model to come up with a computer solution to a particular problem. Build an application model on top of a domain model, because the application must ultimately support the underlying semantics of the domain objects, whereas the domain model can stand on its own. Application models contain computer constructs that are not part of the real-world problem domain but that are nevertheless visible to users. I describe this concept of *application classes* in the column "Objects in the Twilight Zone" (page 279). Examples of application classes include graphic images and table views of domain objects, user interfaces, controllers, devices, and external interfaces.

Application classes have no existence apart from an application, so you can't find them in the real world or as part of a domain analysis. They have to be flushed out from the application requirements. They can be identified from the use cases.

Two Prong Analysis

When an application involves real-world expertise (which is normal), it is useful to follow a two-prong analysis approach: first build a *domain model* by capturing domain knowledge, then build an *application model* by examining use cases of the particular application. Figure 3 illustrates this two-prong approach to analysis: solid lines indicate strong influences and dashed lines indicate weaker influences.

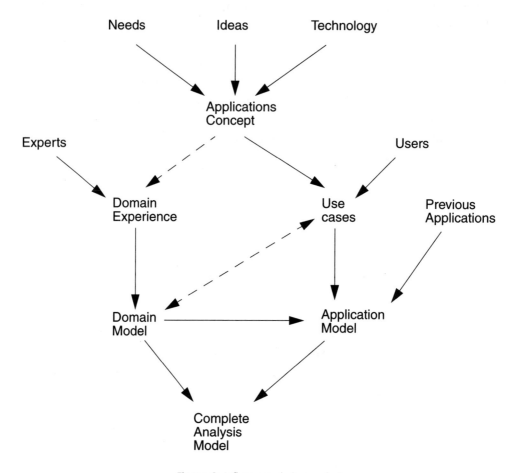

Figure 3. Influences during analysis

Building Domain Models

Build a domain model by considering the problem domain directly. First build an object model by doing one of the following:

1. Think of important real-world concepts, terminology, and jargon in the problem domain. Organize them into a class model showing their relationships.

Then think up useful real-world operations on these objects (Bertrand Meyer's "shopping list operations.") This approach requires a good understanding and internal feeling for the problem domain itself but leads to domain models that can be reused many times for different applications.

2. Write a description of the underlying semantics of the particular problem, from the point of view of the domain expert. Don't worry at all about how users will interact with the application; concentrate on the core semantic operations and the objects they affect. A domain expert can prepare this statement. Then an analyst can extract the classes and their relationships from the statement, but the final model will have to be validated and corrected by the expert. The semantic computations in the statement become the operations on the domain classes. This domain model may be more narrowly drawn to the needs of a particular problem and may not be so reusable unless extra effort is made.

3. Extract the domain objects indirectly from the use cases. This is the most indirect approach, as the domain objects may not appear in the use cases directly and may have to be inferred from their views, which do appear. This approach is probably better as a cross-check for objects that are missed on a more direct approach. Identifying domain operations is also more indirect.

Typically domain objects do not embody much control; most of them are passive data objects, rather than controllers of other objects. It is usually not necessary to build dynamic models of domain objects, although it may be helpful to build a *life history model* showing the operations that take the object between fundamentally different life states.

Building Application Models

Once the domain model is built, then build an application model. Start by listing use cases. Then examine the use cases to identify application objects (plus any domain objects that were overlooked). First determine how underlying domain information will be formatted and presented to the user by visual, aural, mechanical, or other means. Each presentation format is a view class. One domain class may have many views. Also identify devices and interface objects mentioned in the use cases.

Try to separate view classes from the underlying semantic classes that embody the domain information; use the *model-view-controller* framework (page 297). Examine each view class to see if it is a mapping of some underlying semantic object. Some view classes contain only application information, but presumably the purpose of most applications is to actually do something, so at least some of the view classes should be views of domain objects. If the domain classes have not already been identified from a domain analysis, add them to the domain model. Try to separate domain classes from any particular way of viewing them and their reusability will be greatly enhanced, even within a single application that may have multiple views of a single domain object.

A *controller* is an object that manages interactions between the system and outside actors to control system objects. It embodies most of the context-dependent decisions in an application, such as user-control options. The controller permits other reusable objects to be hooked together in flexible ways without modifying the objects to be connected. The state diagram of the controller defines the allowable sequences of interactions inherent in a use case. Every application needs at least one controller. Start by assuming one controller per use case and later see if you can combine them.

Construct a state diagram for each controller by examining use cases. Go through the use cases, identify events between the outside world and the system, and organize the states of the controller into legal sequences. The state diagram formalizes the interaction sequences stated informally in a use case, so it becomes the definitive statement of behavior.

Many input events trigger the application to perform system operations. Sometimes the operation returns a value to the actor (or another actor) as an output event, sometimes the operation changes the internal state of the application. Identify the system operations from the use cases. Attach each operation on the controller's state diagram to the transition that triggers it, and also assign each operation to the class that handles it. System operations may be domain operations or application operations. Describe each operation in text at least.

Using Use Cases

This has been a brief overview of using use cases with OMT. I feel that a combination of direct domain analysis and use cases is an effective approach to starting analysis, rather than depending on use cases or a domain model alone. How do use cases affect the rest of the development effort?

On a large project, use cases can be an effective way to partition the analysis into modules in a top-down manner before discovering all the individual classes. (If you can discover the classes first and then organize them into modules, it is not a large problem!) This is generally equivalent to partitioning the problem by functionality, because each use case normally embodies a certain kind of functionality. If you have a lot of use cases, you may be able to group them at a higher level.

Are use cases still important during design? They are primarily an approach to discovering requirements from a user-centered viewpoint, so the immediate answer is no. The state diagrams for controllers should incorporate, in a more formal way, the requirements expressed informally in use cases.

Classes and state diagrams describe a system in a reductionist manner, one class at a time. It can be difficult to design a system from such a narrow viewpoint. The design concept of object interaction diagrams (page 167) is the design-time correlate of use cases: they both follow the flow of a thread of control from object to object within a system for a single holistic transaction, so indirectly use cases are useful even during design.

References

1. Kenneth S. Rubin and Adele Goldberg. Object behavior analysis. *Communications of the ACM 35,* 9 (Sept. 1992), 48-62.

2. Ivar Jacobson, Magnus Christerson, Patrik Jonsson, Gunnar Övergaard. *Object-Oriented Software Engineering: A Use Case Driven Approach.* Addison-Wesley, Workingham, England, 1992.

3. James Rumbaugh, Michael Blaha, William Premerlani, Frederick Eddy, William Lorensen. *Object-Oriented Modeling and Design.* Prentice Hall, Englewood Cliffs, N.J., 1991.

4. James Rumbaugh. Objects in the twilight zone. *Journal of Object-Oriented Programming* 6, 3 (June 1993), 18-23.

5. James Rumbaugh. Modeling models and viewing views. *Journal of Object-Oriented Programming* 7, 2 (May 1994), 14-29.

6. James Rumbaugh. Going with the flow. *Journal of Object-Oriented Programming* 7, 3 (June 1994), 12-23.

The Life of an Object Model
How the Object Model Changes During Development
March 1994

Same Notation, Different Uses

One of the advantages of OMT and many other OO methodologies is that they are *seamless*, that is, the notation does not impose rigid boundaries between various steps. The same notational constructs and syntax are used throughout the entire development cycle, avoiding the need for translating notations and the consequent loss of information that accompanies any translation, among natural languages or computer languages. This does not mean, however, that the content of a model is fixed during the development cycle. As a model progresses from analysis through design to implementation, it changes in several ways: it gains much more detail; it takes on a more specific form suited to a particular application and language; and its organization may be transformed into a more efficient and convenient form. These changes can be shown in several different ways: by the addition of additional elements to the model (classes, associations, methods, etc.); by the use of naming conventions; by the use of graphical conventions, possibly in conjunction with textual comments; by the use of textual annotations to the model that are typically maintained in the background by an editing tool; and by the addition of new notation specifically intended for representing design or implementation issues. These techniques are listed in a rough order indicating their invasiveness. Textual conventions can be adopted within existing tools, but they require some discipline on the part of users; however, it is often easy to write simple consistency checkers for them. New notational constructs require extensions to tools and impact the portability of the notation, so they should be added only after deliberation.

Writing a book is an example of the evolution of a model. The general model of a book is a tree of parts written in English (or your own favorite language). During the first draft the tree is expressed as an outline of chapter, section, and subsection headings with sketchy descriptions of each part. During later drafts the outline is expanded into paragraphs, but its overall form is still a tree of parts consistent with the outline (as modified during editing). There is no sharp line between the outline and the full text; it is possible to add more and more detail to the outline until it slips slowly into a prose form. Although English words and phrases are used throughout the entire process, they are used in a distinctly different way in an outline and in prose text.

I make a distinction among analysis, design, and implementation. Analysis is understanding a problem; design is devising a strategy to solve the problem; implementation is building the solution in a particular medium. This does not mean that these stages are rigidly defined, but I think they are useful mileposts along the way, just as we distinguish an outline and a book, although some of the intermediate steps may overlap.

We have used OMT object-modeling notation for all stages of development, including analysis, design, coding, reverse engineering, and enterprise analysis. In this column I will explore the differences in form and content between object models for different stages of the development cycle, but keep in mind that the boundaries are flexible.

Analysis Models

Analysis is the process of understanding a problem and capturing the understanding in a clear, precise manner. Constructing an object model is usually the most important part of analysis because it provides the framework for everything else in an object-oriented methodology. The analysis object model should capture the information in the problem *and no more*. By "problem" I mean the actual problem to be solved, not somebody's initial statement of it in some document. An analysis model should be a minimal model of the situation that captures its essential structure and semantics but that does not attempt to implement it.

An analysis model should not contain implementation constructs, optimizations, or packaging features, as these are aspects of the design that are not inherent in the problem. Note that most software engineering concerns, such as visibility, encapsulation, or information hiding, are techniques of organizing a design for human use and are *not* logical issues needed in analysis. I will explain these guidelines in more detail:

Associations—use them rather than pointers. Treat all references between objects as associations; don't embed pointers from one object to another. Don't worry about whether one class "knows" about another class; during analysis everything is bidirectional. Don't worry about access control on traversing associations. Don't use linked lists or invent classes to hold sets or lists of objects; instead represent collections as associations with multiplicity *many*, with the indication *ordered* if the ordering of elements matters. Collection classes are design issues, needed to optimize the program, not to understand the problem or the logical model; they should be addressed during design by specifying an implementation for each association.

Attributes—capture the object state, no more. In many cases there are a lot of different ways to represent the attributes in a class, for example, rectangular or polar coordinates for positions. Pick enough attributes to capture the degrees of freedom in the problem. It usually doesn't matter which ones you pick; either polar or rectangular coordinates are good for points, for example, but don't use both. (You can later write operations to retrieve the coordinates in either form, however.) Strive to capture the minimal description of the system state. Think in terms of data, not in terms of abstract operations on stateless classes. (I know, I know—this is rank heresy from the point of view of many OO fans, but a data-driven approach works pretty well for finding objects.)

Encapsulation—ignore it during analysis. During analysis work from a bird's-eye view, during implementation work from a worm's-eye view. The purpose of encapsulation is to protect future developers (including the original developer six months later) against excessive interdependencies in the design that make the model difficult to modify. During analysis your goal is to understand a problem, so don't "hide" information from yourself. Once you know what exists, you can decide how to encapsulate it during the design stage. Make up classes, attributes, and associations to capture the system state. Make sure that the information needed to perform operations is available, but don't worry about efficiency of access (yet). Don't model attribute, operation, or association visibility during analysis. Assume everything is visible when planning operations. All of these important issues should be addressed during design.

Optimization—don't worry about efficient access, just capture the information state of the system. During the design stage, design data structures in conjunction with algorithms. It doesn't matter during analysis how efficient the access path is; you can fix it up during design.

Support classes—don't show support classes, such as container classes, strings, dates, and so on. All data-structure classes are part of the implementation substrate for a system; they are not semantically meaningful at the application level. When is the last time you saw a linked list in the real world? (Well, maybe for forwarding mail at the post office, but that's it.)

Methods—it is not so important to include methods in an analysis object model. It is more important to get the data information correct. There are an infinite number of methods possible on a class but only a finite amount of information in it. Most high-level operations appear on the dynamic model. If you nevertheless do want to show operations on the object model, then don't worry about inheritance of methods during analysis. Just represent each operation at the highest level in the class hierarchy at which it applies. Whether and when to override a method are design issues; the semantics of the operation itself (across *all* classes) are what matters during analysis.

Logical Design Models

Design is the process of organizing a model for efficient execution on a computer without actually programming it. It is similar to a detailed outline of a book. Usually the design model should proceed directly from the analysis model in several ways. Extensions to the model come in two forms: those that support the detailed design separately from the implementation language and those that specialize the design toward a particular implementation language. First we will look at use of design notation independently of language. Although I treat them separately, you would usually not want to bother keeping separate models for design and implementation unless you were going to port to different programming languages, which would probably be a bad idea anyway.

The typical design model has many more elements than the analysis model. Most of the additional elements support the implementation of procedures. No change in form is necessary to add the new elements to the model.

During design the elements in the model should be optimized for efficiency and convenient execution. The design model is *not* a minimal model; it may contain redundant elements for efficiency. These often take the form of additional associations to permit more efficient access and searching. For example, an *index* is an association sorted by some attribute value in a class of objects. An index can be represented as a qualified association, in which the qualifier value is the index key. Redundant attributes can also be introduced to hold derivable information so that it need not be recomputed every time it is needed. No new notation is necessary to represent transformations of the model and redundant information.

A design model makes physical distinctions that are not important at the logical level taken during analysis. During design, for example, we no longer want to assume that all associations are implemented as two-way links between classes; normally associations will be implemented as pointers embedded in objects. In most cases these distinctions represent *additional* information that further specifies the implementation but does not contradict anything in the original analysis model. I call these refinements *annotations*, because they represent additional notes imposed on top of and consistent with an existing model. There are several ways to represent annotations:

1. Annotations can be stated by textual comments on a diagram. This approach is easy to implement but cannot be used for semantic checking or code generation. However, it is fine for planning stages and requires no extension to a modeling tool. We recommend that comments in OMT notation be enclosed in braces to set them off: {**This is a comment.**}

2. Annotations can be represented by textual conventions applied to strings. For example, we represent class attributes (as opposed to instance attributes) by prefixing a '$' symbol to the attribute name (the dollar sign is not usually needed in C code, some VAX code notwithstanding). Similarly, I indicate public, private, and protected access by prefixing '+', '-', and '#' symbols to the attribute or operation names. This approach requires no extension to a modeling tool (provided it accepts punctuation marks in names) and can be handled by a code generator with a few simple tests.

3. Annotations can be represented by extensions to the graphical notation or by employing conventions in the use of existing symbols. For example, I use an arrowhead on an association in a design model to indicate that the association must be implemented in the direction of the arrow; an association could have 2, 1, or even 0 arrowheads, the last case indicating an association that is to be suppressed in the code. This approach requires an extension to a modeling tool, unless it already has a few spare symbols available that have not been assigned semantic meanings. When I designed the OMT, I left the arrowhead without a semantic meaning, because it seemed like a useful symbol to use for various purposes.

4. Annotations can be omitted from the graphical notation and instead can be accessed using a background text panel window associated with an element, such as a class, an association, an attribute, or a method. Typically the panel would not be visible all the time but would be popped up on demand. An annotation panel can contain information already present in the graphical view, such as class names, lists of attributes, and so on, but it can also contain additional information, some of which may be language dependent.This is a good place to attach a brief text description to an element, as well as to specify language issues such as whether a method is constant, abstract, etc. Using an annotation panel requires explicit support in a tool and isn't very useful without a tool, but it is an effective way to

work on-line. The contents of the annotation panel can easily be extended and can be used by code generators.

I regard the various kinds of annotations to models as being on the borderline between methodology and tools. I don't think it is necessary to standardize all of these usages in an "official" methodology. A methodology should not be a strait jacket but should contain some flexibility. An organization should adopt style guidelines, similar to style rules for formatting and naming program code, for example. All organizations don't have to use the same style, but people working on a large project should be consistent. Tool support can help a lot in enforcing consistency.

Different tools may handle some of these secondary modeling issues differently. That's all right. Tools can also provide other kinds of graphic

markers, such as color, that can be used by users to designate various kinds of things as they see fit. Portability need not be a problem, because tools can easily convert between various kinds of symbols (even clouds and crow's feet).

Another important design issue is packaging of models. During analysis it is convenient to structure large models into modules using some kind of tree structure, but this is just for convenience. During design a breakdown into well-chosen modules is much more important, because it will drive the packaging of the implementation into separate pieces. Normally it is sufficient to group modeling elements into modules. If you want, you can draw a tree to show the aggregation of modules into high-level modules, but it usually isn't necessary. We find it convenient to assign each class to a *home module*. We adopt the rule that to edit a class you need to check out to the home module; only one designer may have write access to a module at a time. In other modules the class can be referenced in associations but its attributes and operations cannot be modified. To indicate the home module, we adopt the convention of showing all the attributes and operations in the home module; references to the class in other modules only show its name in a box.

Implementation Models

Every model must eventually be implemented in some programming language. As development progresses, the language casts a longer shadow over the model. Although the overall form of the model doesn't change, the contents must observe the syntax and restrictions of the language.

Many language issues can be resolved by adopting naming conventions on names, types, and so on. In other cases language-dependent issues can be handled using annotations. The goal is to be able to generate all of the declarations and some of the procedural code for a program directly from the object model. In our C++ work, we work directly from object models using OMTool to edit methods and generate header files. We find this more convenient than dealing with the often arcane rules of C++, such as restrictions on ordering declarations. Working from an OMT model also gives a better overview of the program.

Some of the language modeling issues include the following:

You must observe the syntactic rules for the target language as well as the normal conventions and idioms. For example, in C++ you cannot have embedded spaces in names (mandatory) but you should capitalize class names (by convention). You must avoid name conflicts or use of keywords. No extensions are needed to tools or notation to support these rules, because they are just conventions. A tool *could* enforce style rules and check for name conflicts, but this is not essential.

In the sample applications, I didn't have to change any names between analysis and design, because I was careful to make the original names C++ compliant.

Types must be specified for attributes, arguments, and methods in a strongly typed language such as C++. (I think it is also not a bad idea to specify them for a weakly-typed language, even though they will not be used in code generation.) We simply treat a type as a string expressed in the syntax of the target language. No extensions to the tools or notation are needed.

Hybrid languages, such as C++, have nonclass types, such as enums, unions, typedefs, and so on. It is also necessary to specify global variables, functions that exist outside of any class (such as "main"), and other language-dependent features, such as "#include" files and macros. The nonclass types can be represented directly in the textual code (in which case it is not a modeling problem) or some slight extension to the syntax can be adopted to permit them to be shown on the object model. I find it convenient to see both class types and nonclass types on a single diagram.

There are usually a number of peculiarities of each language that don't fit within a general framework for all languages. In C++, these include specification of virtual methods, virtual base classes, "const" attributes and methods, abstract methods, friends, and so on. These can be handled in a tool using annotations but there is little reason to consider them part of the general methodology applicable to all languages.

One of the noticeable changes in going from design to implementation is a vast increase in the number of "junk" methods, methods that don't really add much semantic information, but are present for encapsulation or modularity. In this category I would lump most constructors, destructors, attribute accessors, initializers, and association maintainers. These methods don't do much of interest but they are needed to prevent outside methods from reaching inside a class to grab its attributes. Most of them can be generated automatically by a tool.

Usually there are also a large number of "buck-passer" methods needed to pass control from a requestor object to a target object that is not directly accessible. It is bad form (and a violation of Lieberherr's "Law of Demeter" design rule) to traverse paths in the object model to send a message to an indirectly connected object; you should instead pass a message to a neighboring class and let it forward the message to one of its neighbors. But this can result in a lot of methods that don't do anything other than forward operations to other classes. There is no notational problem with these methods, but they clutter up the model and prevent you from understanding it clearly, so I recommend not adding them during the logical design stage but deferring them until you begin coding. They are trivial to write anyway.

Philosophy

A seamless notation permits a model to be developed and evolved from stage to stage without any sudden discontinuities. Different developers can apply their own guidelines about how early to bring in language-dependent considerations, such as naming rules. Much of the specificity that is needed in later development stages can be obtained by simply adopting naming and usage conventions, without having to extend the notation or even make the conventions part of the formal methodology. Other techniques include background annotations using textual spreadsheets to show language-dependent features, textual comments on the object diagram, and nonsemantic symbols (such as arrows) that can be pressed into service by convention. In any case, a good notation and methodology should be flexible and easy to use.

Objects in the Twilight Zone
How to Find and Use Application Objects
June 1993

What Kind of Object Is the Application?

Most applications serve some real-world purpose, so their analysis object models concern real-world objects. Understanding the real-world situation and constructing models containing real-world objects drawn from the problem domain is the best way to ensure that the application does the right thing. Such models should be constructed in the language of the problem domain, such as physics, engineering, finance, business, medicine, or whatever else motivates the problem. On the other hand, the internal details of the program are not of interest during analysis. During analysis we seek to understand and model the problem to be solved so we should avoid making any premature commitments to any particular implementation. An analysis model should not contain internal objects that represent computer constructs or implementation details.

But what about the application itself as an artifact? When we start out, the application doesn't exist, so it can hardly be considered a real-world object, but when the program is written users can interact with it and use it. Its external details are not hidden from the users, in fact, they should be clearly specified and documented in user manuals. What is the application itself, a real-world object or an internal object? Is it an object at all?

My answer is that the user-visible part of an application falls into a twilight zone between the real-world and the internal world of the computer. I call the application–dependent objects that are visible to the outside users *application objects*. We cannot look to the real world for guidance in constructing the application objects, but neither are they merely internal design details.

Application Objects

Application objects represent user-visible aspects of an application. They have no meaning outside of the context of an application, unlike the real-world objects, or *domain objects,* which represent the semantics of a problem domain and that have semantics independent of any application.

An example may help to clarify the differences among the three different kinds of objects. Consider an airline reservation system. A *flight* is a domain object; it is meaningful in the real world apart from any particular application. A *flight reservation display screen* is an application object; it is meaningless apart from an application, but it is an important part of the application specification and cannot be changed without altering the user's view of the application. Finally, a *window event callback table* is an internal object; it may be part of a particular implementation of the reservation system, but it is by no means required and is invisible to the users.

Although the application objects cannot be found by looking at the problem domain, they should be present in the application specification or in the user manual, if it is complete. The application objects must be invented as part of the process of designing and specifying the application interface (as opposed to the design of the program itself). When should they be discovered? There are various approaches, but I would recommend finding them during analysis after finding the domain objects but before beginning the design of the system implementation.

Kinds of Application Objects

There are several different kinds of application objects. The line between them is not always clear-cut, but this does not much matter anyway, because the purpose of the list is mainly to help you think of them all. I can think of the following kinds:

- presentations
- formats
- controllers
- devices
- boundary objects

Presentations

A *presentation* is a view of semantic data that a user can perceive and interact with. Semantic data cannot be seen directly, of course; it must always be presented in some form or another. It can be a picture, text form, video, audio, or other format.

Consider a molecular modeling package that simulates the physics of interacting atoms in a molecule. The package would be written in terms of the domain objects, such as atoms, electron clouds, and forces, using the equations derived from physics. The solution might be defined in terms of positions of atoms over time. But there are many ways in which this result can be shown to a person. Each view represents a different presentation. Each presentation can be derived from the solution to the equations.

One presentation might be a 3-D view of the atoms as space-filling balls with shading and hidden line removal. Probably everyone has seen such images of DNA and other molecules. Another 3-D presentation consists of sticks representing the atomic bonds, with no attempt at hidden line removal, so this view will be much faster to compute. A variation on the 3-D presentations would be an animated image that changes with time. Still another view would be a 2-D chemical formula. Finally, perhaps the simplest presentation is a text report of the positions of the atoms. Text is a presentation too. It provides a medium for outputting and inputting information.

Fundamental to all presentations is that they represent underlying domain information, so it is necessary to identify the domain objects before constructing the presentation objects. Sometimes presentation objects can be completely derived from domain objects without supplying additional information. The various views of a molecule fit that description, although the user must specify some presentation parameters, such as angle of view and scale factor.

In other presentations the view contains additional nondomain information that tells how to construct the view itself. For example, the semantic information of a circuit diagram is contained completely in the connectivity of the diagram; the actual location of the symbols and lines on the page conveys no additional domain information. But the positions of the symbols may nevertheless contribute greatly to aesthetics and to understanding the model, because the visual arrangement adds a level of organization to the information. By the way, a picture of a circuit diagram can be used to input a circuit as well as output one.

The steps in making presentation objects are therefore as follows: Make up the domain objects and determine the domain information that must be perceived or supplied by the user. Then decide the way or ways to present the information to the user and make up presentation formats for each view. Don't forget text input and output as legitimate views. Typically a model-view architecture will work best. Make a one-to-many association from domain objects to presentation views. When a domain object changes, it sends an *update* message to each of its views. Each presentation object is responsible for updating itself by examining the domain object and modifying itself as needed. The presentation objects understand the content of the domain objects but the domain objects know nothing about their views except for their existence. If the user edits a presentation object, it is responsible for mapping the edit operations into modifications to the underlying domain object and sending a *notify* message to the domain object, which then broadcasts the *update* message to all of its views. In this way changes to any view are propagated to all views. This architecture is typical of most of today's better document editors, spreadsheets, computer-aided design (CAD) editors, and financial packages.

Formats

A format is the syntax for communicating information to an application, so this is really a kind of presentation, but I will single it out for uses such as input/output file formats, command-line formats, save formats, and so on. A format can usually be characterized as a grammar. During early analysis, it is not all that important to pin down the exact syntax of a format, because it usually has only a local effect on the design. Generally it is sufficient to identify what information must be transmitted and to leave the details until later. When you can design a format, keep it simple, preferably a regular grammar; you can implement it with a parser-generator but if it is simple enough it can also be parsed directly.

Controllers

A *controller* is an object that controls an application and its interactions with the outside world. Examples include user interfaces, schedulers, dispatchers, and spoolers. Most applications have a single controller that represents the main control loop of the program, although an application could have multiple controllers if it has multiple independent threads of control.

    Unlike a presentation, which at least could be conceived half apart from the application (although the connection to the domain model is crucial), a controller embodies the essence of an application itself. From the viewpoint of the user, the controller *is* the application. Most important, a controller is a bearer of a dynamic model that defines the interaction sequences permitted to the application. The state variables of the dynamic model are the attributes of the controller. These are the "current state" of the application, such things as global flags and settings, current selection or anything else with "current" in it, and various defaults for the user interface. The operations on controller state transitions are the high-level commands that drive the application.

The steps in making controllers are as follows: Consider the various interactions sequences between the application and the outside world. Generally there will be one controller for each outside actor, such as a user, an operator, or an outside computer. If the interactions with a single actor divide into several independent threads, then there can be several controllers, but this is not the usual case. Generally you don't have to include the controller in the initial object model, because it doesn't usually associate with anything else, but add it to the object model after making up the dynamic model. The dynamic model for the controller is the user interface for the application, so think up the various commands that the user can issue and attach them to the controller. Often a controller is the only class with a significant dynamic model.

Devices

A *device* is a piece of hardware that a user can interact with, usually to supply input or receive output. Examples include printers, display screens, keyboards, mice, speakers, microphones, and disks. Unlike presentations, devices are obvious in the application environment and cannot be invented arbitrarily. You can't do much with a device; you have to take it pretty much as it comes, although you can build an object-oriented wrapper around a non-object–oriented device interface. During analysis, identify the devices used by the application and their relevant characteristics within the application. You can also make a list of the operations that the device provides.

Boundary Objects

In building interfaces to external actors, you should attempt to encapsulate and isolate the dependencies on the external formats and protocols within *Boundary object objects* that exist on the boundary of the system. A boundary object mediates all communications with an external actor, process, format, or device and provides a layer of independence for the application. A boundary object provides a virtual interface for the application to the outside world in terms of operations that do not vary even when the underlying external interfaces vary. For example, don't write an application in terms of the actual events returned by a windowing system, such as XWindows. Instead construct a virtual interface in terms of logical events meaningful to the application, such as *select, extend,* or *execute.* The boundary object can remap the logical events to the underlying physical events but the application doesn't have to care.

How to Find Application Objects

In developing an analysis model of an application, you can work in two passes. During the first pass, think about the problem domain and find the objects in it. These classes will have names meaningful to practitioners within the problem domain: the jargon of the field suggests names of concepts that are felt to be important by people in the specialty. Domain models can be developed for an entire domain and reused from application to application, because they are not specific to the application but belong to the domain itself.

The domain objects form the semantic core of the application. They define the fundamental information computed and maintained by the application in an application-independent manner that should make sense to a domain expert. The domain objects do not need to know about application objects, so you can write the fundamental core of the application as operations on the core domain objects. Often there is little or no need for a dynamic model on the core objects and operations on them are mostly computational. You can think up "shopping list" operations on the domain objects, as Bertrand Meyer puts it. You can make up state diagrams for domain objects with interesting life histories, but most of them will be passive objects that receive, but do not send, events.

On the second pass of analysis find the application objects. These must be approached in the context of the application. First decide the various ways in which domain objects can be viewed and invent presentation objects to describe each way. Remember to include text forms and text files as well as visual presentations. At this stage it is not crucial to specify the exact formats and syntax of the presentations, although it is a good idea to finish this specification before beginning coding and to define it in a user manual. Each presentation object needs a *parser* and an *unparser,* to convert itself to information on domain objects and vice versa.

When you have identified several views, then consider how the users will interact with them to supply and request information. For each view, make up some scenarios of usage. It may help to consider *use cases,* groups of prototypical scenarios that describe different ways for external actors to use the system (as proposed by Ivar Jacobson). If there is one thread of control for the user, then make up a single controller object to manage it, otherwise make up as many controllers as there are independent threads of control. Develop the state diagram of the controller first, but make sure to note any state variables needed to make decisions or carry out operations.

The controllers gather and hold the execution parameters of the application. Write the core application without using default values or context information, if possible. Let the controllers hold the context information and set up the parameters for the core application.

List any devices required by the system, but attempt to encapsulate them behind interface objects. During analysis think in terms of the logical events and operations needed by the application. Don't let raw events or syntax show through from devices or other processes in most cases.

During analysis, don't include internal objects at all. If an object is not visible to the outside users of the application, then omit it. Such objects are part of the design phase of the system, but first understand the fundamental semantics of the application before starting to make design decisions.

The analysis classes are not derived from the problem domain, so there is not reusability there. However, the same kinds of application objects are often found in different applications, so there is a good chance of reusing application frameworks with similar user interfaces, views, or interfaces.

Substrate Objects

There is another kind of object class: the *substate objects* that implement the mechanisms used to implement programs. In this category I place all the generic collection classes, such as *Set, Array, HashTable,* and *Tree,* as well as generic classes, such as *String* and *Time.* This kind of class is on a totally different semantic level from the domain, application, and internal classes in a typical system and should not be included in the same model. If you must design new data structure classes, isolate them into a separate module.

Within the object model for an application, never model something as a *Set* or other container class. If the identity of the set is important in the application, then make up a class to define it, such as *Book* (an ordered set of *Chapters*). Most of the time it is sufficient to have an association with multiplicity *many* rather than introducing a class to represent the set of objects. At implementation time, you can easily and mechanically map associations with multiplicity *many* into the container class of your choice.

Design of Systems

A separation of objects into domain objects, application objects, and internal objects can help in the discovery of classes and the construction of analysis models. A system can often be constructed as a concentric set of rings: the inner ring is the domain model, which does not need to know anything about the other models; surrounding the domain model are the various views of the domain as represented by presentation objects. The views know about the domain objects and update the domain objects when views of the system are modified. Surrounding the views are the devices, formats, and interfaces that mediate external communications. Surrounding everything is the application controller, which controls the entire application and corresponds to the main loop of the program.

Virtual Worlds
Modeling at Different Levels of Abstraction
January 1994

Levels of Reality

The world can be apprehended on many different levels. A football game can be viewed as a result in the morning paper, a set of scores, a detailed list of plays, a continuous pattern of movement on the field, a social experience involving the audience and snack vendors as well as players, or as a real-world illustration of physics principles. All of these views are valid and each is appropriate in a particular context. In constructing a model, you must select from the many possible views of the world the ones that are most helpful to understanding some problem at hand. Sometimes it is helpful to look at the same problem at more than one level of abstraction, but it is important not to mix up different levels, or confusion will arise.

Often it is convenient to think in terms of a tower of virtual worlds, each built on the world below it. Each higher level represents a more abstract view of the world, omitting details from the subordinate view but replacing them with new emergent concepts that don't appear or even make sense at lower levels.

Modern science is built on this kind of pattern of layers of virtual worlds. At the bottom is physics, concerned with the (supposedly) fundamental forces that underlay the universe; chemistry is derived, in principle, from the laws of physics but represents a new level of complexity; biology is based on chemistry but brings out new concepts; ecology and sociology are build on biology but once again introduce new emergent ideas.

Why do we need to bother with all these layers? Why not just jump from the top layer directly to the fundamental substrate? In practice it is difficult enough or even impossible to actually compute one layer from another, but at least the connections are comprehensible; to skip layers is just too much of a leap.

Layers of virtual models are familiar in computing. We have sequences such as: transistors, gates, logical units, processors, assembly language, compiler language, operating systems, libraries, applications. Each level defines building blocks for the level above it. Intercomputer messaging standards are explicitly built as layers of protocols, from low-level bit protocols up to complex messages with delivery and error recovery mechanisms. The XWindows system has a similar structure: complex interactors at the top layer, basic window operations in the middle, and raw screen operations at the bottom.

In constructing a model for a problem, it is important to choose the appropriate level of abstraction. Choose too high a level and the things of interest are invisible because they are too fine; choose too low a level and the things of interest are so large that they become, in effect, invisible again. In this column I will illustrate some OMT models at different levels of abstraction.

Granularity of Time

Perhaps the best guide to the appropriate level of abstraction is the dynamic model. Scenarios illustrate typical interactions between an application and outside actors. Scenarios can be constructed on different semantic levels. Choose the level that best matches the concerns of the problem at some particular stage of development.

A *scenario* is a sequence of events in an execution of an application. An *event* is an occurrence at a point in time, a transmission of information from one object to another. In principle an event has no duration. But this is somewhat misleading; what I really mean is that an event is atomic at a particular level of abstraction, a particular granularity of time. At the given level of granularity, nothing can interrupt an event; not because we forbid interruptions, but because they don't make sense at a given level. At some other level of detail, an event might be decomposed into pieces.

Consider an airplane flight. This can be modeled on different levels. For the flight status board in the airport, the only relevant events are *departed* and *arrived* (and maybe *delayed*); the event *landed* is not relevant, because it does not affect the status until the airplane arrives at the gate. Relevant states include *in flight, arrived,* and *boarding*.

An air traffic controller sees more events and states. Relevant states include *parked, taxiing, on runway, taking off, landing, in the pattern,* and *cross country*. Relevant states include *landed,* as well as others such as *arrived, exited the runway,* and *transferred from tower to cross country control.*

A flight simulator operates at a much lower level of time granularity. At this level, *landed* may be expanded into a series of more specific events: *entered ground effect, rear wheels down, front wheels down, speed under control.* To the flight simulator, entering different phases of traffic control are irrelevant; the physics of flight works the same no matter whether a plane is going cross country or is in the pattern.

We could go to an even higher level of abstraction. From the point of view of a travel itinerary, the entire flight could be considered an event: "Joe traveled from New York to Chicago."

Which level of granularity is the "right" one? Any of them, depending on the purpose of the model. There is no one "right" model for all purposes.

Shifting Semantic Levels

A user interface can be viewed at several different levels of granularity. At the top level the events are defined in terms of user-level commands: *open old file, open new file, save, print, quit,* and so on. At this level, we think in terms of semantic operations meaningful to a user, not in terms of keystrokes or menu entries. Commands may have parameters. For example, *open old file* has *filename* as a parameter. At the logical semantic level, it is unimportant how the file name is entered. In fact, it may be entered in several different ways, such as by typing it in or by selecting it from a menu of existing files. The logical semantic level is the appropriate level for most high-level analysis, as it is neither necessary or desirable to focus on the syntax of data entry when trying to understand the logic of an application. In fact, the binding between high-level commands and low-level syntax can and should be deferred until run time in a modern GUI (graphical user interface).

Figure 1 shows a fragment of a document processing system. The input events represent logical commands, such as opening an old file or creating a new file. The details of obtaining the parameters, such as *filename,* are not shown. The operations correspond fairly closely to the events. The states are high level and meaningful to a user.

A user interface can be viewed at a lower level, the interactor or "widget" level. This level is concerned with the various sequences of entering input and interacting with widgets. For example, to invoke the *open old file* command and specify the parameters on a Macintosh, we can select the **"Open..."** command from the menu; we can type the command-O accelerator key; or we can double-click the file itself to open it with its bound application. In the

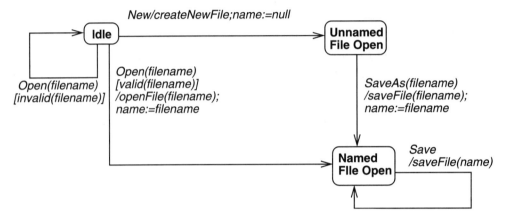

Figure 1. Dynamic model at logical semantic level

first two cases, a dialog box appears to select the actual file name from a menu. The widget level model is appropriate when designing the details of the user interface, particularly to check for consistency of input.

Figure 2 shows a fragment of the widget-level dynamic model for the document processor. Now we see the input sequences that the user performs to invoke a command, but not the exact keystrokes that selected the open command from the menu, for example. At this level, the parameter entry mechanisms are shown, such as the dialog box that gathers the file name. This medium-level state machine is shown as terminating with two possible output events: **Open** and **Launch.** These represent events at the next higher level of abstraction; the lower-level machine is a filter to transform low-level events into high-level events. In the upper-level machine, the *launch* command may invoke the *open* command, depending on the application type, but we can't tell at the lower level.

The lowest level interface of a user interface is the keystroke level. This level is concerned with the individual keystrokes to initiate a command, such as selecting a command from a menu by depressing the mouse button over the menu bar, sliding the mouse down the pop-up list of choices, and releasing the button over the name of the desired command. At this level, the individual commands such as *open* or *quit* do not even appear, as they are what is being selected from the menu. We have shifted to the metalevel of command selection itself, and the commands are just entries in a list.

Figure 3 shows the dynamic model for the menu processor. Here we see the details of popping up menus and making selections from them. This mechanism is so generic that it is applicable to any application, but it does not have any of the semantics of the actual ap-

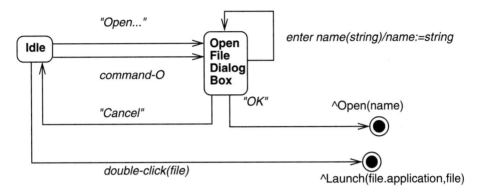

Figure 2. Dynamic model at widget level

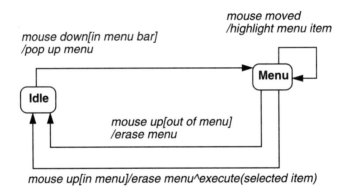

Figure 3. Dynamic model at syntax level

plication in it. The actual commands only show up as "selected items" to be executed when they are picked. On the other hand, because it is so generic, we don't normally need to worry about it when designing a new application; it is just part of the support mechanism.

This shift in meaning is characteristic of a "semantic stack" of virtual levels. Each level is the ground on which the next higher level is built, with the emergence of new levels of meaning on each new layer and the submergence of formerly meaningful concepts to become mere mechanisms, cogs in the machine.

In developing a computer application, it may be necessary to model all the layers, but the successively lower layers are needed later in the development cycle, so all the layers need not be modeled at once. Start with the semantic level, with high-level parameterized commands meaningful to users. Early analysis should be performed at this level. Later the sequences of inputs for the user interface should be determined, in terms of menus, dialog boxes, text inputs, and the like. It is unnecessary to get to the individual keystroke level just yet, as the binding of keystrokes to inputs is supplied by most GUIs and moreover can be rebound at run time in many cases. The implementation of a particular input mechanism (a "widget") represents the lowest level of granularity, a level that the normal application need not worry about.

How to represent the connection between two semantic levels in a dynamic model? Two state machines are required, one for each level, because it is not desirable to mix semantic levels in one model, as the items in the different models are at different levels of reality. The lower level state machine takes as input the raw events and produces as output logical events accepted by the higher level state machine. The output of the lower level state machine is the input of the higher level state machine. The purpose of each machine is to translate the input events to a higher abstract level. The process can be repeated to reach even higher levels. Each machine represents the substrate for the machine above it.

Object Model Levels

We can also build an object model as a series of semantic layers. The objects in each layer are *implemented from* the objects in the next lower layer. This is not aggregation, which is a meaningful relationship between things at the same semantic level, such as a company and its divisions. Each level shifts the meaning to a different and incompatible level. It makes sense to model a system at more than one level, but not in a single model.

Each lower level is more general than the one above it and can be used to model many different higher level models. For example, a desktop publishing program deals with objects such as *documents, fonts, formats,* and *paragraphs* at its outer semantic level. Figure 4 shows a fragment of an object model for a document containing paragraphs, each with its own format. Each format has a font that must be chosen from the font library.

At a lower level these semantic concepts are implemented in some physical organization. The physical organization for a document is shown in Figure 5, in which a document contains various physical sections, such as font descriptions, format descriptions, and layout descriptions. A document contains both paragraphs and physical layout into pages, columns, and lines. A paragraph is implemented as an array of characters, but each character has a location within a text line. This is the typical kind of design data structure found in an application.

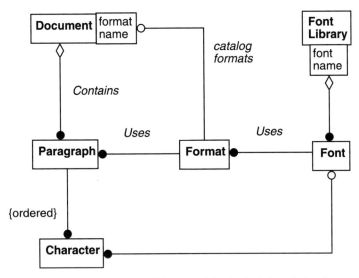

Figure 4. Object model at logical domain level

At the lowest level container classes and other basic mechanisms are implemented in terms of the underlying computer machinery. Figure 6 shows the structure of a variable-length array that contains a pointer to a memory block, as well as both a nominal length and an allocated length (to avoid excessive reallocations). The array is generic; it contains the size and type of its elements as well. This level is so generic that it has no trace of the actual application.

In the protocol for the communications standard, each level of the protocol has a different model for the messages that are sent and maintained at that level. Each message is constructed from pieces that are defined at the next lower level. Each logical level becomes the implementation medium for the level above it.

Functional Levels

Functions are normally implemented in terms of other functions at a lower semantic level. It is common to implement a function ultimately as a series of layers of functions.

For example, many engineering problems require the calculation of forces on a mechanical structure; this can be formulated as setting up and solving a set of linear equations; solving the equations can be formulated as forming a matrix, solving the matrix, and back

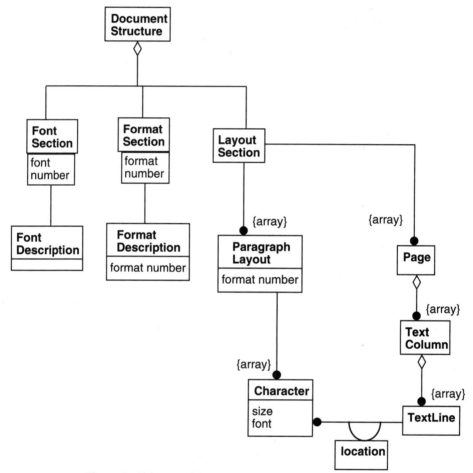

Figure 5. Object model at application implementation level

substituting the values into the equations; solving the matrix can be formulated as iterating over a pivot step, multiplying a row of the matrix and subtracting from another row to reduce the leading term to zero; subtracting two rows can be formulated as a vector sum on real (or complex) numbers. As we go from the top to the bottom, the functions become more generic and lose their connection to any specific problem.

In the document processing system, the top level classes, such as *Document*, have semantic operations, such as *openFile, print,* or *buildIndex.* These are high-level operations directly meaningful to humans.

Figure 6. Object model at library implementation level

At a medium level, the document system deals with physical structure in an implementation-dependent manner, such as converting its own internal representations of text containing characters and fonts into a layout on a line and thence to a PostScript text description to actually generate the output. The operations at this level deal with the physical structure of the system.

At the lowest level are library functions on basic data structures, such as arrays, hash tables, or files. These are again so generic that they are independent of any single application.

Each step drops to a lower virtual level of function. But each lower level function is a design choice that represents one possible way to implement the higher level function. Other choices are possible so it is important to keep the levels separate.

Architectural Levels

Designing a system as a stack of virtual layers is a standard approach that yields both portability and reusability. Semantic level shifting occurs at each interface between two levels. Each lower level is more primitive and therefore more reusable as well. The upper levels hide the details of the specific implementation and permit other implementation to be used.

During initial analysis it is unnecessary to think in terms of semantic levels. Analysis is the process of understanding a problem, which should be approached in terms of the problem semantics itself and not in some more primitive level. For example, during analysis it is inappropriate to think in terms of container classes or data structures, because these are not found in real-world problem domains.

Some aspects of the implementation are nevertheless visible to users; these are the *application objects*. Because application objects represent both user-visible behavior and implementation decisions, they must be *designed* as part of the requirements specification process (not a contradiction in terms, but a recognition that the development process is iterative and not a simple waterfall). An application object, such as a visual presentation or a controller, usually involves a semantic level shift from the problem domain level to a computer domain level.

Each shift from one level to another requires a design step. The requirements at one level are implemented using facilities at a lower level. This may impose requirements on the lower level, so the design process may repeat. If the lower level functionality does not already exist, it has to be developed, which means determining its requirements, designing its implementation, and actually constructing it.

Even the levels themselves are a design choice, of course. Often all the lower levels are already implemented, so only the top level must be created. Sometimes, however, the lower levels don't provide quite all the functionality needed and must be extended. For example, a complicated user interface using XWindows might require the addition of a new kind of widget. Once the extensions are made, they can often be reused in the future.

Working with Levels

You will work with different semantic levels in developing an application; it is a normal part of software design. The main thing to remember in modeling is to keep the different levels separate. Don't mix classes from different levels, events, or functions. Instead you may use entities from one level in the implementation of the next level. The top level is the domain semantics; the bottom level is the predefined system and the foundation libraries. The goal of software construction is to bridge the gap between them with additional reusable levels.

Modeling Models and Viewing Views
A Look at the Model-View-Controller Framework
May 1994

User Interfaces

No one can see the bits inside a computer, so a major part of most software systems is devoted to ways of presenting information to users and allowing them to manipulate it. User interfaces seem as if they should be straightforward to build, but if they are poorly designed they can introduce enormous interdependencies that can undermine a system. A good software, architecture avoids unnecessary dependencies by separating the user interface from the rest of the system and dividing it into several loosely coupled parts. The Model-View-Controller (MVC) framework, developed within the Smalltalk community, is a popular object-oriented framework for user interface architecture. The actual Smalltalk MVC code is fairly convoluted and varies somewhat among implementations.

In this column I will explain a high-level user interface architecture that incorporates the key ideas from Smalltalk MVC as well as certain other user interface models, such as the Seeheim graphics model. The details of these frameworks differ considerably, and I don't intend to compare them but rather to examine the fundamental ideas that transcend all of the programming implementations.

Subjects, Views and Controllers

The fundamental idea is to separate the underlying semantic information of a problem—the *subject*—from the various ways of presenting the information to a user—the *view*. We

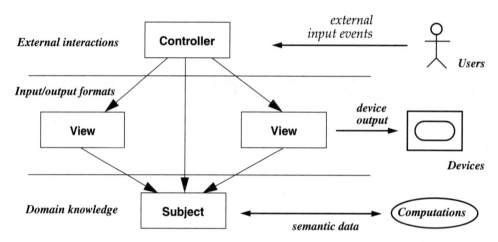

Figure 1. Layers and dependencies in subject-view-controller framework

further distinguish the interactive aspect of the problem—the *controller*—from the data re-lationships implicit in the subject and its views. Subject objects know only about semantic information, so they can be designed first by understanding the problem domain. Views must be aware of subjects and the mapping between subjects and views, so they can be de-signed after the subjects, but they don't have to interpret user interactions. Finally, control-lers convert user inputs into operations on views and subjects, so they must be aware of ev-erything and must be designed last. Because the dependencies are one-way, a system can be constructed a layer at a time without circularities (Figure 1).

The *subject* is the information that is inherent in the problem domain itself, indepen-dent of user interface, user interactions, and so on. For example, in a flight simulator the subject model includes the airplane flight parameters, the atmospheric conditions, and the terrain. A *view* is a format of presenting information to a user. Views are often visual but can include other modalities, such as sound, touch, or mechanical actions. Two different views in a flight simulator include a top-down map of the countryside with an icon of the airplane superimposed and the image that the pilot sees from the cockpit window. The sound of the engine would be another possible view. The controller in the flight simulator interprets user inputs, such as mouse clicks, keyboard entries, and joystick movements, and translates them into operations on the subject and views.

[I use the word *subject* in place of the Model-View-Controller word *model,* which I use in its more standard meaning of "an abstract description of a system," such as an object model, a dynamic model, or an analysis model. The word *subject* has been used extensively

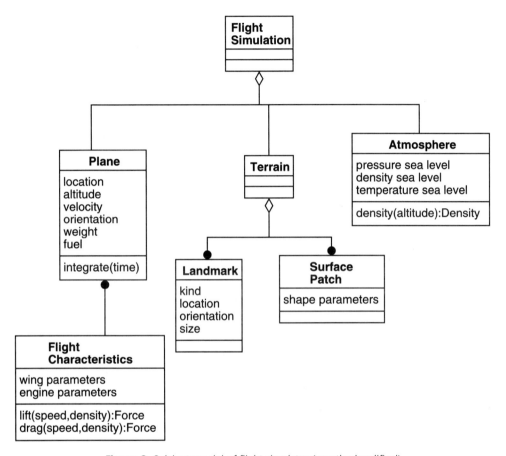

Figure 2. Subject model of flight simulator (greatly simplified)

in graphic systems. A standard graphic term for *view* is *presentation,* which is neutral regarding modality, but *view* is shorter and in common usage, so I will use it here.]

Subjects

The subject model describes the underlying information and computations within a domain of interest. Figure 2 shows a subject model of a flight simulator. Subject information is usually meaningful in the real world and would be understandable by a domain expert,

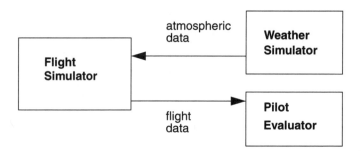

Figure 3. External batch programs process subject data

such as a pilot or aeronautical engineer, chemist, stockbroker, or whatever. It can be numerical data, such as engineering data or physics data; logical data, such as the parse tree of a computer language; or mixed, such as the information about a stock market trade.

Typically there are many kinds of semantic computations that can be applied to subject data, such as circuit calculation, heat flow analysis, common subexpression evaluation, or stock ownership update. The equations for computations can be taken from textbooks in the subject domain or other expert knowledge. For the flight simulator, we would need the formulas for lift and drag as well as Newton's laws of motion, temperature and pressure at different elevations, and other equations. It doesn't matter how the subject data is viewed; subject data is meaningful in itself. In particular, it is often useful to write process subject data using batch programs, so it is important to keep subject data separate from view information (Figure 3).

Views

A *view* is an external format for presenting or visualizing subject information. There are usually many different possible views of a piece of subject information. Figure 4 shows some views for a flight simulator. There can be different formats of presenting the same information, such as a terrain map and an image from the cockpit window. Second, there can be different instances of the same view format of the same subject. For example, the flight simulator could show the image from a side window as well as the front cockpit window. A view is a *projection* of its subject; that is, it may select some of the subject data and suppress the rest. Each view shows different aspects of the subject and organizes the information differently. It may take several views (concurrently or over time) to see everything.

Image through front cockpit window
Image through side cockpit window
3-D external view of plane and background
Top-down map of terrain with planes superimposed
Radar scan from control tower
Image of cockpit gauges and controls
Text form with simulation parameters
Sounds of engine and wind noise
Mechanical motion actuator (as in a military trainer)

Figure 4. Some different views of a flight simulator

Views can be textual as well as graphical. A table of numbers, names, or symbols is as much a presentation format as a picture. Text views can be individual strings, tables, forms, or text files. The process of parsing is really a mapping from a text view to some underlying subject. (I like the word *unparsing* to represent the reverse process of formatting data.)

Generating views generally has little to do with the semantics of a subject and a lot to do with graphic techniques, which is why we separate views from the subject. A single subject can have many views, graphical and textual, and the number of views can vary at run time, which is another reason to keep subjects and views distinct.

This separation is the key to the subject-view framework: views must know about subject data (but not subject operations), but subjects do not have to know anything about views. Views don't have to know about other views either. The dependencies are all one way. If the architecture is laid out correctly, new views can be added either at run time or during the design process without modifying the subject objects or subject operations. For example, we could add gauges to show the altitude, ground speed, etc., without affecting the flight simulation or the other views.

View operations may involve complicated graphic mechanisms that are reusable. By keeping domain semantics out of the views, they can inherit from generic graphic classes.

Mapping subject to views

In general, we can think of a view as a static mapping of the data in the subject. Figure 5 shows an abstract model for the subject-view framework using abstract superclasses **Subject** and **View**. Each subject object maps into many view objects. Each view object maps into

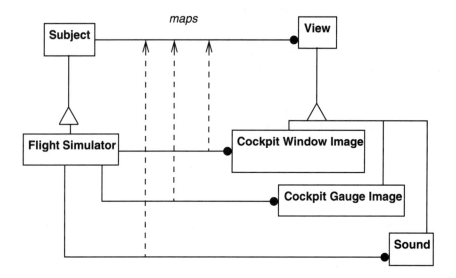

Figure 5. Relationship of subjects and views

a single subject object. (It is possible to think of views that mix information from several subjects, but applications are simpler if this mixing is avoided. As a compromise, input to a view might affect a single subject, but the construction of the view itself might depend on additional subjects.)

The generic subject-view mapping does not permit just any subject to match just any view. Individual view classes match corresponding subject classes. This represents a constraint on association. An individual association between a subject class and a view class can be regarded as a specialization of the association between abstract classes **Subject** and **View**. Figure 5 indicates association generalization by a dotted arrow from a specific subject-view association to the generic association.

Often a subject object is an aggregation of components. Frequently a view on such a subject can also be modeled as an aggregation of view components. For example, the overall flight simulation object consists of terrain, a set of landmarks, and a set of planes. Each of these objects has a counterpart view object in the flight **CockpitWindowImage** object. The overall model consists of many subject-view pairs, organized in two (or more) parallel generalization hierarchies. The job of coordinating changes to a high-level subject or view can be recursively delegated to its components.

Maintaining Subject-View Consistency

The mapping between subject and view objects has a dynamic component: subjects and views must be kept consistent. A change to a view must be reflected in the subject, and a change to the subject must be reflected in all of its views. Where do the changes come from originally? The controller responds to such external events by changing one of the views or sometimes the subject directly. The controller is not responsible for maintaining the subject-view mapping, however. We place responsibility for maintaining consistency on the views, not the subject. Why shouldn't a subject directly update its views? Because then the subject would have to know about all its views, which makes it more complicated and precludes adding new views easily. Instead we let the views handle both view-to-subject updates and subject-to-view updates.

When a view is changed, it must update its corresponding subject. Subjects don't know about views, but views have to know the content of their subjects. A view is a format for subject data and must know how to map itself into the underlying subject data. For example, an input view might show the image of the throttle. As the throttle position is changed, the throttle view must update the engine speed in the simulation. To do this, the throttle view must know the proportionality constant from pixels to engine speed.

When a subject is changed, all of its corresponding views have the responsibility for updating themselves. Because each view knows itself and its subject, it can determine how to map a subject change into its own format. For example, as the engine speed changes an image of an engine speed gauge would update itself to show the new speed (Figure 6).

The simulation uses the new engine speed to calculate thrust. It doesn't know or care how the speed was changed. It simply computes its values according to the flight equations. As the thrust increases, the plane goes faster. An airspeed gauge is another view of the plane that would be updated as a result.

How does a view know that a subject has changed? In principle each view could "watch" its subject continuously for changes, but in practice there are several ways to implement the updating. Perhaps the simplest and cleanest is simply to maintain an explicit association between subjects and views. When a view is created, it links itself to its subject; the view uses this link to find its subject. Whenever a view changes, it updates its subject by sending it messages and then notifies the subject that it has changed (by sending a **notify** message, for example). The abstract **Subject** class catches the message and notifies each view to update itself (by sending an **notify** message, for example). Each view then examines the subject to see what has changed and updates itself accordingly. The mechanism is totally generic for the subjects; no **Subject** subclass needs to do anything and new views can be added freely.

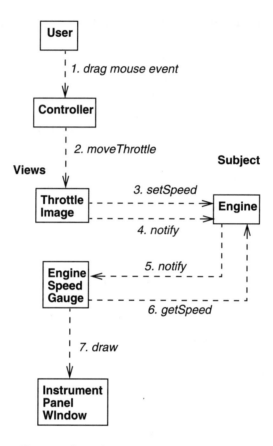

Figure 6. Flow of control to keep the model consistent

There are many possible variations on this general implementation scheme. The notification messages can indicate exactly what has changed to save work at run time, but then adding a new view may require modifying some existing code. Some Smalltalk MVC implementations have eliminated the explicit subject-view dependency links with a more indirect and diffuse notification scheme that binds update actions directly to logical changes.

Controllers

Generally a user controls an application by interacting with views. How are external events, such as button clicks, keyboard entries, and joystick motions, converted into operations on views and thence into operations on subjects? A *controller* is an object that receives events from outside actors, such as users or external devices, and translates them into operations on other objects, such as views and subjects. A controller interprets input events according to the current control context of the application; we call this context the *control state* of the controller and model it by a state diagram. Controllers are the most important application of the OMT dynamic model.

Why separate out the control aspect of views and subjects? Typically application control is highly context dependent and involves a lot of policy decisions, assumptions, and default values that are likely to change during design or deployment. Control is highly dynamic. The same views can be invoked in many different ways, so it pays to separate the views themselves from the ways in which they are used in an application; the controller determines *how* and *when* to initiate actions.

One responsibility of the controller is to direct input among several different windows. In small one-user applications there is only one user, so one controller is usually enough. Large distributed systems, such as a command-and-control system or an airline reservation system, have many users and might have many controllers.

How to Design a System

First design the subject classes without regard to the views. Examine the application domain, extract classes from it, and define semantic operations on them. Don't worry about how to format or control the output. The operations should be meaningful to the domain specialist and should represent the expert knowledge of the domain.

Then consider the different ways of presenting the data to the user; design a view around each presentation format. Specify how each view depends on its subject. Determine how each change to the subject is mapped into a change to the view. If the view can be manipulated by the user, make a list of operations on the view, and determine how each view operation maps into a change to the underlying subject. Because the different views of a subject interact only through the subject itself, it is unnecessary to specify how views affect other views.

Finally decide how the different view operations will be invoked in terms of external events, such as mouse clicks, menu selections, and button pushes. Build a state diagram mapping input events into operations on views (or occasionally operations directly on the subject). The controller is the owner of the state diagram. Determine all of the context variables in the application, such as parameters, default variables, and control switches. Make these attributes of the controller and use their values as inputs to the operations that the controller invokes.

The controller is responsible for initializing the subject and views. Often the subject is initialized at start-up; other times it is initialized in response to some command received by the controller, such as *load file*. The controller must also create views and attach them to the subject. One of the benefits of a subject-view-controller architecture is that the number and kind of views can vary at run time. The controller can create and destroy views in response to user commands at run time, without affecting the underlying subject.

Views with Extra Data

Some views can be automatically generated from their subjects, making them easy to maintain. For example, we might present subject information as a table in a standard format. An organization chart could be automatically drawn as a tree in a window.

Other views, however, require some additional view-only information beyond what can be derived from the subject. For example, the flight simulator might show a 3-d view of the plane itself flying over the countryside. This view would require the position of the "camera" in addition to the location of the plane.

Or consider an OMT object diagram. The underlying semantic information (the classes, associations, attributes, etc.) is represented by the topology of the diagram; the actual positions of the boxes and lines on the page carry no semantics, but they are needed to draw the diagram. The arrangement of boxes on the page may help a user to organize the diagram in an understandable manner, so it is not irrelevant, but it is peculiar to the view itself, that is, the diagram. The layout information is not needed by a code generator, for example, and is not meaningful in another view, such as a textual class browser.

The presence of additional nonsemantic data makes updating views more complicated. If a subject is changed, how should its view be changed? Where does the view-specific information come from? There are several possibilities.

The information could be generated automatically, following some algorithm or heuristic. For example, there are algorithms to lay out networks (such as OMT diagrams) in two dimensions. If the layout is not satisfactory, then the user can modify it. Such layouts would capture the semantics of the subject, but they might fail aesthetically or might fail to emphasize the right things. Also, we do not want to redo an entire view every time the subject changes. Not only might this require a lot of computer time but it would be disconcerting to the user.

In general, we want some kind of hysteresis with the view information. In other words, a small change to the subject should result in a small change to the view. This is sometimes called the *continuity principle*. We might generate view information when necessary, but if it already exists we don't want to disturb it unless it becomes inconsistent. For example, if we add a new class to an OMT diagram, then we might have to generate a location for it on other diagrams on which it appears, because the location information doesn't exist yet; but we would not expect to modify the locations of any existing class boxes or lines.

The final alternative is to force the user to supply the view information when it must be generated. This is not so good in general, but there are times when it makes sense.

Widgets

What kind of thing is a user-interface widget, such as an input form with text boxes, toggle switches, and push buttons? It would seem that a widget combines subject information, view information, and control into a single package. How should it be used in a subject-view-controller architecture?

You can think about a widget at two different semantic levels. At the low level, it is a complete subapplication, with its own prepackaged subject, view, and controller components. At the high level, it is a black box that generates input events along with a view of data. Because a widget comes ready to use in an application, think of it at the high level when designing an application. The internal events of entering data into the form are irrelevant, because they are invisible. All that matters to the application is that the widget generates events (such as **accept** or **cancel**) and that view information is available on demand. Typically the widget would be encapsulated in a view object that maps the contents of the widget to and from the underlying subject.

If you are designing a new widget, however, then the widget itself is the application. In that case, you must look inside the widget and use the subject-view-controller model to make it work.

Commercial Applications

A number of commercial desktop applications incorporate a subject-view mapping at the user level. I use a personal finance package on my home Macintosh. You can have several windows open at once: checkbook register, net worth, current month's expenses, and so on.

If you write a new check or modify an existing one, all of the other windows are immediately updated to reflect the new values. Changes in any window affect all the other windows, so consistency is always maintained.

I use a desktop publishing program for writing books and columns. It has a window for WYSIWYG (what you see is what you get) text, optional windows for setting parameters, such as paragraph format, character format, and status windows showing page number, paragraph type, and so on. Clicking the mouse moves the cursor within the text and also updates all the other windows to match the new location. Modifying a parameter window affects the text and other windows immediately.

These applications and many others use the concept of multiple views that automatically update the subject data and indirectly other views as changes occur. Users don't have to worry about synchronization, because it is automatic, and can work in different windows in any convenient order.

Using the Framework

The basic concepts that I have described here are a good guide to the architecture of an interactive application. They can be used to partition the system, to find classes in an order that avoids two-way dependencies, and to provide a flexible run-time architecture that permits changing the user interface as the design evolves or even at run time. However, the concepts must be implemented in a particular language. In Smalltalk, the Model-View-Controller framework is part of different Smalltalk environments, but it is complicated and difficult to learn. It also varies somewhat between implementations. In C++ you currently have to implement your own framework, although I know of one or more support tools under commercial development. I have used variations on this framework for several projects over a number of years and found it a powerful approach to producing flexible, extensible, user-friendly interfaces.

Controlling Code
How to Implement Dynamic Models
May 1993

Implementing Models

Converting a class model to a set of declarations in a typical object-oriented language is relatively straightforward for most programmers. Class declarations correspond directly to class models, because object-oriented languages provide syntax to declare classes with their attributes and operations. Associations can be implemented as stand-alone objects or as pointers from object to object, and languages differ in the details of inheritance, object creation, and metaclasses, but the mapping from concept to language declarations is still relatively clean.

A large fraction of programmers would have trouble implementing a dynamic model, however. This is not because the dynamic model is fundamentally new or difficult, but because most languages do not provide syntactic support for it and most programmers are unused to dealing with it. In this column I hope to dispel some of the mystery surrounding control implementation and show that it is straightforward.

State Machines and BNF

Dynamic models are not new. The concept of state machine has been around for a long time in computing and is one of the basic concepts of computer science. The development of compilers and parsers has pushed the invention of languages and algorithms for representing state machines. A grammar is a way to represent a state machine and tie it to computations. The BNF (Backus-Naur Form) grammar representation is a way to represent the syntax of a language as a series of transformations (called *productions*) that operate on portions of the input. For example, in an arithmetic grammar a *term* could be replaced by *expression * expression* or *expression / expression*.

What do grammars have to do with state machines? There is a well-developed theory of parsing that allows a grammar to be replaced by a state machine, in which the various states represent the language constructs found so far in the input and the events represent new input symbols. Although the transformation from grammar to state machine can be automated, it is very tedious to do by hand, so few programmers have experience with it.

Why do I bring this up? I want to point out that many programmers have experience using parser-generators, such as *yacc* under Unix, but that fewer programmers have experience actually constructing state machines by hand. This is why it seems difficult.

Controllers

The most frequent use of dynamic models is to represent the control aspect of a system, typically the user interface or other high-level control. Only a fraction of the classes in a typical system require dynamic models, because most classes are passive, that is, they don't act unless acted on, and many of them are stateless, that is, they always respond to a stimulus in the same way. Although many real-world objects have autonomous behavior and generate their own spontaneous events, the objects that are part of an application program are often just internal representatives, or *surrogates*, that capture the system's knowledge of the external real world. For example, an air traffic control system would have surrogates for airplanes. Surrogates must not be confused with the real thing; in particular, they rarely have autonomous behavior but instead are usually acted on to match changes perceived in the external world. The airplane objects in an air traffic control system do not generate spontaneous events. Although the real-world objects have autonomous behavior and generate events, they are not part of the system, and the internal surrogates do not generate events but just respond to them.

If the real-world objects are not major contributors to the dynamic model, where does it come from? In a typical program, the user interface provides the connection between the external real-world agents (the users) and the passive objects that are part of the application, such as the real-world surrogates and other objects. The user interface is not part of the real world, but it is not a purely internal object either, because it is visible to the external agents and in fact defines the functionality of the application program itself and must be considered during analysis.

It is useful to think about the design of an application system as containing three kinds of objects: real-world objects that exist independently of any application; application objects that represent the externally visible aspects of the application itself; and internal objects that are purely arbitrary implementation constructs invisible to the outside world. Real-world classes can be found by a domain analysis that tries to identify concepts common to an entire domain. The application objects can only be found in the context of a particular application, so a top-down approach is often useful. Purely internal objects should be omitted during analysis, as they do not affect the functionality of the system. The internal objects should be added during the design phase whereever they are helpful.

Application objects include *devices* (such as file systems, displays, audio), *formats* (file formats, command formats, etc.), *presentations* (views) to visualize semantic concepts and manipulate them (pictures, text forms, etc.), and *controllers*. A controller is the interface between an external agent (such as a user) and the application. Controllers embody the control state of the interaction, including all the context variables. In practice, we often think of the controller as *being* the application.

In many or even most cases, an application has a single controller, because most applications have a single user. Multi-user applications may have multiple controllers, and even a single application might have several independent parts, although too much parallelism can be confusing to users. Each independent thread of control should have a controller.

A controller's purpose is to represent control, so its dynamic model is very important. The controller also holds the state variables for an interaction, so it is useful to think of it as an object whose attributes are the state variables. All of this is easier to understand using a simple example.

State Machine Interpreter

The straightforward approach to implementing a state machine is perhaps the best: represent the state diagram as a table and write a small interpreter to "execute" it. This is the traditional approach to state machines that has been used in computer science for 30 years. State machine interpreters are good object-oriented applications.

Figure 1 shows the object model for a state machine interpreter. I have left out some aspects of state diagrams, such as guard conditions or sending events to other objects; these could be added later. The *superstate-substates* relationship defines a tree of states, where each

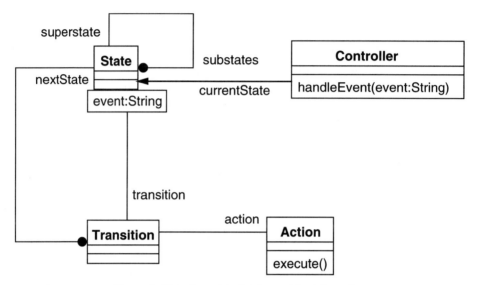

Figure 1. Object model of state machine interpreter

substate inherits the transitions of its ancestors. Each state has a table of transitions indexed by event name. Each transition has an action, which can be executed, and a next state. All events are processed by the *handleEvent* operation on the controller object.

C++ code for the handleEvent operation is shown in Figure 2. The controller starts with the current state and then searches up the tree of superstates looking for a state that has a transition on the given event. If a transition is found, it is executed. (Actions can be implemented in various ways that I will not elaborate now.) If a transition is not found, the search continues up the tree of states. If no transition is found on any state, then the event is ignored.

States As Objects

Another implementation of control takes advantage of the inheritance mechanism in an object-oriented language to find transitions. Because transitions relate to states in a state diagram exactly as operations relate to classes in an object diagram, the fact that we can use method inheritance is not surprising.

In an *object model* implementation of the state machine each state maps into a class. The states are all descended from the *Controller* class, the class that implements the controller

```
Controller::handleEvent (String event)
{
    for (State* state=currentState;
            state=state->superstate; state!=0)
    {
        Transition* transition = state[event];
        if (transition != 0)
        {
            transition->action->execute(this);
            currentState=transition->nextState;
            break;
        }
    }
}
```

Figure 2. Code for state machine interpreter

itself. Each input event is represented by an operation. The callback function that handles system events maps operating system or windowing system events into operation calls on the controller object. Each possible event is defined as an empty virtual operation on the root state which is overridden by any substate that has a transition on the event. The inheritance mechanism in the language finds the right method and executes its action as the method body.

You can take advantage of a feature of C++ to simplify writing action methods without having excess indirections. The controller itself corresponds to the entire Controller class, rather than an instance of it. In many applications there is only a single instance of the controller. Therefore we can store its state variables as C++ static members (class variables in Smalltalk), which are common to all instances of the class (indicated in the diagram by dollar sign symbols). Class variables persist as instance are created and destroyed, but they can be accessed within instance methods by just their names. The states are subclasses of the Controller class, so they can access its class variables using only the name, but they have no instance variables to copy, because the state information is stored by the static members. The state subclasses exist for their methods only.

It would be a reasonably simple matter to extend C++ to permit an object to change its class within a subtree provided it did not add new attributes. This facility would greatly simplify the implementation of control, but I doubt the powers that be would go along with this.

OMT Summary

THIS SECTION summarizes the OMT method. Since the publication of *Object-Oriented Modeling and Design* in late 1990, OMT has undergone an evolution. The basic ideas were sound and changed less than many other methods, but there were many holes in both modeling concepts and process. When possible, I borrowed ideas from other methods so as to avoid unnecessary duplication of ideas. In late 1994 I joined Rational Software Corporation and began working with Grady Booch to unify the OMT and Booch methods into a single method. In 1995 we were joined by Ivar Jacobson to unify the OOSE method as well. Our goal was to completely unify the modeling language of these three methods, but we wanted to include good ideas from other methods as well.

In late 1995 we produced a first draft of the Unified Modeling Language (UML) which we completed in 1996. The Unified Modeling Language serves as a basis for representing most methods using a common set of modeling constructs and a common notation. It captures the concepts from the OMT, Booch, and OOSE methods, but we hope that other methodologists will adopt it also, so that users can understand models from any method without confusion. The ideas that went into the UML came directly and indirectly from scores of different individuals; it is truly the product of the entire object-oriented community.

We did not attempt to standardize a common process. The important thing was to develop a common language, so that everybody could understand everybody else. It is not desirable that everybody use the language in the same way; different people and different organizations need different processes. The models and notation of the Unified Modeling Language are usable with many different methods, including (by a process of back projection) the original OMT, Booch, and OOSE methods.

This section summarizes the OMT method as it had evolved by 1995 before it merged into the Unified Modeling Language. I have translated some of the notation into the Unified Modeling Language but I have not included new concepts or models that were not present in the extended OMT method, and I have left unchanged some of the main features of the original OMT. This summary is necessarily brief; therefore detailed explanations and fine points are omitted. Major differences with the UML notation are indicated in paragraphs set in italics.

OMT Object Model

January 1994

THE object model is the core of an OMT model. This view shows the structure of a system: its contents and their relationships to each other. In its most fundamental form, it shows the state of a system, that is, those elements that must be remembered from moment to moment and not transient "uses" relationships. (Uses relationships can be shown, but they should be regarded as a summarization of information that appears in a more essential form somewhere else.)

Diagrams for object models come in two varieties, *class diagrams* showing generic descriptions of possible systems and *object diagrams* showing particular instantiations of systems. Class diagrams contain classes and object diagrams contain objects, but it is possible to mix classes and objects when dealing with various kinds of metadata, so the separation is not rigid. Normally you will build class diagrams plus occasional object diagrams illustrating complicated data structures or message-passing structures.

Classes

A class is drawn as a three-part box, with the class name in the top part, a list of attributes (with optional types) in the middle part, and a list of operations (with optional argument lists and return types) in the bottom part (Figure 1). During analysis the types can be vague; during later design they should have the syntax of the target language.

The attribute and operation sections of the class box can be omitted to reduce detail in an overview. Omitting a section makes no statement about the absence of attributes or op-

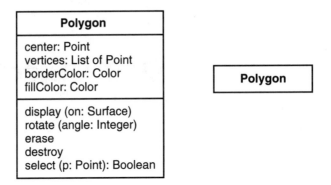

Figure 1. Class

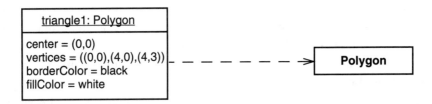

Figure 2. Object

erations, but drawing an empty section explicitly states that there are no elements in that part (or at least none visible with any filters in effect). Normally I draw each class once in full detail; if it must appear more than once in a model I use only a box with a name for subsequent references.

An object is also drawn as a box with two parts: the top part contains the object name followed by the class name, the bottom part contains a list of attribute names with their values (Figure 2). No operations are needed as they are the same for all instances of a class (I suppose a third section would make sense for a delegation-based language such as *self*.) The object name can be omitted for anonymous objects. You can show instantiation with a dotted arrow from the object to the class, but generally the class name in the object is sufficient. *In the UML the name and type of the object are underlined to distinguish it from a class.*

A class can have a multiplicity indicator, drawn as a small expression in the upper right corner (Figure 3). This indicates how many instances of the class can exist at a time. The

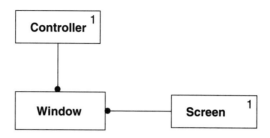

Figure 3. Class multiplicity and singleton class

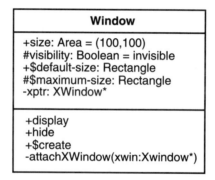

Figure 4. Visibility and scope of attributes and operations

default is *many*, i.e., an unlimited number. The most important special case is 1, a *singleton class* with exactly one instance.

Various refinements are useful when class diagrams are used for detailed design and coding (Figure 4). Initial values for attribute values can be specified in the format *name : type = expression*. Attributes and operations can be global to the entire class (*$name*). The external visibility of an element can be public (+), protected (#), or private (-). To accommodate other features needed by programming languages, annotations in braces can follow the affected element (*{note}*). These can be used in a language-dependent way, such as {**const**}. In particular, {**abstract**} indicates an operation whose implementation is deferred to a subclass (an abstract operation).

Parameterized classes (templates) can be specified by including a list of formal parameters and types in the definition: *classname<arg:type>* (Figure 5). Instantiated classes replace the formal parameters with actual values (*classname<value>*), usually class names. In-

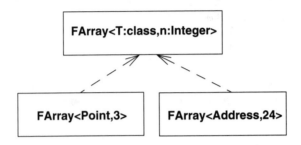

Figure 5. Parameterized classes

stantiated template classes can be connected to their templates by dotted arrows (which can also be used to show instantiation of ordinary classes as objects).

In the UML a template is specified by placing the template parameters in a dotted box in the upper right hand corner of the main rectangle, rather than enclosing them in angle brackets. An instantiated class is specified as described above, so that the template and its instantiation are readily distinguishable.

Associations

Associations (Figure 6) represent structural relationships between objects of different classes, information that must be preserved for some duration and not simply "calls" relationships. The individual instances of an association are called *links;* each is a tuple of object references. Most associations are binary, drawn as lines between pairs of classes. An association can have a name with an arrow showing which way it is read. An association could have different names in each direction, but this would be tedious in practice and is not recommended. Each end of an association is a *role*. Each role can have a name (*rolename*), showing how its class is viewed by the other class. The rolenames opposite a class must be unique. Each role indicates the *multiplicity* of its class, that is, how many instances of the class can be associated with one instance of the other class. Multiplicity can be 1 (no marker), 0-1 (hollow ball), 0 or more "many" (solid ball), or some other integer range value indicated by an expression, such as 1+ (one or more), 3 (exactly three), or 2-4 (two to four inclusive). Use a solid ball for any multiplicity greater than one. If multiplicity is more than one, the annotation {**ordered**} may be placed on the role, indicating that the elements have an explicit or-

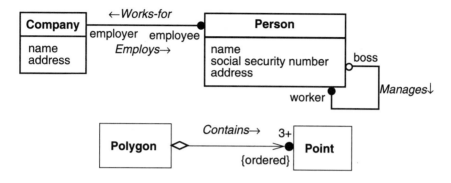

Figure 6. Association notation

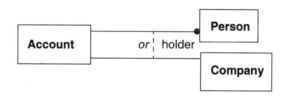

Figure 7. Or-association.

der; otherwise they are an unordered set. The order in which elements are added must be specified for operations that update an ordered association. Note that sorting by a fixed rule is a design decision that does not add any semantic information and is *not* the same as ordered; it makes sense to indicate {**sorted**} during design but not during analysis.

In the UML all multiplicities are specified using the text notation, rather than using balls as adornments. A role with no adornment and no text multiplicity has an undefined or unspecified multiplicity, rather than exactly one. This change allows undefined multiplicity to be clearly distinguished from multiplicity of exactly one.

Self-associations and multiple associations between a pair of classes are possible and common. It is important to use rolenames to tell them apart. Note that two associations between class A and class B do not mean that the same A and B objects are related twice; a given A object may be linked to different B objects through each association.

Occasionally one class can participate in two associations, with the restriction that each object can only participate in one of the associations at a time. This can be shown by placing an "or" constraint between the pair of associations (Figure 7).

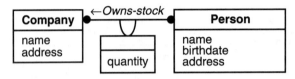

Figure 8. Link attribute

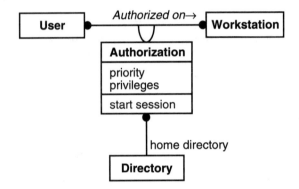

Figure 9. Link class

A link attribute is a value held by an association and not belonging to either class by itself. It is drawn as a box hanging from an association. The box can contain multiple link attributes. Each link in the association has the indicated values (Figure 8).

A link attribute is a degenerate case of a *link class*, an association considered as a class with its own possible attributes, operations, and associations. The most common use of link classes is to show associations between classes and associations (Figure 9).

In the UML a link class is attached to the association by a dashed line instead of a loop. The name has been changed to association class.

A *qualified association* is a variant form of link attribute (Figure 10). A *qualifier* is a link value that is unique within the set of links associated with an object in the association. In other words, an object and a qualifier value identify a unique object across the association; they form a composite key. The qualifier is part of one role of the association; qualification is not symmetric. Qualification reduces the multiplicity of the opposite role; the multiplicity shows the number of instances of the related class associated with a given combination of an object from the first class and a given qualifier value. During design it is useful to allow qualified associations to have multiplicity *many* to indicate an index that selects sets of objects by the qualifier value, that is, a *dictionary* or *look-up table*. Qualifiers are drawn as small

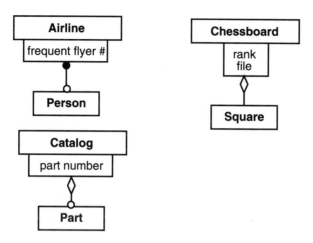

Figure 10. Qualified association

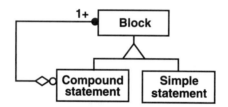

Figure 11. Aggregation in recursive structure

boxes on the end of the association attached to a class. They are part of the association, not the class. A qualifier box may contain multiple qualifier values; the qualification is based on the composite value.

Aggregation is a special form of association with the connotation of "whole-part" relationship. It is indicated by placing a diamond on the role attached to the whole object. Mathematically it indicates that the association is transitive and antisymmetric, normal properties of parts hierarchies. If you are not sure when to use aggregation, ignore it and stick to plain associations. The main semantic use of aggregation is in recursive data structures, where it can be used to forbid cycles among the instances (Figure 11).

The multiplicity of the aggregate role can be one (or optional-one) or many. A multiplicity of one indicates a *physical aggregation*; a part cannot be part of more than one whole. A multiplicity of many indicates a *catalog aggregation*; a part model in a catalog can be used

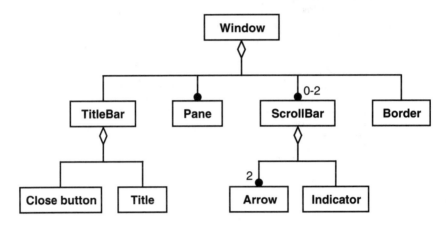

Figure 12. Aggregation tree notation

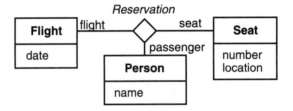

Figure 13. Ternary association

in many different assembly models. Additional notation is not needed to distinguish these two cases; the multiplicity is sufficient.

An alternate way to show aggregation is to combine all of the parts of a given aggregate using an aggregation symbol with one diamond and many tails. Each tail can have its own multiplicity (Figure 12).

Ternary (or higher order) associations are drawn as diamonds with one path to each participating class (Figure 13). This is the traditional entity-relationship model symbol for an association. The binary form is drawn without the diamond for greater compactness, because binary associations are the bulk of associations in a real model. Ternary associations are fairly rare and can also be modeled by promoting them to classes. Ternary associations can have link attributes (attach the arc to the diamond). Roles may have rolenames but multiplicity is more complicated and best specified by listing candidate keys.

Navigation Expressions

We provide a simple expression language for describing class diagram paths. A dot '.' shows accessing an attribute value or traversing an association: **person.employer**. The expression denotes a scalar or a set of values depending on the multiplicity of the association. An expression in brackets shows selection of values from a set: **todaysFlights :=** **flights[flight.date=today]**. For a qualifier, it indicates selecting the associated object with the given qualifier: **aFile := directory.files[filename]**. Note that an array can be modeled as a qualified association with integer qualifiers. A tilde '~' indicates inverse traversal of an association from a class with the given rolename: **pilotFlights := aPilot.~pilot**. This usage requires that the incoming rolenames attached to a class be unique.

An arrowhead on a role indicates that the association is implemented in the given direction; it is used for detailed design and code generation and is unnecessary during analysis. I feel that further details about implementation are best specified in an editing tool as part of a backplane; you should not expect to show everything on a diagram.

Generalization

Generalization is the taxonomic relationship between a superclass and its subclasses. It is drawn as a triangle with a line from the apex to the superclass and one line from the baseline to each subclass (Figure 14). All attributes, operations, and associations of a superclass are inherited by all subclasses.

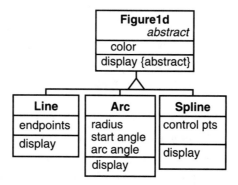

Figure 14. Generalization

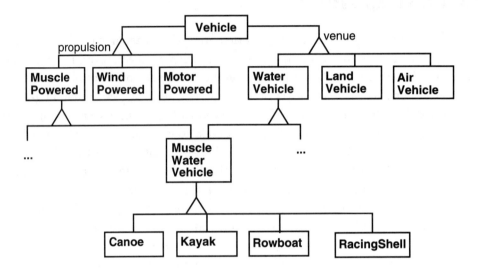

Figure 15. Parallel generalization

In the UML the triangle is moved to the end of the arc attached to the superclass. Multiple arcs may share a single target segment and baseline, or they may be drawn as individual arcs from subclass to superclass.

Generalization is an n-ary relationship, not a binary relationship. In this we differ from most other authors. A superclass can be part of several parallel generalizations, each dealing with a different orthogonal dimension of specialization (Figure 15). Each parallel generalization is drawn as a separate n-ary construct; they all share the same superclass but the subclasses are disjoint. The quality being generalized is called the *discriminator* and can label each triangle. Any instantiable subclass must specify one superclass from each parallel generalization, because they all represent different, necessary aspects of an actual class. This is a kind of multiple inheritance. However, even if the combinations are not explicitly shown, they are implicit.

The rule that subclasses sharing a discriminator must be physically connected is intuitively appealing but unworkable in practice with a model consisting of several physically-distinct submodels. In the UML subclasses in the same group need not be physically connected. Instead each generalization arc may have a discriminator name attached. If two arcs share the same discriminator name, then they belong to the same group of subclasses, that is, grouping is performed by name sharing rather than graphical attachment.

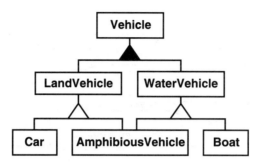

Figure 16. Overlapping subclasses

Generally subclasses are disjoint, indicated with a hollow triangle, but sometimes they can overlap, indicated by a solid triangle (Figure 16). This is a fine distinction that may be omitted. The use of overlapping subclasses implies that they can be combined using multiple inheritance. Note that the common ancestor is inherited even though it may appear on several paths (a virtual base class, in C++ terms).

In the UML this distinction may be specified by a textual constraint.

Multiple inheritance can also occur when a subclass has two superclasses that share no common ancestor. The use of *mixins* is a form of multiple inheritance.

An *abstract class* is one that may not have direct instances (because it has deferred operations, for example). An abstract class can be specified with a keyword as shown in Figure 14. However, many developers prefer to treat all nonleaf classes as abstract. Any concrete intermediate-level class can be easily converted to an abstract class by adding a new concrete subclass equivalent to "none of the other subclasses." If you adopt this practice, then it is unnecessary to indicate abstract classes.

Another use for an abstract class is to organize global parameters into a scoped location. The parameters would be defined as class attributes of the abstract class. All global parameters should be assigned to classes to avoid name conflict and other problems caused by lack of modularity.

Constraints

The symbols I have described together with annotations for particular programming language constructs are sufficient for generating class declarations in most languages. Sometimes you also want to restrict the values that objects or links can assume. A *constraint* is a

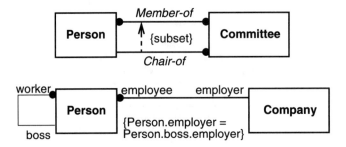

Figure 17. Constraints

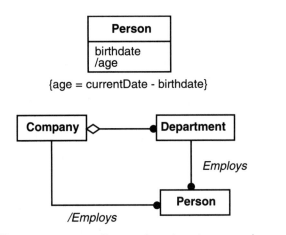

Figure 18. Derived values

restriction on values; it is expressed as an arbitrary expression attached (implicitly on paper) to a class or association. It is enclosed in braces and placed near the elements it constrains. Navigation expressions are handy for writing constraints. Constraints between two elements (usually classes or associations) can be shown by connecting the elements by a dotted line labeled with the constraint (Figure 17).

Generally it is best to avoid redundancy in object models, but sometimes it is useful to show a redundant value or association that can be derived from other elements. To indicate a derived entity, place a slash ('/') in front of the name of the derived entity and write a constraint defining its value (Figure 18).

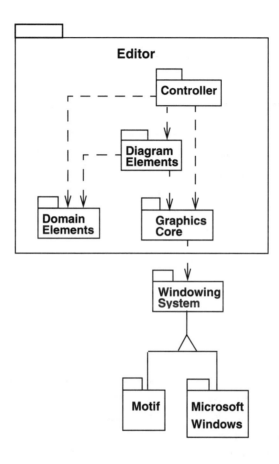

Figure 19. Subsystems (nested form)

Subsystems

Large models require internal organization. A *subsystem* is a subset of the model itself (Figure 19). Each subsystem owns some of the classes, associations, and generalizations of the model, as well as portions of the other model views and the actual code. Subsystems are purely organizational; they have no logical semantics. Subsystems can be nested, so the entire system is the root of the model tree; bottom-level subsystems are called *modules*. Each class has a "home" module in which its internal details are expanded; this module "owns" the class. A class can also appear in other modules, but should appear as a simple box with

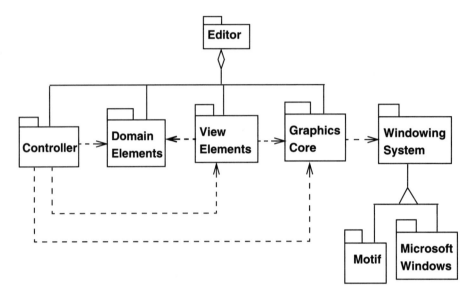

Figure 20. Subsystems (tree form)

classname. The annotation "imported" can be used to signify a class owned by a different module; the module name could be included but is usually best left to an editing tool. Ownership of model elements would be used for configuration control, versioning, and division of work among parallel workers.

A subsystem is drawn as a rectangle with a tab in the upper corner. Dependencies between subsystems are shown by dotted arrows between them, pointing from the dependent subsystem to the independent subsystem (Figure 19). Dependencies may be shown between classes and subsystems but this is usually too fussy.

In the UML the package *is a generic grouping construct for any model or design construct.*

A *subsystem diagram* is a class diagram showing only subsystems (the classes are suppressed). Decomposition of a subsystem into smaller subsystems can be shown in two ways: by nesting subsystems inside larger subsystems (Figure 19) or by using the OMT aggregation tree syntax to externalize the nesting (Figure 20). The OMT generalization symbol is used to show variant implementations of a subsystem.

The external interface of a subsystem can be shown as a diagram showing subsystems and their public classes and public relationships (Figure 21). The public operations can be shown in the class boxes, but usually it is better to simply list them in a table to avoid clutter.

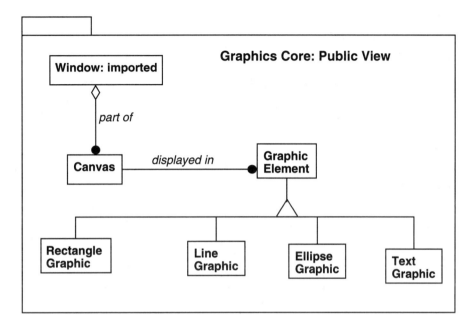

Figure 21. Subsystem interface view

Several subsystems can be shown on one diagram, but then each subsystem can be expanded in its own diagram.

The UML adds constructs for showing interfaces explicitly.

The full details of a subsystem can be shown on a class diagram showing all the contents. Generally it is best to work with one subsystem at a time at the detailed level, but several can be shown at once if necessary.

Composite Objects

A *composite object* is an extended form of aggregation in which the composite is viewed at a higher level of abstraction than the parts. In ordinary aggregation, whole and parts are at the same semantic level and can coexist at run time. Like subsystems, composites really have no additional semantics but instead serve to organize your understanding of a model. A composite is shown as a box surrounding its more atomic components (Figure 22). A composite has identity. All the classes and associations contained within a composite box take

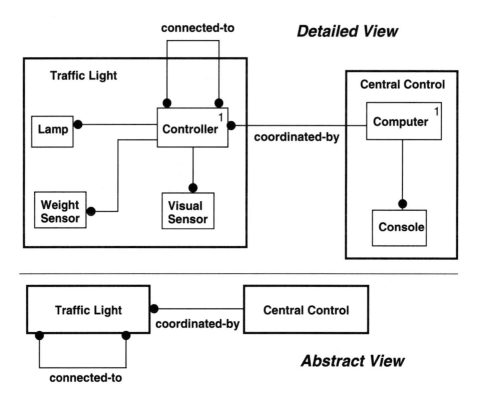

Figure 22. Composites

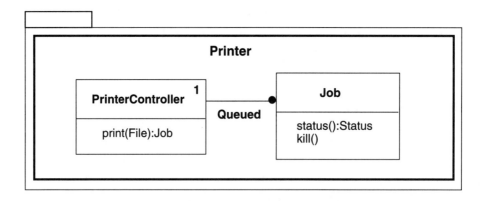

Figure 23. Subsystem object

identity from the composite; their objects and links must all be part of the same composite. However, an association that crosses the composite boundary connects parts from two different composites.

In the UML any class may be composite (although in practice most are not). There is no special symbol for a composite; it is drawn as a class icon containing other class icons.

The multiplicity indicator in a class box shows the number of instances within one instance of the composite object. The default is *many.* You can assume an implicit "system" composite object encloses the entire model.

In an abstract view, the classes and internal associations of composites are suppressed and associations between classes of different composites are subsumed to the composites themselves (Figure 22).

A subsystem that is implemented as a discrete object (or objects) is called a *subsystem object.* It is shown as a subsystem box surrounding a composite box (Figure 23).

OMT Dynamic Model

February 1994

THE dynamic model describes the temporal evolution of the objects in a system in terms of the changes they undergo in response to interactions with other objects inside or outside the system. The dynamic model is defined by state diagrams, each of which describes the life history of objects of a particular class. In practice most of the objects in a system do not undergo significant state changes, so only a minority of classes require state diagrams. (This may not be true for problems that are heavily control-based, in which the dynamic model is dominant.) The state diagram notation that I use was adopted from David Harel with some minor modifications and omissions.

Other views are part of the dynamic model for purposes of understanding, as they can be derived from the state diagrams. These other views, such as use cases and scenarios, can be the main way of developing the state diagrams in the first place, but eventually a full specification of state machines is required.

State Diagrams

A state diagram (Figure 1) is a directed graph of states (nodes) connected by transitions (directed arcs). A state diagram describes the life history of objects of a given class. It describes all possible ways in which the objects respond to events from other objects. Normally state diagrams would be used for objects that receive external events from actors outside

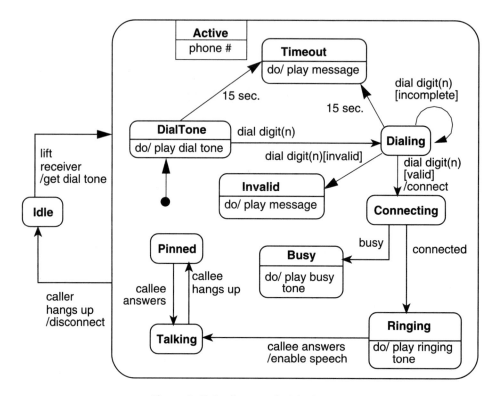

Figure 1. State diagram of a telephone

Event	Condition	Action
pick	[cursor on object]	selection := cursor pick
pick	[cursor not on object]	selection := none
extend	[cursor on object]	selection := selection **or** cursor pick
launch	[single object selected]	selection.launch ()
quit		exit

Figure 2. Modeless event-action table

of a system. Such objects are usually *controllers,* that is, objects whose business is to maintain the system and control other objects.

State diagrams can also be used to show the life history of objects that undergo sequences of operations that take the objects into several fundamentally different states. They can also be used to show the internal flows of control in the implementation of an application, in which case the events correspond to procedure calls. During analysis this level of detail should be avoided.

If an object always responds the same way to external stimuli, then it is *modeless* and can be simply described by a table of events and corresponding operations (Figure 2).

Because there are no states, the different rows in the table are independent of each other, which makes the behavior much simpler. Of course, any graph can be expressed as a table.

Scenarios

A state diagram shows the events and states in the life of an object of a given class; it is generic and describes all possible life histories. A *scenario* shows a particular series of interactions among objects in a single execution of a system; it is an instance of execution of a set of state diagrams and describes a single history without conditionality. Scenarios illustrate interactions that are inherent in the underlying state diagrams but whose overall form is not apparent in the isolated state diagrams. State diagrams are for specification, scenarios are for examples.

Scenarios can be shown in two different ways organized around different dimensions. An *event trace diagram* shows the interactions among a set of objects in temporal order, which is good for understanding timing issues. As an alternative to drawing a diagram, a scenario can be written as a text dialog. An *object interaction diagram* shows the interactions among a set of objects as nodes in a graph, which is good for understanding software structure, because the interactions that affect an object are localized around it.

In the UML the names have been change to sequence diagram *and* collaboration diagram.

An event trace diagram (Figure 3) is drawn as follows: Objects (not classes) in a transaction are drawn as vertical lines. An event is drawn as a labeled horizontal arrow from the sending object's line to the receiving object's line. Time proceeds vertically, so event timing sequences can be easily determined. An object can send simultaneous events to other objects; simultaneous reception of events is not meaningful and should be avoided.

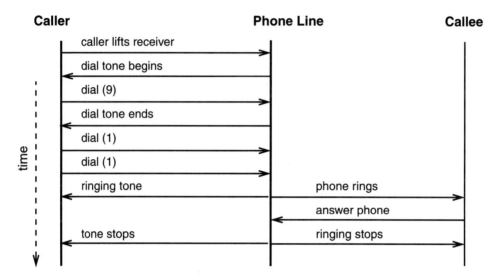

Figure 3. Event trace diagram

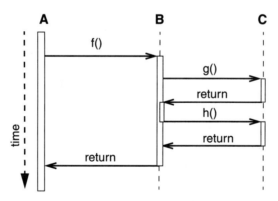

Figure 4. Event trace with control regions

A variant form of event trace diagram shows the period of time when an object has a thread of control as a double line; a single line indicates an object that is blocked waiting for an event (Figure 4). These are good for showing procedure calling sequences in which there is a single locus of control at one time; they are not so useful to fully concurrent systems because all objects are always active.

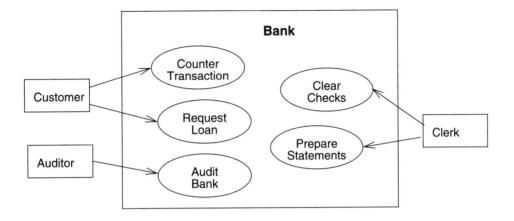

Figure 5. Use case model

Use Cases

Note that a scenario is an instance of a state diagram, the state diagram describing the process or operation itself. A scenario involves many objects.

A scenario is an instance of a use case. A *use case* is a generic description of an entire transaction involving several objects, typically an application system and one or more external actors, but it could also describe the behavior of a set of objects, such as an organization. A use case is typically written as an informal text description of the external actors and the sequences of events between objects that make up the transaction. The specification of a use case can be given as a state diagram whose transitions correspond to message transfers among system objects. Both use cases and scenarios can be regarded as models which cross objects; these holistic diagrams can be derived from more reductionist models. They represent emergent behavior.

Complete information about use cases is easily represented in textual form. A diagram does not add any new information, but many people prefer to have a top-level diagram of a system, so the set of actors and the use cases they interact with can be shown in a *use case diagram* as in Figure 5. The outer objects are the actors and the large object in the system; the use cases are drawn as ellipses within it. Note that a use case diagrams are related to both event flow diagrams and context diagrams, which all show the global interactions between the system and outside actors.

In the UML the actors may be drawn using "stick man" figures.

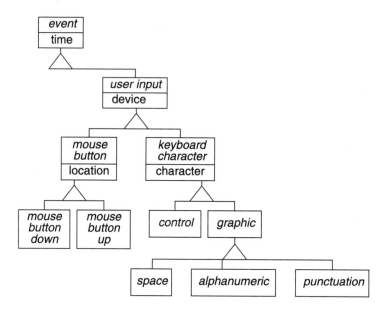

Figure 6. Event taxonomy for keyboard events

Events

Events are the most fundamental concept in the dynamic model; states can be considered as a derived concept. An *event* is a meaningful occurrence at a point in time; a *state* is a period of time during which an object is waiting for an event to occur. The granularity of time depends on the degree of abstraction and can vary at different levels of the same application, but basically an event is something that is atomic, that is, noninterruptible, at the given level of abstraction. A one-way asynchronous transmission of information from one object to another (a *signal*) is an event; the completion of an activity is another kind of event. Events can have parameters with names and types. The general format of an event is:

    eventName (parameter:type, ...)

A two-way information flow (i.e., call-and-return) can always be modeled as two one-way information flows, so there is no need to provide special notation for them, as they are not fundamental. Synchronous transmission is a special case of asynchronous transmission and should be modeled as such; in distributed systems you cannot count on synchronous behavior anyway.

The full specification of an event optionally includes: name, list of parameters, sender and receiver objects, description of event meaning, implementation mechanism, and timing of event delivery.

Events can be arranged into a taxonomy and modeled by a class diagram (Figure 6). The attributes of an event are its parameters. A subevent inherits the parameters of its ancestors and adds its own parameters. A subevent triggers any transitions that depend on any of its ancestor events.

In the UML events modeled as classes would bear a stereotype *called* event.

An event name that is a time period (such as *10 sec.*) is a convention for an *elapsed time event* (Figure 1). This indicates an event that occurs at a given elapsed time after the current state is entered. The mechanism of implementing such an event would involve setting and resetting timers, but there is no need to bother with this internal complexity in the specification, because time-out events are common in practice. The sender of a timer event is the "environment" rather than any individual object.

States

Each state represents a period of time during which an object is waiting for an event to occur. A state is drawn as a rounded box containing the (optional) name of the state. A state box can contain two additional sections, one section containing a list of state variables and the other section containing a list of triggered operations (Figure 7). The sections can be separated by lines for clarity as in a class box.

A state variable is an attribute that is valid while the object is in the state (or any nested substates) and that is meaningless elsewhere. It can have a name, type, and initial value, like any attribute:

```
name: type = value
```

State variables can be accessed and modified by operations within the state, including entry and exit operations.

State variables are attributes of the object described by the state diagram. We single out as state variables those attributes that affect the flow of control, because state diagrams are concerned with control.

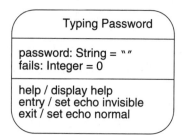

Figure 7. State box with regions

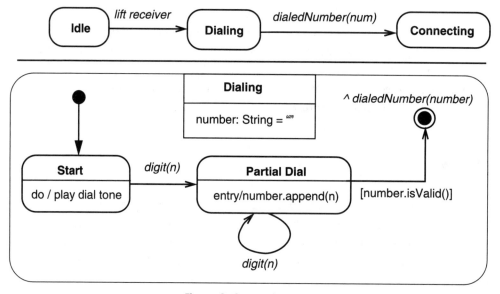

Figure 8. Composite state

Substates

States can be refined into disjoint substates exactly as classes can be refined into disjoint subclasses. The meaning is the same *or-relationship* in both cases: an object in superstate A is either in substate A1 *or* A2 *or* A3 *or* so on. Although the relationships are similar, we draw substates by nesting them inside the superstate box to avoid confusion between substate lines and transition lines (Figure 1). An alternative notation using the generalization tree symbol is possible but generally less clear.

A substate inherits the properties of its superstate: state variables and transitions (internal and external). More precisely, outgoing transitions are inherited. If an event is received by an object in a given substate, all transitions on all enclosing states are potentially applicable, provided they have not been overridden by transitions on inner states. Incoming transitions are *not* inherited, because they point to a specific state.

Composite States

A composite state is like a composite object: a high-level view on a model that can be expanded into lower level detail (Figure 8). At a high level, a composite state is a single state, with one or more transitions entering and leaving it. At an expanded level of detail, a composite state contains several lower-level states responding to lower-level transitions. The lower level events are not visible at the higher level of abstraction.

A composite state may have a starting substate. Any transition to the composite state itself (at the higher level of abstraction) represents a transition to the starting substate. A starting substate is drawn as a circle. A termination substate is drawn as a bull's-eye.

A composite state can "return" an event on a terminal state, using the "send event" notation (Figure 8), because the object is "sending" an event to its higher-level self. This means that the execution of the sequence leading to the termination state is a detailed equivalent of receiving the higher level event in the higher level state diagram.

Although the concepts of state generalization and state aggregation are distinct from the concept of composite states, it is rarely useful to separate them, so nesting in a state diagram for generalization or aggregation also implies a composite state.

Concurrency

Most concurrency arises by aggregation: a composite object contains several parts, each of which has its own state. The state of the overall composite object is the Cartesian product of the individual states. No additional notation is needed in this case.

We also provide an explicit notation for concurrency within a state without using object aggregation. A state can have multiple explicit loci of activity, that is, multiple threads of control. The number of threads can vary among the states of the same object; in other words, the amount of concurrent activity can vary from moment to moment. Concurrent

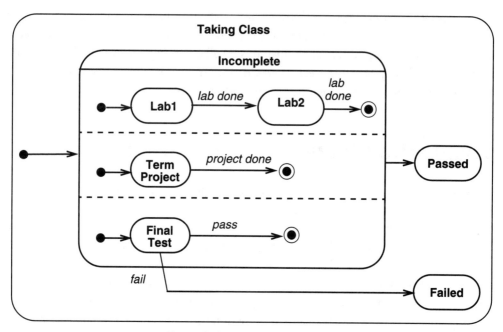

Figure 9. Concurrent substates

substates are shown by partitioning a state into regions with dotted lines (Figure 9). Each region is a concurrent substate. When the enclosing state is entered, there is one thread for each substate.

A transition into an aggregate concurrent state can be shown as a branching arrow with one arrowhead leading to each concurrent substate (Figure 10). An arrowhead can be omitted for a substate that begins in its default starting state, a common occurrence (Figure 9).

A transition from a concurrent substate to a state outside the enclosing superstate terminates any parallel substates by a forced exit (Figure 9). Arrows from several parallel states can merge to indicate that all of the indicated states must hold to enable the transition (Figure 10). An unlabeled transition from the enclosing superstate indicates that all the substates must have reached their terminal substates for the transition to occur (Figure 9).

Concurrent objects can interact explicitly by sending events. They can interact implicitly if one object has a guard condition that depends on the state of another object, such as being in a given state: "object.**in** (*state*)".

A satisfactory model of concurrency is as follows: An atomic object can be thought of as a finite-state machine with a queue for incoming events. New events go on the queue un-

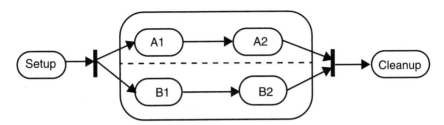

Figure 10. Explicit branching and merging threads

til the object is free to deal with them. Composite concurrent objects contain several atomic objects as parts, each of which maintains its own queue and thread of control.

Transitions

A transition is a response to an event experienced by an object that is in a certain state. A transition may invoke an operation on the object and may cause the object to change to another state. An *external transition* leads to a new state and may invoke an operation. An *internal transition* invokes an operation without causing a change of state.

Transitions leading from the current state of an object are eligible to be triggered by an event received by the object. The trigger for an event includes an event name and an optional guard condition. The event may have parameters, which must be the same for all occurrences of the same event name. The values of the event parameters are available to operations triggered by the event.

A guard condition is a Boolean expression in terms of trigger-event parameters, state variables, and functions of the controlling object. If the event occurs and the value of the expression is true, then the transition occurs, otherwise the transition does not occur. The same event name can be used for more than one transition from the same state, but they must have different guard conditions. In principle no more than one guard condition should evaluate to *true,* but in practice any conflicts can be resolved by specifying the order for evaluating transitions from a given state.

As I have noted, events can be reified and arranged into a class hierarchy (Figure 6). An event triggers any transitions that depend on any of its ancestors in the hierarchy. Events that do not trigger any transitions in a state are simply ignored.

In principle, operations triggered by transitions are instantaneous. In practice they take some time to evaluate in an actual program, so this really means that they are atomic and noninterruptible at some level of abstraction.

A useful convention is to permit transitions without event names. If an unlabeled transition has a guard condition, then it is triggered whenever the condition becomes true; in practice, it need be tested only after an event occurs because something must initiate a change. A state can have a single unlabeled transition without a guard condition; this transition is automatically taken when the internal activity of the state is completed. These so-called *lambda transitions* are not needed in theory, but they permit state diagrams to be factored into simpler pieces that are easier to understand.

The overall syntax for a transition permits all the following elements, each of which is optional:

```
event(arguments)
  [condition]
  ^target.sendEvent(arguments)
  /operation(arguments)
```

During design additional information might be specified, such as the medium (procedure call, input/output event, interprocess message, hardware signal), the transport channel, and the timing of event delivery and response. This kind of information is probably best kept in tables maintained by a tool so that diagrams do not become too cluttered, although it might be exposed for certain kinds of applications.

Operations

Operations on the controlling object are invoked by transitions. I call these operations *actions;* they must be instantaneous, i.e., noninterruptible. They can be implemented as methods on the controlling object. As methods, they have access to the parameters of the trigger event as well as the state variables and other attributes of the controlling object; they can invoke other operations reachable from the controlling object.

To permit modularization of states, we allow *entry* and *exit operations.* An *entry operation* is an operation that is automatically performed whenever the state is entered by a transition. An *exit operation* is an operation that is automatically performed whenever the state is exited by a transition. The same effect could be obtained by attaching the operation to all transitions entering or exiting the state, but this notation permits a separation between the inside and outside of the state. In effect, it makes the state a self-contained module. Entry and exit transitions are shown as internal transitions with the pseudo-event names **entry** and **exit** (Figures 7 and 8).

If a transition enters a nested state, then all the entry operations are performed starting with the outermost state; the reverse is true when leaving a nested state. On an internal transition the entry and exit operations are not performed, because control remains within the state. On a self-transition, the exit and entry operations are performed, because control exits and reenters the state. Therefore there is a subtle difference between an internal transition and a self-transition: the self-transition triggers exit and entry events on the state, whereas the internal transition does not.

Activities

An *activity* is an ongoing operation within a state that takes time to complete. Because it has duration, it cannot be attached to a transition (internal or external) but it can be interrupted by an event that causes a state transition. An activity is indicated as a pseudo-transition with the event name **do.** An activity may or may not terminate by itself. If it terminates by itself, then any unlabeled (lambda) transition for the state is taken. Whether or not an activity terminates by itself, it is forcibly terminated if the reception of an event causes an exit from the state. In principle, one activity per state is sufficient; in practice you could specify a list of operations to be performed in order.

Sending Events

Objects can send events to other objects. In general, an event can be directed to any set of objects known to the sending object. Sending an event to a single fixed object (the most usual case) and broadcasting to the whole system can be considered as special cases of sending an event to a set. Sending an event is an action that can be performed by an object, but we provide special syntax for it because it affects the flow of control so much (Figure 11). Sending an event can be specified as part of a transition as follows:

```
^target.event(arglist)
```

where *target* is an expression designating a set of objects, *event* is the name of an event, and *arglist* is a list of expressions for parameter values. Expressions must be written in terms of

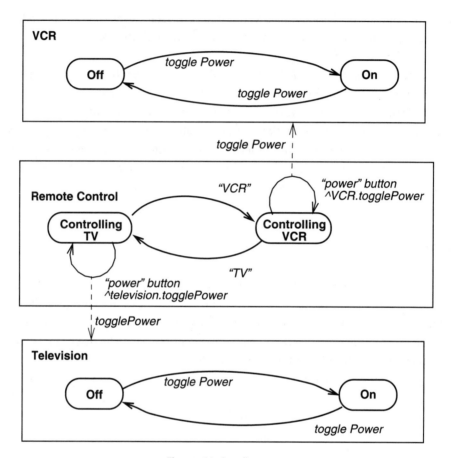

Figure 11. Sending events

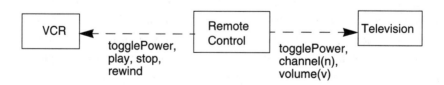

Figure 12. Event flow diagram

parameters of the trigger event, state variables, and functions of the sending object, as well as literal values, such as the target object name. In normal loose practice, the target object may be omitted if it is fixed and well known.

Normally it is sufficient to simply notate sending an event using the text syntax on a transition. Sending an event can also be indicated graphically by drawing a dotted arrow from the sending transition to the target object; the name of the sent event is attached to the dotted arrow.

A diagram showing only objects and the events that they send to each other is called an *event flow diagram*. It can be regarded as a degenerate form of a set of state diagrams with sends (Figure 12). If the events are replaced by their arguments, then the diagram becomes a *context diagram* that shows the data flowing among actors and the system. They are just two different views of the same underlying information.

Creating Objects

Creating a new object of a given class can be thought of as a special case of sending an event to the class itself. The event arguments are used to instantiate the object. When the new object is created, it begins in an initial state in which it receives the creation event as its first "birth" event. This is the way that creator objects pass information to their creations (Figure 13).

A class could have multiple possible birth events, although this makes things more complicated. The initial state would have multiple transitions with different event labels. The creator would specify which event to use.

Destroying Objects

When an object reaches a top-level terminal state, it ceases to exist. (If it reaches a terminal state in a nested state, then the nested state ceases to hold.) As part of the transition to the terminal state, it can send an event to another object (Figure 13). For convenience, an action and an event-sending expression can be attached directly to a terminal state.

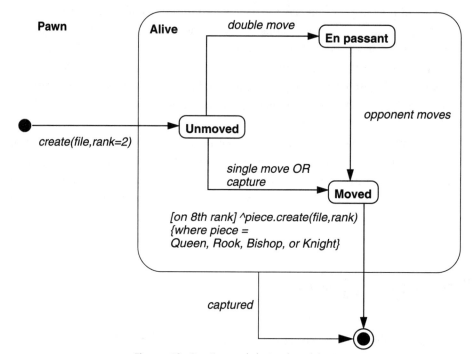

Figure 13. Creating and destroying objects

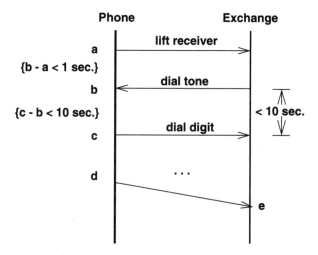

Figure 14. Event trace with timing constraints

Timing Mark

A *timing mark* can be associated with a transition, usually on an event trace diagram. A timing mark is a name designating the time at which the transition occurs (Figure 14). The timing mark can be used to write constraints on the timing of transitions, usually maximum limits on the elapsed time between events. To show the effects of a time-out, use more than one event trace: one to show the normal case and another to show the time-out case. Real-time constraints can be specified using timing marks.

Timing marks can also be used on state diagrams but the control path that they represent in the diagram must be clearly specified.

OMT Functional Model

March 1994

THIS approach to the functional model is a major departure from our book *Object-Oriented Modeling and Design,* which proposed a more conventional use of data flow diagrams that was both misunderstood and poorly accepted. Keep in mind that the OMT division into three "models" (model *views,* rather) is a vague, high-level organization for purposes of understanding; it does not have inherent semantics.

The functional model describes the operations in the system. In particular, it describes how the execution of an operation affects the values of the objects in the system. We can look at operations from two different levels: a black-box viewpoint in which we only look at the results of an operation on the values in the system; and an implementation viewpoint in which we see how the operation works internally. The first viewpoint (nonprocedural) is represented by describing the state of the system before and after the execution of an operation, the second viewpoint (procedural) is represented by describing the flow of control among subordinate operations in various objects effecting the change of state.

The functional model consists of use cases and operation descriptions, as well as object interaction diagrams, pseudocode designs, and actual code to specify how they work.

Operation Specifications

An operation can be specified by giving *before and after conditions* on its execution. A before condition states assumptions on the state of the system at the beginning of the operation. An after condition is a description of the state of a system at the completion of operation

Operation: sort (elements: Array of T)

Responsibilities: organizes the elements of the array (in place) so that
they are in increasing order

Inputs: elements – an array of objects of type T

Returns: none

Modified objects: elements

Preconditions:

All of the elements must be of type T or a subtype.

Type T has an operation *compare(t1:T) returning {LT, EQ, GT}* which
compares two elements and returns whether the first is less than,
equal to, or greater than the second. The operation must define a total
order on the values of T.

Duplicate values of T are allowed.

Postconditions:

The elements are ordered according to the comparison function.

The array contains exactly the same number of occurrences of each
value of T as before.

If two elements compare as equal, then they have the same relative
order before and after the operation.

Figure 1. Operation specification

execution in terms of the state of the system at the beginning of operation execution. Ideally
operation specifications would be in equations or some other formal language, but in most
cases it is satisfactory to express the specification in ordinary words, provided the meaning
is clear. Figure 1 shows a specification of the sort operation.

The implementation of an operation may invoke other operations, but this is a matter
of design and not specification. The functional model for a system analysis model will only
contain descriptions of the top level, system operations that are invoked by interactions
with outside actors. Much of the work of designing a system consists of elaborating the
high-level operations into procedural implementations. Most operations are not complicated but there are a lot of them in most systems, so the bulk of the functional model for
analysis is simply describing them all in words.

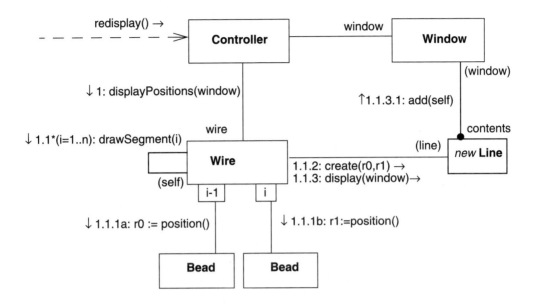

Figure 2. Object interaction diagram

Object Interaction Diagrams

There is a large difference between specifying *what* an operation does and *how* it works. The difference is greater in the functional model than in the object model or dynamic model. It is fairly straightforward to turn an object model into data structures, but often a lot of work is needed to design and implement an operation. For the design process we require an understanding of how an operation works. Ultimately this comes from the algorithm and the code, but an aid to understanding operation behavior is the *object interaction diagram* (OID). Figure 2 shows a sample OID.

An object interaction diagram is an object diagram that shows the sequence of messages that implement an operation. It includes the objects relevant to a particular operation; others can be omitted to avoid clutter. The object diagram shows the objects that exist just before the operation begins and also the objects created during the operation. It is useful to distinguish the two groups by some graphic mark. I show the newly created objects and links with the keyword *new,* but the use of different colors would be clearer when available (in which case you could also distinguish objects destroyed during the operation and temporary objects created and destroyed during the operation).

In UML the distinction between previously existing instances, transient ones, and newly-created ones can be specified using text adornments. A tool could provide alternate means of showing the distinction, such as the use of color.

Changes to an object require control to reach the object, and control flow in an object-oriented system follows data links, so an object diagram contains all the paths that control can follow. Data links include both associations and also more transient relationships, such as procedure parameters and local variables. Transient links are drawn as dotted lines, because they are essentially constrained values that are used for control purposes (for which I also use dotted lines). I indicate temporary knowledge of a link (either transient or association) by placing the rolename in parentheses. Note that transient knowledge in one direction may be persistent knowledge in the opposite direction (as in the **Window-Line** association in Figure 2).

A message from one object to another is indicated by a label consisting of a text string with an arrow showing the message flow direction; the label is drawn next to the link that is used to send the message. Multiple messages can be attached to the same link, in the same or opposite directions. The label contains the following elements (some optional):

1. The label has a sequence number. The numbers show the nested calling sequence in "Dewey Decimal" notation. For example, message 2.1.4 is part of the procedure invoked by message 2.1 and follows message 2.1.3 within that procedure. If the same number is used for two messages, they are concurrent, which means that they are performed in parallel or else they are performed sequentially but the order of execution doesn't matter; a letter can be appended to distinguish concurrent subtrees (such as 1.1.1a and 1.1.1b).

2. The label may have an iteration indicator. This is a star ("*"), optionally followed by an iteration expression in parentheses. Iteration indicates that several messages of the same form are sent either sequentially (to a single target) or concurrently (to the elements of a set). If there is an iteration expression, it shows the values that the iterator or iterators assume, such as "(i=1..n)"; otherwise the details of the iteration must be specified in text or simply deferred to the code.

3. The label may have a return value (or values, if you like multi-valued expressions) followed by an assignment sign (":=" but you can use "=" if you are a devoted C user and can't bear to change). If present, this indicates that the procedure returns a value designated by the given name. The use of the same value

name elsewhere in the diagram designates the exact same value. If the message lacks a return value, then the procedure operates by side effects.

4. The label contains the name of the message. It is unnecessary to specify the class of the message, because this is implicit in the target object.

5. The label contains the argument list of the message. The arguments are expressions built of input values of the transaction, return values of other suboperations, or attribute values of the source object.

Note that my object interaction diagram is essentially the same as Booch's object diagram. You can also draw the messages in a time sequence as an event trace diagram (which Booch calls an object interaction diagram, an unfortunate conflict in names). I find this format useful for addressing timing issues but less useful for designing procedural operations, because it smears out the interactions with a single object for the sake of showing the time sequence clearly.

Concurrent Interaction Diagrams

A concurrent interaction diagram shows the flow of control in the presence of concurrency. In such a diagram more than one locus of control can exist at a given time, each in an active object. An *active object* is an object that maintains its own state and exchanges asynchronous events with other active objects. We indicate an active object by drawing its outline as a heavy line. An active object is a composite object that can contain other objects (including other active objects). Any passive objects in it are under the control of the active object; they are accessed with procedure calls, not true asynchronous events between independent objects.

Messages between active objects follow links just like messages between passive objects. For clarity, such asynchronous messages may be drawn with a half-arrowhead to indicate a one-way flow of control, but this is not really necessary because it is implicit in an interaction between active objects. The sender of an asynchronous message does not wait for a return but proceeds to the next message (if any) or possibly waits for some future message.

The flow of control in a concurrent interaction diagram can branch and merge. It has the form of a partially-ordered graph. The number of loci of control varies at different times. A simple sequential numbering system is not sufficient to represent a partial order, but several other schemes will work. Here is one possible scheme:

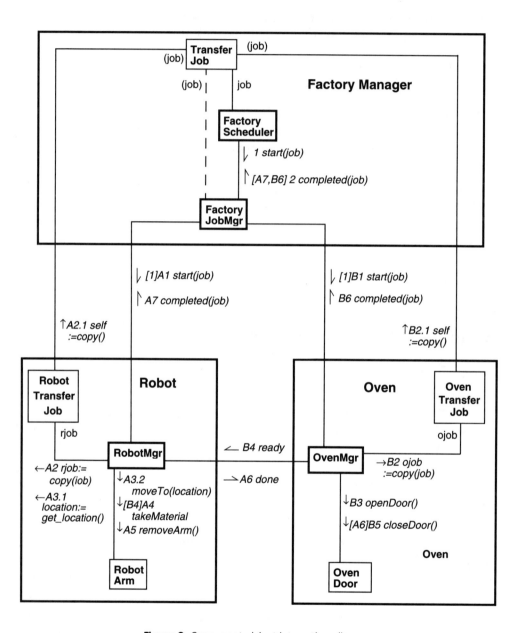

Figure 3. Concurrent object interaction diagram

There can be multiple control subsequences. Each is indicated by an initial letter followed by a sequence number (such as "B3"). Each letter defines a separate subsequence (there is also a "main" subsequence for labels without initial letters). Within a subsequence, messages occur in sequential order, for example, "B3" follows "B4". Different subsequences are potentially concurrent, subject to explicit dependencies. Dependencies between different subsequences are specified explicitly: "[B2]C4" indicates that message "C4" follows messages "B2" (explicitly) and "C3" (implicitly).

Within a concurrent interaction diagram, procedural messages to passive objects can be shown in the usual way using nested numbers. Nested procedural flow of control is part of a single locus of control that eventually terminates at a top level active subsequence.

Figure 3 shows a sample concurrent OID for a factory control system with 3 active objects. The active objects contain passive parts, both hardware parts (such as oven doors and robot arms) and data parts (such as transfer jobs), as well as controllers (such as the manager object in each active object).

Code

Both kinds of interaction diagram illustrate the effect of executing a single high-level operation (or transaction). They are instance examples, not generic descriptions. They show the holistic view of a system as a pattern of interactions among objects, but the detailed specification of behavior is a reductionist activity.

State diagrams specify the behavior of classes from a local point of view. You can specify operation behavior using state diagrams, but in practice state diagrams are best reserved for true interobject events, rather than procedural flow of control, for which they are usually a bit heavy-handed.

Normally the best approach for designing the detailed behavior of operation is that old favorite: code. During design, operations can be sketched out as pseudocode, which addresses algorithmic issues without delving excessively into the details of actual programming languages. Of course, the eventual implementation of operations is as procedural code (plus other mechanisms in certain systems, such as tables and interpreters).

The OMT Process

May 1994

DESCRIBE the development process using fairly traditional lifecycle stages: conceptualization, analysis, system design, object design, implementation. Keep in mind that development is iterative as well as recursive. It has a fractal nature that is hard to describe using a linear medium such as a magazine article, a book, or a lecture. Although I use the traditional words for the stages, I do not imply that they are applied at the same time to all system elements, as in the popular misconception of the "waterfall" approach. Development proceeds on several dimensions simultaneously: the various elements of a system are developed in some order; high-level abstract elements are expanded into low-level concrete elements; elements take on greater implementation specificity as development proceeds through the lifecycle from analysis through design to implementation; and the maturity level of any element increases as it is corrected, polished, and optimized. At the same time, various alternative designs may be explored and the scope of requirements may change. The actual development process requires judgment to choose among many possible paths. A methodology gives guidelines to help the developer make these choices, but it cannot and should not attempt to prescribe a single rigid path for all problems and all developers. There are many correct designs and many correct ways to develop each of them. One of the most popular and successful approaches to system development is *iterative incremental design,* in which a minimal implementation of a system is constructed first and then additional features are added continuously to an existing system.

Strategy

The overall OMT strategy of system development is as follows:

1. Conceptualization: Conceive a problem to be solved and a system approach that solves it. Make an initial cut at the problem statement by writing use cases or listing requirements.

2. Analysis: Describe the external behavior of a system as a "black box" by building OMT models of it in user-meaningful terms. Avoid any internal computer concepts in this user-centered description, unless the computer concepts are directly visible to the users. Avoid making design decisions during this process because they prematurely commit to decisions before the requirements are fully known. Validate the model as well as possible by checking for consistency and by manual simulation. The final analysis models are the true requirements (although they may continue to change as requirements evolve or mistakes are discovered.

3. System design: Make the high-level global decisions about the system implementation, including its overall structure.

4. Object design: Elaborate the analysis models by expanding high-level operations into available operations. Make algorithmic and data structure decisions without getting stuck in the details of a particular language; most design decisions can be expressed in a language-independent manner. Get a logically correct (if inefficient) implementation; then transform the design model step-by-step to optimize it as needed (preferably after measuring performance to see which optimizations are really needed).

5. Object design: Map the design into a particular language. Coding should be a localized process, as all the global design decisions should have been made already. During this stage many additional "junk methods" are added for convenience and information hiding: methods to encapsulate attribute access, traverse associations, construct objects, and provide convenient calls to more basic operations. It is usually best to omit these operations from the design model as they are easily generated automatically or programmed mechanically.

The entire system need not be developed in unison. An iterative development strategy follows the *skeleton* approach: first implement a minimal skeleton of the system with just enough infrastructure to implement a single use case. In a layered system, this typically involves implementing some infrastructure at each level (the "backbone" of the skeleton) together with one or two pieces of application functionality at each level.

Once the initial skeleton system is operational, additional functionality can be added to the skeleton incrementally. This involves mostly implementing additional application features as well as deepening the infrastructure beyond a minimal core. On a large system, it may even be possible to add additional (usually upper) layers to the skeleton. The advantage of an incremental approach is that most development proceeds in the context of an operational system, which simplifies integration and isolates problems. It also allows users to evaluate capabilities and system concepts earlier. This approach requires a solid architectural vision to permit continual expansion. Because the entire system is not developed at once, some rework may be needed as new capabilities are added, but a good object-oriented design will localize and minimize the number of changes needed.

Conceptualization

You must identify a problem to be solved before you can solve it. The first stage of development is *conceptualization*: the identification of requirements and a concept for a solution. Start by identifying a need from the users' viewpoint. Come up with a general approach to meeting the need, taking into account the available technology, market situation, resources, time available, and existing approaches. Describe the requirements, external constraints, and concept in natural language.

Requirements can be stated from various viewpoints, corresponding to the different OMT model views. Requirements include the information in the system (the object model), the feature list (the functional model), and the user-visible interactions (the dynamic model). The information content is usually not stated explicitly but can be extracted from use cases and domain knowledge. Functionality is often stated as a set of requirements. Interactions can be expressed by use cases that walk users through various scenarios.

There is no sharp line between conceptualization and analysis. I use the word "conceptualization" for the initial informal attempt to express the system goals in words and "analysis" for a more rigorous attempt to build and understand models to capture the requirements.

Use Cases

One way to capture a user's view of a system is to construct *use cases* of the system. A *use case* is a category of interactions between the system and an *actor* (an outside object in a particular role) about a particular way or purpose of using the system from the user's point of view. Each interaction starts with an initial event from the actor to the system and proceeds through a series of events between the actor, the system, and possibly other actors, until the interaction initiated by the original event reaches its logical conclusion (this is a matter of judgment). Some people use the word "story" to emphasize that a use case has a beginning, a middle, and an end.

A use case is best specified informally in words. An overly formal approach defeats the purpose, which is to quickly capture system requirements from the user's point of view. State the purpose of a use case, the actors involved, the initial event that starts it, and the termination condition. The sequence of interactions can be specified in words or by one or more prototypical scenarios. Each prototypical scenario represents a separate branch case. It can be described by a series of text phrases, by a scenario diagrams (formerly called an event trace diagram), or by an object interaction diagram.

Follow these steps to produce a use case:

1. Determine the boundary of the system. Determine which objects are part of the system, which ones interact with it, and which ones are disconnected from it. Develop the use case by considering the system itself as a single object, that is, a *black box.*

2. Determine the actors that interact with the system. An *actor* is one role that outside objects play with respect to the system. Start by examining physical objects that interact with the system, but in many cases each one plays multiple roles. For example, a given person might be a User, an Operator, and an Administrator of a computer operating system. Each role is a different actor.

3. For each actor, determine the fundamentally different ways in which the actor uses the system. Each of these is a use case. You must be able to enumerate the use cases. If you have too many, approach things at a higher level.

4. Identify the initial event that starts each use case.

5. Determine the termination condition that concludes the use case. Often a use case can be approached at several different levels, so pick the level of detail that is compatible with other use cases in the system.

6. List a prototypical scenario that describes the typical transaction.

7. If there are variations, list additional prototypical scenarios or describe the variations in words. Feel free to use ordinary language; a use case is not meant to be highly formal.

8. Identify and describe all the exceptions that are logically associated with a given use case.

When you are done, check that the set of use cases encompasses all the functionality of the system.

Kinds of Objects

During development three kinds of objects are encountered: domain objects, application objects, and internal objects. *Domain objects* carry the real-world semantics of the application. They exist independently of any application and are meaningful to domain experts. Find them as part of a general domain analysis or by knowledge of the domain.

Application objects are computer aspects of the application that are nevertheless visible to the users. They do not exist in the problem domain itself; they are meaningful only in the context of an application. However, they are not merely design decisions, because the user sees them and they cannot be altered without modifying the application specification. These *cannot* be found by domain analysis, but they can often be reused from previous applications, even those from different domains. In a sense, they must be "designed" during analysis. Application objects include views, controllers, devices, and interfaces.

Internal objects are internal components of a system that are invisible to the users. They represent the design choices made to implement the system. They should be omitted during analysis. An important part of the design phase is adding internal objects to make the design work.

Analysis Macroprocess

Analysis is the careful examination of the requirements for a system with the intent of understanding them, exploring their implications, and removing inconsistencies and omissions. The end products of analysis are the true system requirements. Typically it will take several passes to build a complete analysis model, because most large systems are circular in nature.

Domain objects and application objects must be approached differently. A two-prong analysis macroprocess works best:

1. First build a domain model that captures real-world classes and relationships in the problem domain.

> **a.** Identify real-world classes relevant to the application. Capture enough, and only enough, information to characterize the state of the system between operations (the *essential model*, as it was termed in "classical" analysis).

> **b.** Identify real-world operations on the domain objects. Most real-world objects appear as *surrogates*, that is, passive information holders *within the system*, so their operations will be primarily passive. Do not confuse the surrogates in the system model with the actual real-world objects. It may be helpful to append the word *Information* to the names of surrogates, for example, *FlightInformation, CustomerInformation,* and so on. The system operations on such information objects are normally access-type operations.

> **c.** Prepare state diagrams showing the life histories of domain objects. Events correspond to the (mostly) passive operations on the objects.

This approach is more "data-driven" than advocated by many object-oriented writers, but it builds on a long and successful history of information modeling. Capture the essential state of the system and the operations will follow. I don't find role playing and message passing to be so helpful in capturing the analysis model of a domain, although they can be helpful during the design phase when we take a more behavioral view of objects.

2. Then build an application model on top of the domain model. The application model is driven by the use cases and problem statement.

> **a.** Identify the system boundary: decide what is part of the system, what is

       supplied by other existing systems, and what are external actors.

b. Identify all the actors that interact with the system. Then identify one or more use cases that show how each actor uses the system. Start with the more common situations and proceed to less common ones. The first 5 or 10 use cases (total) usually capture the important system behavior. If you get too many use cases (say 50 or more) then rethink the purpose of the application; it may be too disjoint. Make sure to subsystem exception conditions with their use cases.

c. By examining use cases, identify the access required of each domain class. Make up one or more views of each domain class to provide this access in a user-friendly way. Add the view classes to the object model. Define the static mapping from domain classes to view classes (this is part of the functional model).

d. From the use cases, identify events between the actors and the system. Define periods between events as states. Build controllers to sequence events with each view. (Separate the static mapping of view objects to domain objects from the dynamics of the views. Let the controllers animate the views.)

e. Identify system commands. A system command is a logical request from an actor to the system to perform some action. Operate at a semantic level, not at the syntactic level of keystrokes, menu picks, or command line syntax (that is, "save file" not 's', 'a', 'v', 'e', filename). Add system commands to the functional model as operations. Assign operations to classes if possible, but if a command has no obvious target object, assign it to a controller.

f. Determine external interfaces, including devices, other systems, persistent storage, and other jobs. Try to surround the core application by a ring of generic interface objects to protect the core from system dependencies.

Object Modeling Microprocess

The microprocess is the series of low-level steps to follow in building a model. These steps may be invoked many times as part of the higher-level macroprocess. Different parts of the model may be built at different times.

1. Identify classes (from the problem domain or use case).

2. Prepare a model dictionary describing every name in the model. Every model element should be entered into the model dictionary by name together with a brief (two or three sentence) description. Elements include classes, associations, attributes, operations, events, states, and any other named entity. Diagrams and text complement each other. This step must be performed at each point in the process, although I will not repeat it explicitly.

3. Identify associations between classes. An association is any connection between objects that must be remembered between operations.

4. Add attributes of classes and associations. Attributes should be pure values (such as strings and numbers).

5. Use generalization and inheritance to organize classes and reduce redundancy. Abstract classes are usually better discovered bottom up, by identifying the concrete classes and then generalizing, so that you don't make premature assumptions about the inheritance.

6. Verify that access paths exist for likely queries. Verify that the multiplicity of each result is correct. Verify that information exists in the model to perform all operations.

7. Group classes into subsystems based on affinity and association coupling. For large systems the subsystems will be developed first in a top-down manner and then populated with classes.

8. Iterate and refine the model.

Dynamic Modeling Microprocess

The microprocess steps of creating a dynamic model are:

1. Identify external events (from use cases and scenarios).

2. Define states as the periods between events. Examine the states to determine which ones are actually the same (as a result of branches joining or loops). Two states are identical if the future behavior of the system is the same for both.

3. Build a state diagram for each dynamic class showing the legal sequences of events and states. Build at least one state diagram for each controller.

4. Identify the operations that are invoked on each transition and add them to the functional model.

5. Validate the model against the original use cases and scenarios. Construct new scenarios from the state diagrams and see if they make sense.

Functional Model Microprocess

The functional model is the description of the operations discovered while building the object and dynamic models.

1. Write a text description of each system operation from the dynamic model and each operation already assigned to the object model.

2. If an operation affects a number of distinct objects in the system, then it may be worthwhile to draw an object-oriented data flow diagram to show its effects. Identify all the source data values (in objects) and all of the target data values (in objects). Express each target value as a function of source values. Assign the functions to classes as operations.

System Design

System design consists of making global decisions about the structure of the design and implementation. Whereas analysis asks *how to do it,* system design asks *what is a good approach to get it done.*

There are a lot of things to think about during system design, but the most important is to define the overall structure of the design. A large system must be decomposed into smaller parts, and there must be some underlying order to the relationship among the parts if the design is to be understood.

We represent the system architecture as a nested collection of subsystems. A *subsystem* is a subset of the model elements: classes, associations, and their corresponding operations. At the top level the system is a single subsystem; at the bottom level it consists of modules (bottom-level subsystems) that represent the physical units of the implementation: files, configuration control units, and so on.

A *dependency* arises when one subsystem depends on another, by one of the following: using a class from it for association or subclassing; instantiating an object from one of its classes; or calling an operation on one of its operations received as an argument. The goal of system design is to reduce the dependencies between subsystems, especially by avoiding circular dependencies and forming some regular pattern of dependencies. A highly-dependent situation can often be changed into a loosely-dependent situation by moving classes to different subsystems, by restricting the knowledge classes need to use other classes, and by introducing new subsystems to break circular dependencies.

Some of the issues to consider during system design are the following:

1. Estimate performance and resource usage. Do "back of the envelope" calculations if necessary to ensure that the resources are adequate.

2. Decompose the system into subsystems, trying to minimize present and future anticipated dependencies.

3. Make a plan for reuse. This includes reuse of existing components (libraries, frameworks, previous programs) as well as planning to reuse parts of the current system in the future.

4. Determine the strategies for dealing with concurrency in the system. If there is concurrency, then you will often have to deal with distribution as well.

5. Decide how global resources will be managed. These include devices, shared objects such as windows, and logical name spaces such as IDs and color maps. For devices and shared objects a *guardian object* can be assigned the sole direct access to the resource; access to the guardian object is managed by software concurrency control. For logical name spaces, blocks of values can be dynamically allocated to different nodes at run time (the "box office" scheme) or the name space can be statically partitioned in advance ("bit slicing").

6. Determine how data storage will be managed. Standard approaches include databases, files, and volatile memory.

7. Determine how the system will be initialized and terminated. Include serious error conditions among these boundary conditions.

8. Specify optimization and trade-off policies for the entire system. If these are not explicit and consistent, then different implementors will optimize different things and cancel out any optimization.

Object Design

Most of the design effort is spent elaborating operations as procedural code. The analysis model shows system operations to be implemented; the design shows how to implement them in terms of lower-level operations and eventually primitive operations (language statements and library operations). If system operations could all be implemented directly in primitive operations, design would be simple, but such procedures would often be many pages long, hard to understand, and lacking all reusability. The problem is to bridge the gap between the desired high-level operations and the available primitive operations by inventing one or more layers of intermediate operations, each of which can preferably be used many times. Unfortunately the real world and the requirements offer no guidance to these intermediate operations, because they are constructed for design structuring reasons and are not directly required by the external requirements. The guidelines for these intermediate operations predate object orientation:

◆ each operation should be well focused ("do one thing well"); and

◆ avoid unnecessary dependencies.

The object design macroprocess is:

1. Start with the analysis model as the skeleton of the design model. Add new elements (classes, associations, operations, etc.) to it for design purposes, and add design adornments to analysis elements to specify their implementation properties. When the design is complete the analysis model will be embedded within the design model, avoiding the need to maintain two separate models. (You could mark or name the classes to distinguish them if you want to, although it is not usually necessary to maintain a sharp line between analysis and design anyway.)

2. Identify the implicit internal system state needed to preserve information between system operations. If the effect of an operation depends on a previous operation, then some object within the system must hold information between the two operations. This state information is usually not explicit in use cases or problem statements, so you have to extract it from between the lines. Make up storage objects (and new classes if necessary) to hold the information. Apply this design rule: do the sets of operations and storage objects cluster into groups? If an operation affects many different storage objects, or a storage object is affected by many different operations, reconsider your system decomposition and choice of storage objects to reduce dependencies.

3. Start with the system operations identified from the use cases, dynamic model, or general thought. Expand each operation into suboperations using the concept of responsibilities: List the responsibilities of an operation in detail; group the responsibilities into affinity clusters; make up a suboperation for each cluster. Repeat until the suboperations are simple enough to implement directly in primitive operations. Role playing may be useful in designing suboperations. Use object interaction diagrams to plan the flow of control in complicated cases, particularly those with reentrant flows.

4. Once the design is logically complete and correct, transform the object model to permit more efficient access and operations. Each transformation should be small and verifiable so that the entire optimization can be verified.

5. Encapsulate external dependencies by using mediator objects to separate the core of the system from the outside world. The core of the system should not directly see outside objects (such as windowing systems, graphics drivers, and machine platforms).

6. Decide how to map classes to language structures. Wait until late in the design to choose the implementation of associations (because their implementation is easy to generate and change). Examine usage patterns before deciding whether to implement associations in both directions (mutual pointers) or in only a single direction. Code generation from associations is easily automated and does not require much forethought during design; it can be changed as circumstances dictate. If you can't modify the participant classes, consider implementing an association as a container class of tuples using hashing; access time using good algorithms is constant at about 10 times the cost of a pointer implementation.

7. Late in the design reexamine the object model to look for more inheritance. Look below the surface for matching operations: sometimes you have to rename them or their arguments, rearrange or revise arguments, or add default arguments to one operation to match another one.

8. Write the code.

Here are some other things that need to be done during object design.

◆ Reify behavior (turn it into an object) when you expect variant algorithms, changes in algorithms as the system matures, or want run-time control over algorithms.

◆ Consider a direct encoding of a state diagram as a table interpreted by a state machine interpreter. For operating system events, the execution cost is minuscule and the flexibility great.

◆ Practice "need to know" with intermediate operations. Restrict their visibility to the class or subsystem that needs them.

◆ Concentrate on the design of substantive operations that modify objects. Queries should be written without causing any side effects. Write convenience operations in terms of other public operations on a class; don't allow them to access private information, even on their own class.

◆ Complete most of the design before deciding how to implement associations.

What Methods Can and Can't Do

Don't expect a method (this one or any other) to be a cookbook. Software development is an engineering process. A method will not tell you everything you have to do. It outlines a process to follow and proposes a format for capturing the work products, but the developer must supply the creativity, insight, and judgment to make it work. As in any discipline, such as music, literature, sports, or engineering, the expert knows when to follow the rules and when to break them, but the beginner is advised to gain some experience before breaking rules. So keep in mind that OMT is a tool to be used and not an edict to be blindly followed. If you want to extend it or hybridize it, fine, but you are responsible for the results.

This summary describes the state of OMT at the time of the integration of OMT, Booch, OOSE, and other methods into the Unified Modeling Language (UML) and Unified Method. OMT no longer evolves as a separate method; it has been merged into the Unified Method and its ideas have been absorbed and enhanced. A newcomer will find that the UML contains most of the OMT concepts in a familiar form but will also find many new concepts that solve problems that OMT and the other older methods could not handle. All of these articles are equally applicable to the UML and Unified Method.

I hope that these insights prove helpful to the readers of this book. They are based on experience, but experience continues to evolve and expand, so let your own experience guide and enhance the future development of modeling and design methods.

Bibliography

THE following books provide insight on various aspects of modeling. I have listed only widely available current books. I have not included references to journal articles or purely academic works, although some of these are included in the individual articles. There are many other fine books on object-orientation available and this is not meant to be a complete list.

Grady Booch. *Object-Oriented Design with Applications, 2nd ed.* Benjamin/Cummings, Redwood City, Calif., 1994.

Grady Booch. *Object Solutions: Managing the Object-Oriented Project.* Addison-Wesley, Menlo Park, Calif., 1996.

Frank Buschmann, Regine Meunier, Hans Rohnert, Peter Sommerlad, Michael Stal. *Pattern-Oriented Software Architecture: A System of Patterns.* Wiley, Chichester, England, 1996.

Peter Coad, David North, Mark Mayfield. *Object Models: Strategies, Patterns, and Applications.* Yourdon Press, Englewood Cliffs, N.J., 1995.

Peter Coad, Edward Yourdon. *Object-Oriented Analysis, 2nd. ed.* Yourdon Press, Englewood Cliffs, N.J., 1991.

Derek Coleman, Patrick Arnold, Stephanie Bodoff, Chris Dollin, Helena Gilchrist, Fiona Hayes, Paul Jeremaes. *Object-Oriented Development: The Fusion Method.* Prentice Hall, Englewood Cliffs, N.J., 1994.

Margaret A. Ellis, Bjarne Stroustrup. *The Annotated C++ Reference Manual.* Addison-Wesley, Reading, Mass., 1990.

David W. Embley, Barry D. Kurtz, Scott N. Woodfield. *Object-Oriented Systems Analysis: A Model-Driven Approach.* Yourdon Press, Englewood Cliffs, N.J., 1992.

Donald G. Firesmith, Edward M. Eykholt. *Dictionary of Object Technology.* SIGS Books, New York, 1995.

Erich Gamma, Richard Helm, Ralph Johnson, John Vlissides. *Design Patterns: Elements of Reusable Object-Oriented Software.* Addison-Wesley, Reading, Mass., 1995.

Adele Goldberg, David Robson. *Smalltalk-80: The Language and its Implementation.* Addison-Wesley, Reading, Mass., 1983.

Adele Goldberg, Kenneth J. Rubin. *Succeeding with Objects: Design Frameworks for Project Management.* Addison-Wesley, Reading, Mass., 1995.

Ivar Jacobson, Magnus Christerson, Patrik Jonsson, Gunnar Övergaard. *Object-Oriented Software Engineering: A Use Case Driven Approach.* Addison-Wesley, Workingham, England, 1992.

Tom Love. *Object Lessons.* SIGS Books, New York, 1993.

James Martin, James J. Odell. *Object-Oriented Analysis and Design.* Prentice Hall, Englewood Cliffs, N.J., 1992.

James Martin, James J. Odell. *Object-Oriented Methods: A Foundation.* Prentice Hall, Englewood Cliffs, N.J., 1996.

Bertrand Meyer. *Object-Oriented Software Construction.* Prentice Hall, New York, 1988.

James Rumbaugh, Michael Blaha, William Premerlani, Frederick Eddy, William Lorensen. *Object-Oriented Modeling and Design.* Prentice Hall, Englewood Cliffs, N.J., 1991.

Bran Selic, Garth Gullekson, Paul T. Ward. *Real-Time Object-Oriented Modeling.* Wiley, New York, 1994.

Sally Shlaer, Stephen J. Mellor. *Object Lifecycles: Modeling the World in States.* Yourdon Press, Englewood Cliffs, N.J., 1992.

Sally Shlaer, Stephen J. Mellor. *Object-Oriented Systems Analysis: Modeling the World in Data.* Yourdon Press, Englewood Cliffs, N.J., 1988.

Rebecca Wirfs-Brock, Brian Wilkerson, Lauren Wiener. *Designing Object-Oriented Software.* Prentice Hall, Englewood Cliffs, N.J., 1990.

Edward Yourdon, Larry L. Constantine. *Structured Design.* Yourdon Press, Englewood Cliffs, N.J., 1979.

Index

SIGS BOOKShelf

Applying OMT
Kurt W. Derr

Applying OMT is a how-to guide on implementation processes and practical approaches for the popular Object Modeling Technique (OMT) created by James Rumbaugh et al. The book begins by providing a thorough overview of such fundamental concepts as modeling and prototyping and then moves into specific implementation strategies using C++ and Smalltalk. By using a typical business application as a case study, the author illustrates the complete modeling process from start to finish.

1995/557 pages/softcover/ISBN 1-884842-10-0/Order# 6S01-2100/$44/£ 34

Object Technology Strategies and Tactics
Gilbert Singer

Designed for both managers and software developers interested in understanding OO concepts, this book will help you make intelligent analysis, design, and management decisions. Language independent, this nuts-and-bolts guide is designed to help minimize the risks and maximize the benefits of OT.

May 1996/Approx. 250 pages/softcover/ISBN 1-884842-38-0/Order# 6S01-2380/$39/£ 26

The Java Source
The Worldwide Guide to Java Companies, Products, Services and Books
Marisa Urgo

For the first time ever: comprehensive information on Java products, vendors, consultants, resources, and more.

1997/approx. 500 pages/softcover/ISBN 1-88-4842-57-7/Order# 6S01-2577/$35/£ 28

The Object Primer
Scott W. Ambler

The Object Primer is the ultimate introductory text on object-oriented technology. By reviewing this easy-to-read book, you'll gain a solid understanding of object-oriented concepts and object-oriented analysis techniques.
The Object Primer provides all a developer needs to know to start using object-oriented technology immediately.

November 1995/250 pages/softcover/ISBN 1-884842-17-8/Order# 6S01-2178/$35/£ 28

What Every Software Manager Must Know to Succeed with Object Technology
John Williams

The two biggest causes of failure of object-based projects are the software managers' lack of understanding of the technology and their inability to recognize that OT projects must be managed differently from other projects. This book shows managers what object technology is and how to manage it effectively. It provides readers with a no-nonsense approach to object technology management, including effective guidelines on how to track the development of projects.

1995/294 pages/softcover/ISBN 1-884842-14-3/Order# 6S01-2143/$35/£ 29

Managing Your Move to Object Technology
Barry McGibbon

Written for software managers, **Managing Your Move to Object Technology** clearly defines and illustrates the management implications associated with the transition to object technology. Although other books may cover the technological benefits of OT, this is one of the few to address the business management issues associated with new technology and the corporate environment. It covers what OT will do to the corporate culture, not simply what it will do for it.

1995/288 pages/softcover/ISBN 1-884842-15-1/Order# 6S01-2151/$35/£ 29

Successful Enterprise Modeling Techniques

Getting Results with the Object-Oriented Enterprise Model

Thornton Gale and James Eldred

Enterprise modeling is the primary tool used in business reengineering. Historically, the number-one problem with enterprise modeling has been the lack of formalism. **Getting Results with the Object-Oriented Enterprise Model** tackles this dilemma head-on and prescribes a formal methodology based on object technology.

1996/650 pages/softcover/ISBN 1-884842-16-X/Order# 6S01-216X/$45/£ 30

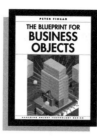

The Blueprint for Business Objects

Peter Fingar

The Blueprint for Business Objects provides a clear and concise guide to making informed decisions about emerging object technology and to mastering the skills you need to make effective use of the technology in business.

Based on the workplace experiences of several major corporations, **The Blueprint for Business Objects** presents a framework designed for business and information systems professionals. It provides the reader with a road map, starting at the level of initial concepts and moving up to the mastery level. It also includes information on how to select and find additional learning resources.

1996/300 pages/softcover/ISBN 1-884842-20-8/Order# 6S01-2208/$39/£ 26

Reliable Object-Oriented Software Applying Analysis and Design

Ed Seidewitz and Mike Stark

Reliable Object-Oriented Software presents the underlying principles of object orientation and its practical application. More than just another text on methodology, **Reliable Object-Oriented Software** focuses on the fundamental concepts of software development and architectural design, and lays the foundation necessary to develop robust, maintainable and evolvable software.

November 1995/425 pages/softcover/ISBN 1-884842-18-6/ Order# 6S01-2186/$45/£ 30

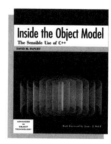

Inside the Object Model

David M. Papurt

Foreword by James J. Odell

Inside the Object Model serves two key functions: it teaches object-oriented analysis and design from first principles and clearly explains C++ mechanisms that implement object-oriented concepts.

With over 100 figures, hundreds of working code examples, and comparisons of coding techniques, this is the book you will need to gain a complete understanding of both C++ and the object model. Professional software analysts, designers, programmers, and advanced computer science students will benefit from reading this book.

1995/540 pages/softcover/ISBN 1-884842-05-4/Order# 6S01-2054/$39/£ 26

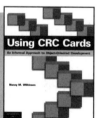

Using CRC Cards

An Informal Approach to Object-Oriented Development

Nancy M. Wilkinson

Using CRC Cards is a comprehensive introduction to CRC (Class, Responsibility, Collaborator) cards. It includes a description of the cards and how they can be used in interactive sessions to develop an object-oriented model of an application.

In this book, the author draws on her years of project experience to describe how CRC cards can contribute at every stage of the software life cycle. It includes practical examples of how to use CRC cards in projects using either formal or informal development techniques.

1995/243 pages/softcover/ISBN 1-884842-07-0/Order# 6S01-2070/$29/£ 19

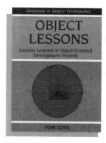

Object Lessons

Tom Love

In this usable guide to developing and managing OO software projects, well-respected consultant and OOP pioneer Tom Love reveals the absolute do's and don'ts in adopting and managing object-oriented technology. **Object Lessons** is filled with applicable advice and practical suggestions for large-scale commercial software projects.

If you are an applications programmer, project leader or technical manager making decisions concerning design and management of large-scale commercial object-oriented software, this book is for you.

1994/275 pages/softcover/ISBN 1-9627477-3-4/Order# 6S01-7734/$29/£ 19

Java as an Object-Oriented Language
Mark Lorenz

Get the latest information on this groundbreaking language from an expert in the emerging field. Clear, crisp, and indispensable, this management briefing compares Java to the most popular OO languages, including C++ and Smalltalk.

This management briefing examines Java in ways not found in today's books, which are mostly reference manuals with some applet examples. **Java as an Object-Oriented Language** examines the same application design as implemented in Smalltalk, C++, and Java (with the emphasis on Java, of course).

June 1996/40 pages/softcover/ISBN 1-884842-40-2/Order# 6S01-2402/$85/ £ 57

The Directory of Object Technology
Edited by Dale J. Gaumer

Find exactly what you're looking for, the moment you need it. This is the only complete guide devoted to OO information worldwide.

The Directory of Object Technology puts the entire OO industry at your fingertips. With over 900 entries, it is the most comprehensive object technology resource guide available. This book will help you define and identify the products and services you need. Divided into five separate sections, the Directory provides a complete listing of vendors, products, services, and consultants.

1995/softcover/385 pages/ISBN 1-884842-08-9/Order# 6S01-2089/$69/£ 46

Next Generation Computing
The Fast Track to Distributed Business Objects
Peter Fingar, Dennis Read, and Jim Stikeleather

The unique format of this white-paper collection is the fastest and easiest way to learn about the next generation of computing. This book covers major topic areas in succinct, yet complete, chapters. Written in a clear and compact style, each of these crisp 30-minute business briefs will be invaluable to your staff, developers, and managers.

1996/300 pages/softcover/ISBN 1-884842-29-1/Order# 6S01-2291/$50/£ 33

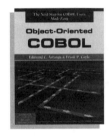

Object-Oriented COBOL
Edmund C. Arranga and Frank P. Coyle

This is the only book that walks COBOL users through the next phase of the COBOL language: object-oriented COBOL (OOCOBOL). Written by experts in COBOL programming, **Object-Oriented COBOL** teaches you how to integrate COBOL with object-oriented methodologies. It provides explanations and roadmaps that will help you understand, navigate, and successfully integrate analysis and design concepts with enabling OOCOBOL constructs.

May 1996/400 pages/softcover/ISBN 1-884842-43-8/Order# 6S01-2348/$39/£ 26

Dictionary of Object Technology
The Definitive Desk Reference
Donald G. Firesmith and Edward M. Eykholt

Dictionary of Object Technology is the only reference of its kind dedicated to the terminology used in the object technology field. With over 3,000 main entries and over 600 pages, this long-awaited and much-needed dictionary is cross-referenced by major components and includes complete appendices specific to industry standards, programming languages, and more.

This fundamental reference will help maintain consistent language usage across the entire spectrum of the object technology field.

1995/628 pages/hardcover/ISBN 1-884842-09-7/Order# 6S01-2097/$55/£ 42

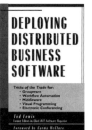
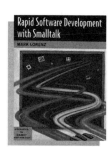